Biodiversity and Native America

Biodiversity and Native America

Edited by Paul E. Minnis and Wayne J. Elisens

University of Oklahoma Press : Norman

Published with the assistance of the National Endowment for the Humanities, a federal agency which supports the study of such fields as history, philosophy, literature, and language.

Library of Congress Cataloging-in-Publication Data

Biodiversity and Native America / edited by Paul E. Minnis and Wayne J. Elisens.
    p. cm.
    Includes bibliographical references and index.
    ISBN 0–8061–3232–9 (cloth)
    ISBN 0–8061–3345–7 (paper)
    1. Indians of North America—Ethnobotany. 2. Indians of Mexico—Ethnobiology. 3. Biological diversity—North America. 4. Human ecology—North America. I. Minnis, Paul E. II. Elisens, Wayne J., 1948–
B98.B54 B56 2000
304.2'089'97—dc21   99–055136
                                                     CIP

2 3 4 5 6 7 8 9 10

CONTENTS

List of Illustrations   ix

Introduction   3
     Paul E. Minnis and Wayne J. Elisens

ISSUES AND OVERVIEWS

1. Native American Management and Conservation
   of Biodiversity in the Sonoran Desert Bioregion:
   An Ethnoecological Perspective   29
        Gary Paul Nabhan

2. Relationships between Mexican Ethnobotanical
   Diversity and Indigenous Peoples   44
        Robert Bye and Edelmira Linares

3. Ethnopharmacology and the Search for
   New Therapeutics   74
        Walter H. Lewis

ETHNOGRAPHIC CASE STUDIES

4. "We Live by Them": Native Knowledge of Biodiversity
   in the Great Basin of Western North America   99
   Catherine S. Fowler

5. "Just Like a Garden": Traditional Resource Management
   and Biodiversity Conservation on the Interior Plateau of
   British Columbia   133
   Sandra L. Peacock and Nancy J. Turner

6. *Iwígara:* A Rarámuri Cognitive Model of Biodiversity
   and Its Effects on Land Management   180
   Enrique Salmón

PREHISTORY AND BIODIVERSITY

7. Human Disturbance and Biodiversity: A Case Study
   from Northern New Mexico   207
   Richard I. Ford

8. Levels of Native Biodiversity in Eastern North America   223
   Gayle J. Fritz

9. Ethnohistory of Aboriginal Landscapes in the
   Southeastern United States   248
   Julia E. Hammett

List of Contributors   301
Index   303

ILLUSTRATIONS

FIGURES

3.1. Achual head of household of the Jívaro linguistic family   77

3.2. Collaborative agreements between parties of the
International Cooperative Biodiversity
Group–Peru program   81

3.3. *Podophyllum peltatum* (May apple) near St. Louis in May   84

3.4. Chemical structures of podophyllotoxin, etoposide,
taxol, and emodin   87

3.5. Flowering branches of *Rhamnus purshiana*
(cascara sagrada), Victoria, B.C.   89

4.1. Collecting prince's plume *(Stanleya elata)* in
Death Valley, California   117

4.2. Mrs. Wuzzie George winnowing pine nuts
(Pinus monophylla) in the Sweetwater Range, Nevada   122

4.3. Mrs. Wuzzie George collecting tule *(Scirpus acutus)*
rhizomes, Stillwater Marsh, Nevada   123

5.1. Nlaka'pamux woman digging roots at Botanie Valley   138

5.2. Balsamroot or spring sunflower *(Balsamorhiza sagittata)*,
a former root staple   139

5.3. Secwepemc elder Mary Thomas holding a
"carrot-sized" balsamroot taproot   149

5.4. Soapberry *(Shepherdia canadensis)* was managed
      through pruning and burning   152
6.1. Rarámuri *yúmari* ceremony   186
6.2. Dancing at *yúmari*   187
6.3. The Rarámuri cultural model of *iwígara*   189
6.4. Olla (clay jar) full of fermenting corn beer   194
6.5. Blessing the fields at *yúmari*   196
7.1. Lithic mulch field in the Rio del Oso Valley, New Mexico 213
7.2. Cobble border grid, northern New Mexico   215
7.3. Lithic mulch grid next to plot without
      surface modification   218
9.1. Seasonal round of subsistence activities for
      coastal Virginia Indians ca. 1607   272

MAPS

4.1. The Great Basin of western North America, showing
      the territories of its principal ethnic/linguistic units 101
5.1. Traditional territories of the Interior Salish peoples
      and neighboring groups   136
6.1. The Sierra Tarahumara   182
8.1. Eastern North America with locations of relevant sites
      and cultural areas   229
9.1. The study area, showing routes of Spanish and
      English explorers and traders   252

All illustrations are from the contributors' collections unless otherwise indicated.

Biodiversity and Native America

INTRODUCTION

PAUL E. MINNIS AND
WAYNE J. ELISENS

Nature herself does not speak with a voice easily understood.

THOMAS BANYACYA (1994:115)

INTRODUCTION

Native peoples have been neither passive consumers of nature's economy nor primitive rapists of pristine natural environments. Nor did concern for the world's biodiversity begin during the final third of the twentieth century. Rather, aboriginal peoples have helped shape environments for untold millennia, and their accumulated ecological expertise and experiences with diverse organisms and varied biotas will be critical for building a sustainable and just future.

Those concerned with biodiversity conservation, resource management, and sustainable development have become more sophisticated in their understanding of the economic, the political, and especially the cultural contexts of these efforts. There is a growing consensus that well-executed, successful projects must involve local populations (e.g., Brush and Stabinsky 1996; Downes 1996; Furze, De Lacy, and Brickhead 1996; Janzen 1997; Kangas

1997; Oldfield and Alcorn 1991; Orlove and Brush 1996; Redford and Mansour 1996; Stevens 1997). This understanding is largely missing from developed regions, where indigenous peoples often are assumed to be disarticulated from their traditional lives and natural environments. "Save the rain forest" is a common mantra for philanthropic and commercial interests in the First World. Ironically, some of the loudest calls for preserving biological and cultural diversity come from temperate areas, which are too often believed irrelevant because of their presumed low biological diversity and acculturated indigenous peoples.

There is no better example of this than North America. Just before European conquest and colonization, North America enjoyed tremendous cultural diversity in numerous distinct environmental settings. Millions of Native North Americans in many hundreds of cultures inhabited this continent, scattered from the Arctic tundra to the neotropical mangroves of southern Florida and northeastern Mexico (Denevan 1992). Theirs is a fascinating record of the creative, ingenious, and practical and of complex adaptive and management strategies in response to varied environmental conditions. Starting in the early sixteenth century, Native North American populations faced dislocation, relocation, and a population loss so large that the word "genocide" is not inappropriate. This essay was written in the state that became home to the largest number of Native Americans displaced by the Euro-American juggernaut. At times, governmental policies actively worked to destroy generational links that sustained cultural heritages and knowledge stretching back thousands of years. Under such historical conditions, it is not surprising that in North America many aboriginal environmental relationships were broken and some lost forever. Some might argue that, because higher levels of biotic diversity are present in tropical regions and because cultural-environmental interactions are often more "intact" in less-developed countries, ethnobiological investigations of indigenous North American peoples are of little significance globally or locally.

We show in this volume how wrong this common perception is. While a small area of neotropical lowland forest may indeed have as many tree species as all of North America north of Mexico (Gentry 1982), it is not a convincing argument for ignoring less diverse areas and for not studying cultural-environmental strategies in "temperate" biomes. Furthermore, the contributors to this volume show that the common assumption that Native North Americans no longer live in ethnobiologically rich cultural traditions is incorrect. We argue that much additional research can and should be focused on North America, particularly given its unique cultural and biotic composition, the significant economic and political resources available for environmental issues, and the numerous examples of the impact of various governmental policies and economic development strategies on cultural and biological diversity.

In this volume, the concept of biodiversity is applied broadly. It includes issues of biotic richness and uniqueness, ecological adaptation and resource management, crop germ plasm diversity, and agroecology. We emphasize the roles that Native North Americans play and have played in these matters, and it is not possible to address these issues without an understanding of the cultural context of human ecology, including its historical dimensions (e.g., Crumley 1994) and belief systems (e.g., Anderson 1996; Rappaport 1979). First, we consider the importance of indigenous ecological experiences for understanding ecosystem dynamics and environmental history and for designing programs to manage and preserve biological diversity and "natural" environments. Second, we examine the value of Native North American ethnobiological knowledge, including crop diversity, agroecology, and medicines.

While much of Native North America is considered in this volume, some regions are more intensively examined. Mexico is only partially represented, because there is a significant amount of research available elsewhere for this ecological and culturally diverse country and because much of Mexico has a neotropical biota (e.g., Rzedowski 1978). Bye and Linares (this volume) provide a Mexican overview, and Salmón (this volume) discusses a specific example from the Tarahumara, or Rarámuri, of northwestern Mexico. The ethnobiology and ethnography of eastern North America (both the United States and Canada) are less extensively studied than those of western North America, owing in no small part to the greater effects of outside groups on traditional lifeways in eastern North America. Consequently, a disproportionate number of chapters focus on western North America.

The contributions of living indigenous peoples have, until quite recently, been slighted in projects for conserving natural environments and crop diversity; human experiences in the ancient past are *still* ignored. Therefore, we have made a conscious effort to include not only current and historically recorded Native Americans but their prehistoric ancestors as well. Just as ecosystem composition and distribution are dependent on paleoenvironmental events, human ecology is historically bounded; what people do is conditioned greatly by what their forerunners did. For all continents of the world, with the exception of Antarctica, most of human history occurred before written records. North America's earliest humans date to at least 15,000 years ago. Because written history does not begin until A.D. 1492 for most of North America, slightly over five hundred years ago, only about 3% of human history in the New World is even touched by archival data. Archival records, even during that 3%, chronicle only a small fraction of Native North American experiences. Consequently, to understand both environmental history and the human ecology of North America one must deal with both the present and the ancient past. To do otherwise impoverishes our understanding of North America and its cultural and biotic heritage.

BIODIVERSITY AND
NATIVE NORTH AMERICA

Many Native North Americans now lead lives little different ecologically from those of their non-Indian neighbors, and their contributions to resource sustainability and conservation may be no different from those of other citizens of North America. A large number of Native Americans, however, maintain cultural traditions of environmental interactions begun millennia ago. Native American ecology of this sort is not simply passive environmental steward-ship maintaining natural, that is, "human-free," ecological patterns. Rather, indigenous/environmental relations are active. Environ-ments that at first appear to be "natural" may have a marked anthropogenic component under closer examination. For example, the ecological role of fire in vegetation dynamics and the human use of "controlled burns" to modify habitats have received much attention from ecologists (e.g., Collins and Wallace 1990; Russell 1983). William Cronon's (1984) study of the environmental history of northeastern North America, as another example, demonstrated to a wide audience the effects of Native and colonial Americans on their environment. Both Fritz (this volume) and Hammett (this volume) deepen our understanding of anthropogenic environ-mental changes in eastern North America.

Many purposes are served by recognizing the value of indige-nous environmental experiences. Here we outline two broad cate-gories. The first is a better understanding of environmental history and the pre–European contact biological landscape. The second involves a multitude of ways in which traditional environmental experiences and knowledge are of essential value, both for Native Americans themselves and for the wider population.

ENVIRONMENTAL HISTORY AND ECOLOGICAL KNOWLEDGE

Ecology is dynamic; environments, ecosystems, populations, and species change, often greatly (Botkin 1990; Brown and Lomo-lino 1998). There are natural oscillations (e.g., Quaternary climatic change), cyclical transformations (e.g., vegetational succession), profound alterations (e.g., ecological disturbance), and other pre-dictable and stochastic events that impact natural environments.

Similarly, human history is not static, and people are an interactive part of their environments. The relationships between culture and nature are, not surprisingly, reciprocal and ever changing in a variety of ways. Humans have been an integral part of New World ecosystems for thousands of years during the Quaternary, a geological period that witnessed the evolution of human societies as well as some of the most rapid climate and ecological changes ever noted in earth's history (e.g., Betancourt, Van Devender, and Martin 1990; Delcourt and Delcourt 1991; Ritchie 1987). Although the degree to which environments are anthropogenically influenced is argued widely, the natural history of North America suggests that "any understanding of contemporary biodiversity change in the Americas is likely to be uninformative and misleading if it employs a prehistoric baseline imbued with pristine characteristics" (Stahl 1996:105). These issues are complex and multifaceted, but they are, fortunately, amenable to research, as the contributors to this volume demonstrate.

Knowledge of environmental history and of the role of people in shaping it is essential today. With increasing political pressure to preserve biodiversity, expand nature reserves, maintain biological communities, and restore previous environments, one must ask the question: what ecosystem models are being used? Why in North America, for example, choose idealized precontact environments as the model for a natural environment? While it is true that contact introduced non-native organisms to the New World, altered land use patterns, modified and fragmented habitats, and changed the environmental character of North America (e.g., Crosby 1986), biological communities were not static in precontact times (Axelrod 1985; Delcourt, Delcourt, Cridlebaugh, and Chapman 1986; Delcourt, Delcourt, Morse, and Morse 1986; McAndrews 1988). "Conservationists often refer to restoring an ecosystem to its condition before it was colonized by technologically advanced people. Choosing this particular time marker makes no sense in the face of climate change; we are always dealing with a moving target" (Hunter 1996:696).

We have many cases of prehistoric human manipulation of North American environments. Perhaps the best known is the argument that the earliest Native North Americans were at least partially responsible for the extinction of megafauna at the Pleistocene/Holocene boundary (e.g., Martin and Klein 1984; Stahl 1996). There are many other studies of the environmental consequences of human history in North America. Ancient agriculturalists, in particular, modified landscapes, and we have many examples of these in western North America (e.g., Kohler 1992; Minnis 1985) as well as in eastern North America (e.g., Delcourt 1987; Fritz, this volume; Hammett, this volume).

If there was an active relationship between precontact Native North Americans and their environments, did these processes occur postcontact and do they continue in some form today? In short, the answer is "yes." Five hundred years after first contact and after centuries of efforts to reduce the viability of Native North American cultures, many still live in intimate and daily interaction with their local environments. Two contributors to this volume in particular emphasize this point. Both focus on cultural areas with historically low human populations of hunter-gatherers, areas where one would have expected scant environmental impact by indigenous peoples. Such is not the case. The degree of environmental manipulation by peoples of the Great Basin (Fowler, this volume) and of the Interior Plateau of British Columbia (Peacock and Turner, this volume) is astonishing. Environmental manipulation extends beyond reasonably large-scale and easily seen actions, such as the purposeful burning of vegetation, to the subtle micromanagement of individual plants and species. Other excellent examples include research in California (e.g., Anderson 1991, 1996). This careful work by dedicated scholars over many years demonstrates the incalculable rewards of in-depth collaboration with Native North Americans, peoples too often assumed to have lost their ethnobiological heritage. But time is short, as many of the contributors indicate. Most indigenous informants are grandparents, and often their grandchildren are not learning the environmental knowledge of their elders.

Aboriginal knowledge is, however, valuable for more than understanding anthropogenic ecology. Traditional knowledge—some call it "indigenous science"—has discovered ecological relationships unknown to Western science (Nabhan, this volume; Salmón, this volume). How could one think otherwise? How surprising it would be to find peoples who inhabited and made a living in an area for hundreds and perhaps thousands of years and yet failed to notice detailed relationships between organisms and their physical environment.

Indigenous Expertise and Experiences

Despite ubiquitous silicon chips, stamped steel sheets, and plastic containers, our industrial and postindustrial world is still dependent upon natural products, as has been the case for all people, now and in the past. Every morsel of food and a surprisingly large number of medicines, as well as numerous materials for clothing and construction, are derived from plants and animals. Many of these resources come from North America; thus, it should be expected that through thousands of years of adaptations to varied environments Native North Americans experimented with and learned to use a large number of plants and animals in ways that might be of value to others. Here we concentrate on only three categories: medicines, foods, and farming.

Medicines

Mark Plotkin (1993), Richard Schultes and collaborators (e.g., Schultes and Raffauf 1990; Schultes and Von Reis 1995), and Walter Lewis and Memory Elvin-Lewis (1977), among many others, point out that tropical forests probably contain numerous medicines still unknown to pharmaceutical companies but used by traditional healers. Drug companies are intensifying their prospecting efforts among local populations, Shaman Pharmaceutical being the best known and most highly focused example (King, Carlson, and Moran 1996).

North America may prove to be a greater storehouse of indigenous medicines than previously thought (e.g., Lewis, this volume). There is much information available about Native American medicines, including a series of regional summaries (e.g., Kay 1996; Kindscher 1992; Moore 1979) as well as classic compilations (e.g., Millspaugh 1892; Vogel 1970). The most comprehensive study is Daniel Moerman's (1986) two-volume, 900-page summary listing over 17,000 medicinal uses of 2,137 plant species in 142 families that are ethnographically documented in North America. While this current documented database provides a tremendous corpus of information to study, there is undoubtedly more knowledge of Native North American medicines still to be recorded.

What about the past? Was knowledge of medicinal plants and animals lost before and after European contact? No doubt much was, but this knowledge may not be lost forever, as some assume. People leave material evidence of their lives—the archaeological record. Although archaeologists and specialists studying organic remains from prehistoric sites focus on foodstuffs, there is increasing interest in the use of prehistoric medicines (e.g., Reinhard, Hamilton, and Hevley 1991). For example, Karl Reinhard, Richard Ambler, and Magdalene McGuffie (1985) note that paleofeces with goosefoot seeds (*Chenopodium* sp.) from a cave in southern Utah seem to have a lower incidence of parasitic infestations.

Crop Diversity

Much concern has been expressed about the erosion of global crop diversity, the end product of 10,000 years of selection, domestication, and farming by local groups throughout the world (e.g.,

Fowler and Mooney 1990; but see Brush 1992). Thousands of regional domesticated species and crop varieties are a rich gene pool for developing higher-yielding, better-adapted cultigens and more nutritious foodstuffs. A critical part of our human inheritance and biological resources could slip away. To reverse this trend, governments and nongovernmental organizations, such as Native Seeds/SEARCH in the Southwest, are working to preserve indigenous heirloom seeds in North America.

The agricultural heritage of southern North America in Mexico is well appreciated, as this region is one of the premier centers of crop domestication. America north of Mexico, in contrast, is not well appreciated but may prove a greater resource than previously thought (see Ford [1981] for a summary of prehistoric crop histories in North America), despite the widespread characterization of North America as a place of little consequence regarding the development of crops. The image is well known: prehistoric Native Americans cultivated crops—mainly maize, beans, and squash—domesticated in Mesoamerica, and they then used Old World crops introduced after contact. The only widely known crop domesticated in North America north of Mexico is the sunflower (*Helianthus annuus*), although some are also familiar with a related domesticate, the Jerusalem artichoke or sunchoke (*Helianthus tuberosus*).

This popular image masks a dynamic history of indigenous agriculture in North America by minimizing two contributions: native crops of North America and Native North American agricultural techniques and strategies. Native North Americans domesticated many indigenous cultigens, although most of them are poorly known. These include extant crops such as Sonoran panic grass (*Panicum sonorum*), Devil's claw (*Proboscidea parviflora*), the gourdy squash (*Cucurbita pepo* var. *ovifera*), various species of the century plant or mescal (*Agave* spp.), and possibly the tepary bean (*Phaseolus acutifolius* var. *acutifolius*) (Fish et al. 1985; Nabhan 1989; Nabhan and de Wet 1984; Nabhan et al. 1981).

Crop diversity should not be limited to noting those that still exist. We have a record of what are now extinct crops, which were domesticated in prehistory but no longer exist in their domesticated form and are known only from the archaeological record. Only the domesticated forms of these species are extinct; the wild forms are still growing. Examples from eastern North America include a knotweed (*Polygonum erectum*), goosefoot (*Chenopodium berlandieri* ssp. *jonesianum*), sumpweed (*Iva annua* var. *macrocarpa*), and little barley (*Hordeum pusillum*) (e.g., Fritz, this volume; Scarry 1993; Smith 1992; Yarnell 1987). In addition, there are dozens of other species that may have been domesticated or at least highly managed by prehistoric people in western North America (e.g., Fowler 1986; Nabhan 1985b; Winter 1974; Winter and Hogan 1986; Yarnell 1977).

The rapidly expanding list of now extinct crops is not simply esoteric knowledge; it may have substantial practical utility. Perhaps we can increase the number of available cultigens and cultivars by redomestication. These crops may now be extinct, but we know that their extant wild progenitors are amenable to domestication by the best evidence possible: they once were crops.

Farming Strategies

Agriculture is more than crops; it is agroecology, including strategies and techniques based on knowledge of ecological conditions and processes (e.g., Altieri 1995; Swift et al. 1996). Native North Americans developed approaches to growing crops successfully in locations that would appear to be marginally suitable or incapable of cultivation by industrial agriculture. Chinampa ("floating garden") fields in the Basin of Mexico (e.g., González 1992) and Hopi sand-dune agriculture of semiarid northern Arizona (e.g., Bradfield 1971; Whiting 1939) are two of the best-known examples. There are many other examples of ingenious indigenous agriculture successfully adapted to local conditions throughout North America (e.g., Ebeling 1986; Hurt 1987; Vecsey and Venables 1980).

Again, the abundant record of prehistoric peoples in North America provides descriptions of agricultural techniques adapted to local conditions (for southwestern examples, see Fish and Fish [1984] and Toll [1995]). Techniques most easily seen in the archaeological record include permanent facilities such as irrigation (e.g., Doolittle 1990), terracing (e.g., Donkin 1979), and rock mulching (e.g., Lightfoot 1996). Following in this tradition, Ford (this volume) emphasizes prehistoric agroecology through a conceptual framework he terms "cultural topography."

Information about prehistoric agricultural techniques and strategies may have practical value, although we know of no example from North America that matches the reintroduction of a prehistoric agricultural technology such as that achieved in South America (Kolata 1996). While it is unlikely that prehistoric techniques will be employed directly in the industrial food production of North America, techniques such as terracing or rock mulching might prove productive for small-scale agriculture, specialty horticulture, or gardening. This is especially true as humans expand into upland and other settings less suited for familiar agricultural and gardening practices. Quite frequently Native North Americans have conducted these experiments, selecting for suitable biotypes and optimizing growth conditions.

Native Foods

In addition to crops, Native North Americans consumed hundreds of different wild edible plants. The large number of popular books describing the edible plants of North America and how to prepare them is evidence that many people are interested in native foods, although one wonders how many of these readers actually consume more than small amounts of wild foods. Nonetheless, knowledge of these foods can increase dietary variety and healthfulness (e.g., Nabhan 1985a). Additionally, these foods can be used in emergencies. While this seems a remote possibility and overly alarmist in the wealthy and overfed countries of northern North America, one should remember that native plants have sustained groups for millennia during times of agricultural abundance and, as importantly, in times of want (Minnis 1991). As recently as a half-century ago, the government of the Netherlands issued a pamphlet identifying and describing the use of wild plants to help feed a starving populace during World War II (Den Hartog 1981).

Storage Technology

Growing crops and gathering naturally available foods are merely the first steps in food use. Edibles must be stored for varying lengths of time, especially in temperate climates with a season not suitable for plant growth. Storage technology is also important, because postharvest lost to predation can reduce available food. A 10% loss during storage is more than equal to the same increase in yields, and storage loss is a problem in some areas of the world. Food can be stored safely and efficiently in a number of ways. Prominent Native American examples include Hidatsa pit storage (Wilson 1917) and granaries in northern and central Mexico (Hernández X. 1949). Some indigenous techniques may be adaptable to industrial and peasant agriculture and facilitate sustainable development strategies, not unlike the modification of aboriginal corn-crib designs by Euro-Americans (Hardeman 1981).

DISCUSSION AND CONCLUSIONS

The contributors to this volume are drawn together by a conviction that the prehistoric, historic, and modern experiences of Native North Americans have utility and value—to themselves and to others—in North America and elsewhere. The struggles of Native Americans to adapt to an ecologically diverse continent resulted in a body of knowledge and experiences providing important information about biological diversity, ecological relationships, resource management, and natural products. Specifically, Native North Americans discovered many medicines, some of which no doubt will be useful beyond their original healing systems. Additionally, a number of extant and now extinct plants of North America were domesticated, and their role in filling the world's larder and expanding agroeconomic strategies might increase. Ancient North Americans also developed a number of distinct cultivars of what were originally Mesoamerican domesticates. Their value is well known, since modern hybrid dent corn was derived largely from Native North American varieties (Mangelsdorf 1974). Agriculture is more than crops; creative farming techniques adapted to often suboptimal conditions extend our knowledge of agricultural practices. Native American storage technology, as well, might prove valuable for reducing postharvest loss.

Indigenous peoples have been and are keen observers of their natural setting and of ecological processes; they have to be, since their livelihoods often depend on their knowledge. The collective view of the contributors to this volume is that "folk" and "scientific" ecology are complementary. The long tradition of experimentation, manipulation, and experiences in native North American ecosystems by indigenous peoples should not be overlooked by Western-trained scientists in developing ecological paradigms and management protocols (e.g., Collins and Wallace 1990; Kay 1995; Pina and Covington 1994). In studying biogeographical patterns and ecological processes among the extant North American biota, we should consider both paleoenvironmental change during the Quaternary (e.g., Tausch et al. 1995) and the fact that Native peoples managed natural resources and deliberately altered ecosystems for thousands of years (Delcourt, Delcourt, Cridlebaugh, and Chapman 1986). This is in marked contrast to the "traditional" view that North America was a vast "wilderness" untouched by humans prior to the arrival of Europeans; it has direct implications for establishing ecological "baselines" (Hunter 1996) and for developing conservation, restoration, and management strategies of biological resources (e.g., Gadgil 1996; Jordan 1997; Martinez 1994; Snape 1996).

The chapters in this volume show unambiguously how Native Americans were and are active participants in their environments. Understanding their ecological role is the first step. Political and cultural empowerment, however, is a necessary component for continuing the adaptation of Native North Americans in an age of powerful nation states and a globalized economy. Maintaining biodiversity—whether organismic, ecological, or agricultural— necessitates a concomitant concern for the loss of cultural and linguistic diversity (Brush 1996; Johnson 1994; Kemf 1993; Oldfield and Alcorn 1991; Orlove and Brush 1996). This is as true for Native North America as it is for groups elsewhere. The point is not to dictate that indigenous peoples live frozen in time and in ways assumed by outsiders to be "traditional," but rather to acknowledge their self-determination and the dynamic nature of human and biological adaptations. This can present challenges when the goals of indigenous peoples and conservationists do not mesh completely (e.g., Conklin and Graham 1995; Prybyla and Barth 1996; Redford and Mansour 1996).

A central concern for empowerment is control of intellectual property rights and compensation for knowledge. These issues are culturally, legally, and ethically complex (e.g., Snape 1996) and are not the focus of this volume. Nonetheless, Lewis (this volume), who has experience with these issues in South America, considers the application of intellectual property rights procedures for North America. The issue gets more complicated; no one, to our knowledge, has seriously considered the relationships between intellectual property rights and prehistoric ethnobiological resources. Do aboriginal peoples, for example, have special privilege regarding the biological efforts of their ancestors if they themselves have no knowledge of these plants or animals in their living cultural traditions? What if one of the now-extinct crops of eastern North America is redomesticated and used?

All peoples of the world can benefit from a more sophisticated understanding of the contributions of Native North Americans; our knowledge is expanded by knowing about available resources and how to use them wisely, as well as by knowing how to manage the environments and biological resources of North America better. Preservation and increased use of Native North American expertise, however, have benefits for the people who generated this knowledge. Active Native American participation in Native Seeds/ SEARCH's efforts to preserve traditional land races and to reduce horrendous rates of diabetes by increasing the use of traditional food of the Sonoran Desert is but one example (e.g., Nabhan et al. 1996). The 1995 workshop "Building Bridges between American Indians and Conservation Organizations," cosponsored by the World Wildlife Fund and the Native American Fish and Wildlife Society, represents a similar collaborative effort (Prybyla and Barth 1996). Lastly, within weeks of writing this essay, a working conference, "Native American Traditional and Sustainable Agriculture," was sponsored by the Sac and Fox Nation and by the Thâkîwa Foundation in Stroud, Oklahoma. Active participation by aboriginal peoples is essential, not only for ethical and practical reasons, but simply because this participation keeps the tradition of adaptation to changing circumstances alive. Native North American ecology is not dead; it is an ongoing process crucial for environmental and cultural sustainability.

ACKNOWLEDGMENTS

All of the chapters in this volume but one (Hammett) were prepared for the workshop "Biodiversity and Native North America," held at the University of Oklahoma at Norman, on February 21–22, 1997. We are grateful to R. P. Stephen Davis, Jr., and Vincas Steponaitis for granting permission to reprint Hammett's chapter, originally published in *Southern Indian Studies*. The Associates of the College of Arts and Sciences are thanked for financial support. Kate Held, Gail Jones, Melissa Rickman, Jennifer Nisengard, and Warren Lail assisted greatly during the workshop. Patricia Gilman, Ross Hassig, David Levy, and Donald Pisani commented on this introduction. We appreciate the professionalism of John Drayton, Jo Ann Reece, and Randolph Lewis, at the University of Oklahoma Press, who helped produce this volume. Thanks to all for your suggestions and efforts.

REFERENCES CITED

Altieri, Miguel. 1995. *Agroecology: The Science of Sustainable Agriculture.* Boulder: Westview Press.

Anderson, E. N. 1996. *Ecologies of the Heart: Emotion, Belief, and the Environment.* Oxford: Oxford University Press.

Anderson, M. Kat. 1991. California Indian Horticulture: Management and Use of Redbud by the Southern Sierra Miwok. *Journal of Ethnobiology* 11:145–57.

————. 1996. The Ethnobotany of Deergrass, *Muhlenbergia rigens* (Poaceae): Its Use and Fire Management by California Tribes. *Economic Botany* 50:409–22.

Axelrod, D. I. 1985. Rise of the Grasslands Biome, Central North America. *Botanical Review* 51:163–201.

Banyacya, Thomas. 1994. Address. In *Voices of Indigenous Peoples: Native People Address the United Nations,* edited by A. Ewen, pp. 112–18. Santa Fe: Clear Light Publishers.

Betancourt, J. H., T. R. Van Devender, and P. S. Martin. 1990. *Packrat Middens: The Last 40,000 Years of Biotic Change.* Tucson: University of Arizona Press.

Botkin, Daniel. 1990. *Discordant Harmonies: A New Ecology for the Twenty-first Century.* Oxford: Oxford University Press.

Bradfield, Maitland. 1971. *The Changing Pattern of Hopi Agriculture.* Occasional Papers No. 3. London: Royal Anthropological Institute.

Brown, J. H., and M. V. Lomolino. 1998. *Biogeography.* Sunderland, Mass.: Sinauer Associates.

Brush, Stephen B. 1992. Reconsidering the Green Revolution: Diversity and Stability in Cradle Areas of Crop Domestication. *Human Ecology* 20:145–68.

————. 1996. Whose Knowledge, Whose Genes, Whose Rights? In *Valuing Local Knowledge*, edited by S. Brush and D. Stabinsky, pp. 1–24. Washington, D.C.: Island Press.

Brush, Stephen B., and Doreen Stabinsky. 1996. *Valuing Local Knowledge: Indigenous People and Intellectual Property Rights.* Washington, D.C.: Island Press.

Collins, S. L., and L. L. Wallace. 1990. *Fire in North American Tallgrass Prairies.* Norman: University of Oklahoma Press.

Conklin, Beth A., and Laura A. Graham. 1995. The Shifting Middle Ground: Amazonian Indians and Eco-Politics. *American Anthropologist* 97(4):695–710.

Cronon, William. 1984. *Changes in the Land: Indians, Colonists, and the Ecology of New England.* New York: Hill and Wang.

Crosby, Alfred W. 1986. *Ecological Imperialism: The Biological Expansion of Europe, 900–1900.* Cambridge: Cambridge University Press.

Crumley, Carole L. 1994. *Historical Ecology: Cultural Knowledge and Changing Landscapes.* Santa Fe: School of American Research Press.

Delcourt, Hazel R. 1987. The Impact of Prehistoric Agriculture and Land Occupation on Natural Vegetation. *Trends in Ecology and Evolution* 2:39–44.

Delcourt, Hazel R., and Paul A. Delcourt. 1991. *Quaternary Ecology: A Paleoecological Perspective.* London: Chapman and Hall.

Delcourt, P. A., H. R. Delcourt, P. A. Cridlebaugh, and J. Chapman. 1986. Holocene Ethnobotanical and Paleoecological Record of Human Impact on Vegetation in the Little Tennessee River Valley, Tennessee, USA. *Quaternary Research* 25:330–49.

Delcourt, P. A., H. R. Delcourt, D. F. Morse, and P. A. Morse. 1986. History, Evolution, and Organization of Vegetation and Human Culture. In *Biodiversity of the Southeastern United States,* edited by W. H. Martin, S. G. Boyce, and A. C. Echternacht, pp. 47–79. New York: J. Wiley and Sons.

Denevan, William. 1992. *The Native Population of the Americas in 1492.* Madison: University of Wisconsin Press.

Den Hartog, Adel P. 1981. Adjustments of Food Behavior during Famine. In *Famine: Its Causes, Effects, and Management,* edited by J. Robson, pp. 125–62. New York: Gordon and Breach.

Donkin, R. A. 1979. *Agricultural Terracing in the Aboriginal New World.* Tucson: University of Arizona Press.

Doolittle, William E. 1990. *Canal Irrigation in Prehistoric Mexico: The Sequence of Technological Change.* Austin: University of Texas Press.

Downes, David R. 1996. Global Trade, Local Economies, and the Bio-diversity Convention. In *Biodiversity and the Law*, edited by W. J. Snape III, pp. 202–16. Washington, D.C.: Island Press.

Ebeling, Walter. 1986. *Handbook of Indian Food and Fibers of Arid America.* Berkeley: University of California Press.

Fish, Suzanne K., and Paul R. Fish. 1984. *Prehistoric Agricultural Strategies in the Southwest.* Anthropological Research Papers No. 33. Tempe: Arizona State University.

Fish, Suzanne K., Paul R. Fish, Charles Mikesicek, and John Madsen. 1985. Prehistoric *Agave* Cultivation in Southern Arizona. *Desert Plants* 7:107–13.

Ford, Richard I. 1981. Gardening and Farming before a.d. 1000: Patterns of Prehistoric Cultivation North of Mexico. *Journal of Ethnobiology* 1:6–27.

Fowler, Cary, and Pat Mooney. 1990. *Shattering: Food, Politics, and the Loss of Genetic Diversity.* Tucson: University of Arizona Press.

Fowler, Catherine S. 1986. Subsistence. In *Handbook of North American Indians, Vol. 11, Great Basin*, edited by W. d'Azevedo, pp. 64–97. Washington, D.C.: Smithsonian Institution Press.

Furze, Brian, Terry De Lacy, and Jim Brickhead. 1996. *Culture, Conservation, and Biodiversity: The Social Development and Conservation through Protected Areas.* Chichester: John Wiley and Sons.

Gadgil, M. 1996. Managing Biodiversity. In *Biodiversity: A Biology of Numbers and Difference*, edited by K. J. Gaston, pp. 345–66. Cambridge, Mass.: Blackwell Sciences.

Gentry, A. H. 1982. Patterns of Neotropical Plant Species Diversity. *Evolutionary Biology* 15:1–84.

González, Carlos Javier. 1992. *Chinampas prehispánicas.* Mexico City: Instituto Nacional de Antropología y Historia.

Hardeman, Nicholas P. 1981. *Shucks, Shocks, and Hominy Block: Corn a Way of Life in Pioneer America.* Baton Rouge: Louisiana State University Press.

Hernández Xolocotzi, Efraím. 1949. *Maize Granaries in Mexico.* Botanical Museum Leaflet 13, No. 7. Cambridge, Mass.: Harvard University.

Hunter, M. 1996. Benchmarks for Managing Ecosystems: Are Human Activities Natural? *Conservation Biology* 10:695–97.

Hurt, R. Douglas. 1987. *Indian Agriculture in America, Prehistory to the Present.* Lawrence: University Press of Kansas.

Janzen, D. H. 1997. Wildland Biodiversity Management in the Tropics. In *Biodiversity II*, edited by M. L. Reaka-Kudla, D. E. Wilson, and E. O. Wilson, pp. 411–31. Washington, D.C.: Joseph Henry Press.

Johnson, B. A. 1994. *Who Pays the Price?: The Sociocultural Context of Environmental Crisis*. Washington, D.C.: Island Press.

Jordan, W. R. 1997. Ecological Resortation and the Conservation of Biodiversity. In *Biodiversity II*, edited by M. L. Reaka-Kudela, D. E. Wilson, and E. O. Wilson, pp. 371–87. Washington, D.C.: Joseph Henry Press.

Kangas, P. 1997. Tropical Sustainable Development and Biodiversity. In *Biodiversity II*, edited by M. L. Reaka-Kudla, D. E. Wilson, and E. O. Wilson, pp. 389–409. Washington, D.C.: Joseph Henry Press.

Kay, C. E. 1995. Aboriginal Overkill and Native Burning: Implications for Modern Ecosystems. *Western Journal of Applied Forestry* 10:120–26.

Kay, Margarita A. 1996. *Healing with Plants in the American and Mexican West*. Tucson: University of Arizona Press.

Kemf, Elizabeth. 1993. *The Law of the Mother: Protecting Indigenous Peoples in Protected Areas*. San Francisco: Sierra Club.

Kindscher, Kelly. 1992. *Medicinal Wild Plants of the Prairie*. Lawrence: University Press of Kansas.

King, Stephen R., Thomas J. Carlson, and Katy Moran. 1996. Biological Diversity, Indigenous Knowledge, Drug Discovery, and Intellectual Property Rights. In *Valuing Local Knowledge*, edited by S. Brush and D. Stabinsky, pp. 167–85. Washington, D.C.: Island Press.

Kohler, Timothy A. 1992. Prehistoric Human Impact on the Environment in the Upland North American Southwest. *Population and Environment* 13:255–68.

Kolata, Alan K. 1996. *Tiwanaku and Its Hinterland: Archaeology and Paleoecology of an Andean Civilization: Agroecology*. Washington, D.C.: Smithsonian Institution Press.

Lewis, Walter H., and M. P. F. Elvin-Lewis. 1977. *Medical Botany: Plants Affecting Man's Health*. New York: John Wiley and Sons.

Lightfoot, Dale R. 1996. The Nature, History, and Distribution of Lithic Mulch Agriculture: An Ancient Technique of Dryland Agriculture. *Agricultural History Review* 44:206–22.

McAndrews, J. H. 1988. Human Disturbance of North American Forests and Grasslands: The Fossil Pollen Record. In *Vegetation History*, edited by B. Huntley and T. Webb, pp. 673–97. Boston: Kluwer Academic Publishers.

Mangelsdorf, Paul C. 1974. *Corn: Its Origins, Evolution, and Improvement*. Cambridge, Mass.: Belknap Press of Harvard University.

Martin, Paul S., and Richard G. Klein. 1984. *Quaternary Extinctions: A Prehistoric Revolution*. Tucson: University of Arizona Press.

Martinez, D. 1994. Back to the Future: Ecological Restoration, the Histor-
    ical Forest, and Traditional Indian Management. In *Proceedings of the
    Fifteenth Annual Forest Vegetation Management Conference*, pp. 121–46.
    Redding, Calif.: Forest Vegetation Management Conference.

Millspaugh, Charles F. 1892. *Medicinal Plants*. Philadelphia: John C.
    Yourston.

Minnis, Paul E. 1985. *Social Adaptation to Food Stress: A Prehistoric
    Southwestern Example*. Chicago: University of Chicago Press.

———. 1991. Famine Foods of the Northern American Desert Borderlands
    in Historical Context. *Journal of Ethnobiology* 11:231–57.

Moerman, Daniel E. 1986. *Medicinal Plants of Native America*. Museum of
    Anthropology Technical Reports No. 19. Ann Arbor: University of
    Michigan.

Moore, Michael. 1979. *Medicinal Plants of the Mountain West*. Santa Fe:
    Museum of New Mexico Press.

Nabhan, Gary P. 1985a. *Gathering the Desert*. Tucson: University of Arizona
    Press.

———. 1985b. Native Crop Diversity in Aridoamerica: Conservation of
    Regional Gene Pools. *Economic Botany* 39:387–99.

———. 1989. *Enduring Seeds: Native American Agriculture and Wild Plant
    Conservation*. Berkeley: North Point Press.

Nabhan, Gary P., Angelo Joaquin, Jr., Nancy Laney, and Kevin Dahl. 1996.
    Sharing the Benefits of Plant Resources and Indigenous Scientific
    Knowledge. In *Valuing Local Knowledge: Indigenous and Intellectual
    Property Rights*, edited by S. Brush and D. Stabinsky, pp. 186–208.
    Washington, D.C.: Island Press.

Nabhan, Gary P., and J. de Wet. 1984. *Panicum sonorum* in Sonoran Desert
    Agriculture. *Economic Botany* 38:65–68.

Nabhan, Gary P., Alfred Whiting, Henry Dobyns, Richard Hevley, and
    Robert Euler. 1981. Devil's Claw Domestication: Evidence from
    Southwestern Indian Fields. *Journal of Ethnobiology* 1:135–64.

Oldfield, Margery L., and Janis B. Alcorn. 1991. *Biodiversity: Culture,
    Conservation, and Ecodevelopment*. Boulder: Westview Press.

Orlove, Benjamin S., and Stephen B. Brush. 1996. Anthropology and the
    Conservation of Biodiversity. *Annual Reviews of Anthropology* 25:329–52.

Pina, V. Y., and W. W. Covington. 1994. Conservation Biology, Restoration
    Ecology, and a Navajo View of Nature. In *Sustainable Ecological Systems:
    Implementing an Ecological Approach to Land Management*, edited by
    W. W. Covington and L. F. DeBano, pp. 122–24. Rocky Mountain Forest

and Range Management Experiment Station, General Technical Report RM 247. Fort Collins, Colo.: USDA Forest Service.

Plotkin, Mark. 1993. *Tales of a Shaman's Apprentice.* New York: Viking.

Prybyla, D., and S. Barth. 1996. *Building Bridges between American Indians and Conservation Organizations.* WWF Topics in Conservation Report. Washington, D.C.: World Wildlife Fund.

Rappaport, Roy A. 1979. *Ecology, Meaning, and Religion.* Berkeley: North Atlantic Books.

Redford, Kent H., and Jane A. Mansour. 1996. *Traditional Peoples and Biodiversity Conservation in Large Tropical Landscapes.* Arlington, Va.: America Verde Publications.

Reinhard, Karl J., J. Richard Ambler, and Magdalene McGuffie. 1985. Diet and Parasitism at Dust Devil Cave. *American Antiquity* 50:819–24.

Reinhard, Karl J., D. J. Hamilton, and R. I. Hevley. 1991. Use of Pollen Concentrations in Paleopharmacology: Coprolite Evidence of Medicinal Plants. *Journal of Ethnobiology* 11:117–32.

Ritchie, J. C. 1987. *Postglacial Vegetation of Canada.* New York: Cambridge University Press.

Russell, E. W. B. 1983. Indian-Set Fires in the Forests of the Northeastern United States. *Ecology* 64:78–88.

Rzedowski, Jerzy. 1978. *Vegetación de México.* Mexico City: Editorial Limusa.

Salmón, Enrique. 1996. Decolonizing Our Voice. *Winds of Change* (Summer): 70–72.

Scarry, C. Margaret. 1993. *Foraging and Farming in Eastern Woodlands.* Gainesville: University of Florida Press.

Schultes, Richard E., and Robert F. Raffauf. 1990. *The Healing Forest: Medicinal and Toxic Plants of the Northwestern Amazonia.* Portland: Timber Press.

Schultes, Richard E., and Siri Von Reis. 1995. *Ethnobotany: The Evolution of a Discipline.* Portland: Timber Press.

Smith, Bruce D. 1992. *Rivers of Change: Essays on Early Agriculture in Eastern North America.* Washington, D.C.: Smithsonian Institution Press.

Snape, William, III. 1996. *Biodiversity and the Law.* Washington, D.C.: Island Press.

Stahl, Peter W. 1996. Holocene Biodiversity: Archaeological Perspective from the Americas. *Annual Review of Anthropology* 25:105–26.

Stevens, Stan. 1997. *Conservation through Cultural Survival: Indigenous Peoples and Protected Areas.* Washington, D.C.: Island Press.

Swift, M. J., J. Vandermeer, P. S. Ramakrishnan, J. M. Anderson, C. K. King, and B. A. Hawkins. 1996. Biodiversity and Agroecosystem Function. In *Functional Roles in Biodiversity: A Global Perspective*, edited by H. A. Mooney, J. H. Hall, E. Medina, O. E. Sala, and E. D. Schulze, pp. 261–98. Chichester: John Wiley and Sons.

Tausch, R. J., R. S. Nowak, and C. L. Nowak. 1995. Climate Change and Plant Species Responses over the Quaternary: Implications for Ecosystem Management. In *Interior West Global Change Workshop*, edited by R. W. Tinus, pp. 14–19. Rocky Mountain Forest and Range Experiment Station, General Technical Report RM 262. Fort Collins, Colo.: USDA Forest Service.

Toll, H. Wolcott. 1995. *Soil, Water, Biology, and Belief in Prehistoric and Traditional Southwestern Agriculture.* Special Publication No. 2. Albuquerque: New Mexico Archaeological Council.

Vecsey, Christopher, and Robert W. Venables. 1980. *American Indian Environments: Ecological Issues in Native American History.* Syracuse: Syracuse University Press.

Vogel, Virgil J. 1970. *American Indian Medicine.* Norman: University of Oklahoma Press.

Whiting, Alfred F. 1939. *Ethnobotany of the Hopi.* Bulletin No. 15. Flagstaff: Museum of Northern Arizona.

Wilson, Gilbert L. 1917. *Agriculture of the Hidatsa Indians: An Indian Interpretation.* Studies in Social Sciences No. 9. Minneapolis: University of Minnesota.

Winter, Joseph C. 1974. Aboriginal Agriculture in the Southwest and Great Basin. Ph.D. dissertation. Department of Anthropology, University of Utah, Salt Lake City.

Winter, Joseph C., and Paul F. Hogan. 1986. Plant Husbandry in the Great Basin and Adjacent Northern Colorado Plateau. In *Anthropology of the Desert West: Essays in Honor of Jesse D. Jennings*, edited by C. J. Condie and D. D. Fowler, pp. 117–44. Anthropological Papers No. 10. Salt Lake City: University of Utah Press.

Yarnell, Richard I. 1977. Native Plant Husbandry North of Mexico. In *Origins of Agriculture*, edited by C. Reed, pp. 861–75. The Hague: Mouton Press.

———. 1987. A Survey of Prehistoric Crop Plants in Eastern North America. *Missouri Archaeologist* 47:47–60.

Issues and Overviews

Native American Management and Conservation of Biodiversity in the Sonoran Desert Bioregion

An Ethnoecological Perspective

GARY PAUL NABHAN

The claim that Native Americans were "the first ecologists" has been hotly debated; unfortunately, there have been few longitudinal studies conducted that could confirm or deny the premise that, over time, indigenous management practices based on traditional ecological knowledge have positively benefited local or regional biodiversity. One approach to this issue is the analysis of intensively documented case studies of indigenous perception, use, management and/or conservation of particular plant and animal resources within a particular biome. Within the Sonoran Desert region straddling the U.S./Mexico border, some twenty indigenous cultures continue to interact actively with the native biota, using orally transmitted perceptions and management techniques to influence vegetation and faunal densities. For example, Sonoran Desert peoples have translocated, hybridized, and managed populations of animals such as the Piebald Chuckwalla (*Sauromalus varius*), the Black Chuckwalla (*Sauromalus hispidus*), and the spiny-tailed iguana (*Ctenosaura hemilopha*) (Nabhan in press). Basketry, food, and medicinal plants are harvested, pruned, and sometimes transplanted or actively managed by controlled burns. Other plants such as the Hohokam agave (*Agave murpheyi*) were prehistorically domesticated and transplanted on hundreds of thousands of hectares of desert-scrub uplands and riparian forests on floodplains. More recently, selected plants such as a basketry fiber, devil's claw (*Proboscidea parviflora* var. *Hohokamiana*), were domesticated entirely within the region, and a number of food and medicinal plants such as saiya (*Amoreuxia palmatifida*) and yerba mansa (*Anemopsis californica*) have been brought into cultivation in Yoemem and O'odham Indian villages because of their diminished access to wild populations.

Among the extant Sonoran Desert cultures, farmers and hunter-gatherers recognize, name, and in some cases manage ecological interactions between dozens of rare native plants and animals, which are the focus of this discussion, since they are the component of biodiversity most likely to be lost. It is my hope that a fuller understanding of their knowledge of ecological interactions involving threatened species may offer Western-trained scientists and resource managers better ways to manage and conserve threatened species and their ecological associates.

Slowing the loss of diversity is currently a major preoccupation both of conservation biologists concerned with disappearing species (Wilson 1992) and of linguistic anthropologists concerned with disappearing languages (Hale 1992; Wurm 1991; Zepeda and Hill 1991). In the Sonoran Desert region, over five hundred endemic plants and at least seventy-five endemic vertebrates are faced with a variety of land use pressures of unprecedented magnitude, since the human population of the region has grown sevenfold within just the last fifty years. Similarly, cultures such as the Mayo, Lowland Pima, Cocopa, and Maricopa have a low percentage of the entire communities that speak their native languages (Hinton 1994; Zepeda and Hill 1991), while other groups such as the Seri retain a higher percentage of native speakers in their population, but population size overall is small (ca. 550). Of course, cultural and environmental changes are inevitable (Spicer 1980). The concern is that such changes have accelerated. Both native desert species and cultures have so many new pressures upon them and their habitats that interventions on their behalf must be implemented or dramatic losses will occur. And yet the intervention strategies chosen will vary greatly depending on how one defines biodiversity and linguistic diversity and on how one identifies proximate and ultimate causes of these losses (Nabhan 1994).

In practice, biodiversity has been discussed largely in terms of "species richness," although most conservation biologists recognize the contribution of other levels of biological organization (genetic variation within populations, variability between populations, habitat heterogeneity, ecosystem diversity) that are more difficult to monitor or measure (Harmon 1996; Office of Technology Assessment 1987). As J. N. Thompson (1996:300) has recently argued, there is another, often overlooked element of diversity: "the diversity of life has resulted from the diversification of species and the interactions that occur among them . . . nevertheless, the focus of studies on the conservation of biodiversity has often been primarily on species rather than interactions." Of course, the ways in which plants' and animals' interactions with their ecological associates are modified by persistent uses by Native Americans are part of this interaction diversity. However, ignorance of such biotic interactions has led to the decline of particular plant species that have lost their mutualists (and in some cases their human harvesters and pruners) even though they occur within a formally protected area such as a national park or forest (Tewksbury et al. 1999).

Similarly, most assessments of linguistic diversity focus merely on how many extant languages there are ("language richness"), on the declining abundance of living speakers of indigenous languages ("speaker richness"), or on the erosion of idiomatic vocabularies ("lexical richness"). Relatively few studies have looked at inter-actions within or among languages, such as the deterioration of structural differentiation within a language (Hill 1995).

A related dilemma has plagued ethnobiology, the study of cultural perceptions of and interactions with the earth's biodiver-sity. Recognizing that both cultural traditions and lifeforms are rapidly disappearing, some ethnobiologists have gone into certain biomes among imperiled cultures to "salvage" their ethnopharma-cological knowledge for posterity by pressing plant samples, recording names, then tallying up how many medicine plant species remain culturally utilized. However, most of these salvage ethnobotany missions only scratch the surface of "indigenous knowledge about the natural world" by simply recording indige-nous names for plants and cataloguing their uses, rather than assessing how human interactions affect the plants. Such descrip-tive, purely utilitarian ethnobotanical surveys hardly tell us anything about how "the natural world works" from an indigenous perspec-tive or how indigenous extraction and management decrease or enhance local biodiversity. In this way, ethnobotanists mirror "biodiversity systematists" who ignore ecological interactions but demonstrate how "species can be counted and classified, preserved as voucher specimens, and mapped in the search for regions of high population abundance or hotspots of overall species richness" (Thompson 1996:300).

At the same time, many evolutionary ecologists have become skeptical when ethnobiologists speak of indigenous peoples as "the first ecologists" because these scholars are unaware of any truly ecological knowledge derived from ethnobiological field studies. Published inventories of useful plants named in native languages typically appear to be lacking any ecological or evolutionary context.

I propose a strengthened or renewed focus on traditional ecolog-ical knowledge of plant-animal interactions for ethnobiological field studies to overcome the above-mentioned methodological and philosophical inadequacies. I suggest that indigenous cultures retain a wealth of linguistically encoded empirical knowledge about ecological relationships among plants and animals, based on observations of interspecific interactions that may have escaped notice by field biologists. Although some indigenous observations may seem irrational or counterintuitive when one first looks at ethnoecological accounts, they may in fact be linguistically encoded means of validly explaining certain relationships between plants and animals (Anderson 1996). I demonstrate that some indigenous hypotheses about the nature of plant/animal interactions can be tested by Western scientific means, resulting in insights of significance to ecological and evolutionary theory. I also address how ethnoecological studies of interaction diversity can contribute to the conservation of biodiversity, particularly when the relationships that indigenous peoples recognize and describe are between rare or endemic species. Finally, I suggest a few ways in which such knowledge itself can be conserved and integrated into endangered species and habitat recovery programs.

METHODS

I will use examples from just two cultural groups within the Sonoran Desert with whom I have studied for two decades: the Comcáac or Seri, a subset of Hokan speakers of Sonora, Mexico; and the O'odham (Desert Papago, Sand Papago, River Pima, and Lowland Pima), a subset of Uto-Aztecan speakers of Arizona, USA, and Sonora, Mexico. The Seri, as they are commonly called in Mexico, number less than 600 individuals residing in two permanent villages and several temporary fishing camps on the Sea of Cortez coast of Sonora, near Tiburón Island, which is also part of their aboriginal territory. The O'odham or Northern Piman speakers number 18,000 to 21,000 individuals living in south-central Arizona and adjacent Sonora. I have interviewed between 50 and 100 individuals among older generations in these two tribal communities. Interviews were typically accomplished in Spanish and English, with native Seri and O'odham terms used as prompts; when interviewing monolingual speakers, I was usually accompanied by bilingual relatives of the person(s), who translated and verified my understanding of the responses. On several occasions, sightings of the rare plant or animal elicited commentary; in most cases, however, because of the rarity of the organisms, photos and drawings of the organisms in question were utilized to elicit discussion. Folk taxonomic information for the O'odham and Seri was corroborated by consulting recently completed linguistic and ethnographic works (Felger and Moser 1985; Rea 1983, 1997) as well as my own Seri ethnoherpetological overview (Nabhan in press).

DEFINING ETHNOECOLOGY

One of the earliest definitions of ethnoecology was published by Robert Bye, Jr., and Maurice Zigmond (1976): "the area of study that attempts to illuminate in an *ecologically* revealing fashion man's interactions with and relationship to his environment." Despite the many ethnobiological books and journal articles published since that time, only a few scholars have sought to reveal how human cultures recognize and influence the ecological relationships between plants and animals in their environment (Rea 1983, 1997; Peacock and Turner, this volume). Fewer still have chosen to focus their research on indigenous knowledge of specific ecological interactions between plants and animals. Nevertheless, a range of indigenous knowledge of biotic interactions can be demonstrated in the following examples, taken largely from my work with colleagues in the Sonoran Desert of Arizona and Sonora, Mexico.

Imbedded in any folk taxonomy are numerous references to interactions among taxa. Plant names may make evident a particular animal's use of a particular plant: for example, *hap oacajam*, 'what mule deer flay antlers on' (Felger and Moser 1985). Among the Seri, this name refers collectively to three shrubs used by a particular subpopulation of mule deer stags to scrape velvet off their new antlers (*Caesalpinia palmeri, Echinopterys eglandulosa,* and *Thryallis angustifolia*). Analysis of the folk taxonomy of the Seri (Felger and Moser 1985) indicates that 10% of the terminal ethnotaxa for plants have faunal referents within them. However, my follow-up interviews with the Seri reveal that only 4% of the lexemes for these terminal ethnotaxa specifically refer to plant/animal interactions.

A word of clarification on terms may be necessary here. Keep in mind that a compound lexeme may include an animal name within it such as 'Coyote's Tobacco,' but this refers to the inferior quality of *Nicotiana trigonophylla* for smoking brought about by the mythic trickster Coyote, not to foraging of this plant by coyotes (*Canis latrans*) (Nabhan 1982). In contrast, there are at least nineteen plant names used by the Seri that refer to interactions between flowers and their pollinators, fruits and their seed dispersal agents, foliage and its herbivores or foragers, larval host plants and their larvae, brushy canopy-providers and dormant or reclusive animals, algae associated with sea turtle carapaces, and nest-providing canopies and their nesting birds. In such cases, it is reasonable to assume that plant names that recognize their faunal associates are derived from empirical observations of plant/animal interactions.

Similarly, animal names may include references to particular plants. For example, the O'odham call the Phainopepla (*Phainopepla nitens*) by the name *kuigam,* meaning 'mesquite dweller' (Nabhan et al. 1982; Rea 1983). Not only do Phainopeplas dwell in mesquite (*Prosopis* spp.), but they are the major dispersal agents of parasitic mistletoe (*Phoradendron* sp.) to mesquite.

In special cases, the same lexeme is polysemic for both a plant and an animal, generally when the relationship between the two is unusually robust. One such case of polysemy comes from the Chontal Maya, whose name for the Great Kiskadee (*Pitangus sulphuratus*) and for the wild Chiltepín (*Capsicum annuum*) is the same lexeme. The Chontales and their mestizo neighbors recognize the Great Kiskadee as an important seed dispersal agent of wild chiles in secondary growth emerging after milpa (field) abandonment. In the Sonoran Desert region, Amadeo Rea and I have recorded the same wild chile taxon associated with two *Cardinalis* species, the Northern Cardinal and the Pyrroloxia, by elderly O'odham harvesters of wild chiltepines. These chiltepines seldom grow in abandoned milpas but are often found associated with ancient, shade-providing nurse plants (Nabhan 1997; Tewksbury et al. 1999).

Such perceived differences in faunal associates of one ecologically variable species are a critical reason why ecological interactions should not simply be looked at within one locality alone or through the lens of just one cultural community. As Thompson (1996:300) has argued, "Many species are composed of populations specialized to different interactions . . . some [of which] can evolve rapidly under changed ecological conditions." To fathom a cultural community's understanding of such interactions, it is critical to go beyond mere taxonomic inquiries, to interview indigenous specialists about particular plants and animals in the habitats where those species occur. Ethnobiologists should not confine themselves to taxonomic inventories, but should devote more time to eliciting truly ecological knowledge from folk practitioners.

Conversely, sometimes "Western scientists" claim they have discovered an ecological interaction that was previously well known by indigenous peoples. Among the O'odham, this is true both for winter hibernation of poorwills (*Phalaenptilius nuttalii*) in the Sonoran Desert (Rea 1983) and for the intoxicating effects of thorn-apple (*Datura*) alkaloids on nectar-feeding hawkmoths (*Manduca* spp.).

Verne and Karen Grant (1965) were the first to report in biological literature that hawkmoth pollinators demonstrated intoxicated behavior after several visits to *Datura* flowers, a behavior that they attributed to the hallucinogenic alkaloids in this plant. University of Arizona pollination ecologists Rob Raguso, Karen Kester, and Stephen Buchmann are now attempting to verify this empirical observation experimentally, since alkaloid levels in *Datura* nectar itself should be minimum or negligible. However, neither the Grants nor the University of Arizona team were previously aware of the following O'odham song excerpt, no doubt about *Manduca* moths and their hornworms, recorded by José Luis Brennan in 1901, first published in translation by F. Russell (1908) and recently retranslated (Nabhan 1997):

> Sacred datura leaves, sacred datura leaves,
> eating your greens intoxicates me,
> making me stagger, dizzily leap.
> Datura blossoms, datura blossoms,
> drinking your nectar intoxicates me,
> making me stagger, dizzily leap.

From this song, we may infer that there is valuable ecologically encoded information about hawkmoths, datura, and phytochemicals known to the O'odham; however, such oral traditions remain an undervalued source of knowledge about native biodiversity.

MANAGEMENT OF THREATENED AND ENDEMIC SPECIES

It is clear from a number of studies, summarized elsewhere (Nabhan 1992, in press), that indigenous communities are reservoirs of considerable knowledge about rare, threatened, and endemic species that has not to date been independently accumulated by Western-trained conservation biologists. What may be less obvious is that indigenous knowledge of biotic relationships with rare plants or animals can help guide the identification, management, protection, or recovery of habitats for these species. Native Americans certainly are aware of details of the diets, nesting, and refuge cover requirements of endangered species that have not necessarily been recorded in the literature of conservation biology.

Take as examples the following details regarding the autoecology of four endangered animals: the Desert Tortoise, the Green Sea Turtle, the Sonoran Pronghorn Antelope, and Desert Bighorn Sheep. For the Desert Tortoise (*Gopherus agassizi*), a key issue in its conservation management has been providing protected habitat where sufficiently diverse forages are available for its dietary use. Despite sixty years of incidental reports on Desert Tortoise feeding behavior and stomach contents, knowledge of the species' dietary needs remains fragmentary since most observations were made incidental to fieldwork (Nabhan in press).

In contrast, there are four species of desert plants known for centuries to the Seri as *xtamoosn(i) oohit*, 'Desert Tortoise forage.' These include three species not otherwise identified in tortoise diets elsewhere in the Sonoran Desert (*Chaenactis carphoclinia, Fagonia californica*, and *F. pachyacantha*), although another species of *Chaenactis* has been identified in Sonoran Desert Tortoise diets and *Fagonia* may be found in Mojave Desert Tortoise diets (Van Devender, personal communication, 1998). A fourth species, *Chorizanthe brevicornu*, has only recently been verified as an important component of Desert Tortoise diets even though it is an inconspicuous, ephemeral wildflower. The Seri also identify a fifth forage consumed by Desert Tortoises, the False Purslane (*Trianthema portulacastrum*) (Nabhan in press).

The same is true for the Seri association of the endangered Sonoran Pronghorn Antelope (*Antilocapra americana sonoriensis*) with an ephemeral legume, *Phaseolus filiformis*, which they call *hamooja ihaap*, 'pronghorn-its-wild-bean.' Although this plant is occasionally abundant where the remnant pronghorn population occurs in northwestern Sonora, it is seldom abundant where the northernmost Seri bands lived, some 60–80 km south, in a poorly documented area of the Sonoran Pronghorn Antelope range. To date, this forage has not been recorded by members of the Sonoran Pronghorn Antelope recovery team in their dietary studies, although it is a likely candidate. Sadly, this subspecies of Pronghorn has declined to less than 300 individuals in Arizona and to less than 50 in Sonora, perhaps due to lack of access to habitats where this forage is in abundance.

A wild onion (*Allium haemotochiton*) is called 'Desert Bighorn's forage,' referring to *Ovis canadensis mexicanus*, another threatened subspecies. Although this winter-blooming onion has not been recorded in Desert Bighorn Sheep diets to date, it also seems like a good candidate to wildlife dietary ecologists (Paul Krausmann, personal communication, 1998).

Several species of algae are noted by the Seri as habitat, carapace cover, or forage for the endangered Green Sea Turtle, *Chelonia mydas: Cryptomeria obovata, Halymenia coccinea, Gracilaria textorii,* and *Rhodymenia divaricata.* The most intimate association is with the red alga *Gracilaria,* 'sea turtle's membranes,' which grows up to 30 cm tall on the carapaces of the endangered sea turtle population that overwinters, dormant, in a shallow channel of the Sea of Cortez adjacent to Seri villages (Felger and Moser 1985). The Seri claim that this alga attracts feeding on carapaces by another ecological associate, the Bumphead Parrotfish (Nabhan in press). Knowledge of this overwintering behavior among the *moosni hant koit* population was once unique to the Seri, but after non-Indian fishermen learned of it, they rapidly wiped out this population (Felger, Cliffton, and Regal 1976). Brent Berlin (1992) recently used the Seri as the clearest counterexample to the hypothesis that only farmers "overclassify" economically important plants and animals into "folk species," but the recognition that they also associate a particular alga with a named folk species (or distinct population) of sea turtles is even more remarkable. Unfortunately, my recent interviews with former Seri sea turtle specialists indicate that they hardly ever see individuals of this sea turtle population anymore (Nabhan in press).

INDIGENOUS PEOPLES AS
FULL PARTICIPANTS IN
PROTECTING BIODIVERSITY

In surveys of Native Americans involved in wildlife management, hunting, fishing, and endangered species conservation, these resource managers lament that so many culturally important species have been lost from their homelands during their own life-times. The O'odham and the Seri are aware of recent declines in native fish such as the Razorback Sucker, which once thrived in their irrigation ditches; in plants such as Sandfood, which once proliferated with their "pruning" or disruption of apical domi-nance; and in White Packrats, which not only thrived around their fields but offered caches of foodstuffs to those humans brave enough to seek mesquite pods and fruits in their cholla-covered middens (Rea 1997; Rosenberg and Nabhan 1997).

Many Native American elders in the Sonoran Desert are also aware that their children have diminished exposure to both common and rare species and to the oral traditional knowledge about them, which is also rapidly disappearing, as has been documented among the O'odham (Nabhan and St. Antoine 1993) and among the Seri (Nabhan in press; Rosenberg and Nabhan 1997). This "extinction of experience" of rare and endemic species breaks mutually rein-forcing connections between cultural and biological diversity that have functioned over the last eight to ten millennia in the Americas and longer elsewhere (Nabhan and St. Antoine 1993). In particular, it appears that traditional ecological knowledge about relationships between plants and animals is being lost more rapidly than the native names for these taxa (Nabhan in press; Rosenberg 1997). In interviews with photos of plants and animals, Seri children knew Seri names for 70% of the taxa presented to them, whereas adults averaged 90%; however, the children were far less cognizant of plant-animal interactions such as predation, commensalism, and foraging relations that most adults were intimately conversant with

(Rosenberg 1997). My own interviews with twenty-seven O'odham children may indicate why this trend is so pronounced in the U.S. side of the Sonoran Desert. Whereas only 41% of the children interviewed had noticed wild animals in their yard or garden, 78% had spent time watching "nature shows" on television and 56% had read books about wild animals—they are probably learning more about wildlife living elsewhere than they are about that in their own backyards.

As a solution to this problem, I am working with sixteen Seri Indian "para-ecologist" trainees who learn both from their elders and from visiting conservation biologists how to provide better protection not only for cultural resources but for natural resources such as endangered species as well. This course can be a model for other indigenous communities, for it honors both Western scientific and traditional ecological knowledge about biodiversity. It is critical that Native American youth be given such training opportunities for careers in endangered species and habitat conservation, becoming competent in traditional ecological knowledge as well as Western science. If the links between cultural and biological diversity are to be maintained, strengthened, or restored, indigenous peoples must be included in the management and conservation of the world's remaining biological riches. Otherwise, biodiversity conservation will be relegated to being a concern of an elite few, and indigenous communities will become further disenfranchised from their rich traditions of interactions with native plants and animals.

REFERENCES CITED

Anderson, E. N. 1996. *Ecologies of the Heart.* New York: Oxford University Press.

Berlin, B. 1992. *Ethnobiological Classification.* Princeton: Princeton University Press.

Bye, Robert A., Jr., and M. L. Zigmond. 1976. Book Review: *Principles of Tzetzal Plant Classification. Human Ecology* 4(3):171–75.

Felger, R. S., K. Cliffton, and P. Regal. 1976. Winter Dormancy in Sea Turtles: Independent Discovery and Exploitation in the Gulf of California by Two Local Cultures. Science 191:283–85.

Felger, R. S., and M. B. Moser. 1985. *People of the Desert and Sea: Ethnobotany of the Seri Indians.* Tucson: University of Arizona Press.

Grant, V., and K. Grant. 1965. Behavior of Hawkmoths on Flowers of *Datura metaloides. Botanical Gazette* 144(2):280–84.

Hale, K. 1992. On Endangered Languages and the Safeguarding of Diversity. *Language* 68:1–3.

Harmon, D. 1996. The Converging Extinction Crisis: Defining Terms and Understanding Trends in the Loss of Biological and Cultural Diversity. Keynote presented April 1, 1996, at the colloquium "Losing Species, Languages and Stories: Linking Cultural and Environmental Change in the Binational Southwest." Arizona–Sonora Desert Museum, Tucson.

Hill, J. 1995. Language Decay: The Loss of Structural Differentiation in Obsolescent Languages. Paper presented at the American Association for the Advancement of Science annual meetings, Albuquerque, July.

Hinton, L. 1994. *Flutes of Fire.* Berkeley: Heyday Books.

Nabhan, G. P. 1982. *The Desert Smells Like Rain: A Naturalist in Papago Indian Country.* San Francisco: North Point Press.

———. 1992. Threatened Native American Plants. *Endangered Species Update* 9:1–4.

———. 1994. Proximate and Ultimate Threats to Endangered Species. *Conservation Biology* 8:928–29.

———. 1997. Why Chiles Are Hot. *Natural History* 106:24–27.

———. In press. *Singing the Turtles to Sea: Reptiles in Seri Indian Arts and Sciences.* Berkeley: University of California Press.

Nabhan, G. P., A. M. Rea, K. L. Reichhardt, E. Mellink, and C. Hutchinson. 1982. Papago Influences on Habitat and Biotic Diversity: Quitovac Oasis Ethnoecology. *Journal of Ethnobiology* 2:124–43.

Nabhan, G. P., and S. St. Antoine. 1993. The Loss of Floral and Faunal Story, the Extinction of Experience: Ethnobiological Perspectives on Biophilia. In *The Biophilia Hypothesis,* edited by S. Kellert and E. O. Wilson, pp. 232–56. Washington, D.C.: Island Press.

Office of Technology Assessment. 1987. *Technologies to Maintain Biological Diversity.* Washington, D.C.: U.S. Congress/U.S. Government Printing Office.

Rea, A. R. 1983. *Once a River: Bird Life and Habitat Changes on the Middle Gila.* Tucson: University of Arizona Press.

————. 1997. *By the Desert's Green Edge.* Tucson: University of Arizona Press.

Rosenberg, J. 1997. *Documenting and Revitalizing Traditional Ecological Knowledge.* Tucson: University of Arizona Press.

Rosenberg, J., and G. P. Nabhan. 1997. Where Ancient Stories Guide Children Home. *Natural History* 106:54–61.

Russell, F. 1908. *The Pima Indians.* Twenty-sixth Annual Report of the Bureau of American Ethnology, 1904–5. Washington D.C.: U.S. Government Printing Office.

Spicer, E. 1980. *The Yaquis: A Cultural History.* Tucson: University of Arizona Press.

Tewksbury, J., G. P. Nabhan, H. Suzan-A., D. Norman, and J. Donovan. 1999. In Situ Conservation of Wild Chiles and Their Biotic Associates. *Conservation Biology* 13: 98–107.

Thompson, J. N. 1996. Evolutionary Ecology and the Conservation of Biodiversity. *Trends in Ecology and Evolution* 11(7):300–303.

Turner, R. M., J. E. Bowers, and T. L. Burgess. 1995. *Sonoran Desert Plants: An Ecological Atlas.* Tucson: University of Arizona Press.

Wilson, E. O. 1992. *The Diversity of Life.* Cambridge, Mass.: Belknap Press/Harvard University Press.

Wurm, S. 1991. Language Death and Disappearance: Causes and Circumstances. In *Endangered Languages,* edited by R. H. Robins and E. Uhlenbeck, pp. 1–18. New York: Berg.

Zepeda, O., and J. H. Hill. 1991. The Condition of Native American Languages in the United States. In R. H. Robins and E. Uhlenbeck, *Endangered Languages,* pp. 135–55. New York: Berg.

CHAPTER TWO

RELATIONSHIPS BETWEEN MEXICAN ETHNOBOTANICAL DIVERSITY AND INDIGENOUS PEOPLES

ROBERT BYE AND EDELMIRA LINARES

INTRODUCTION

The richness of the life on earth, according to Mesoamerican cultures, is of sacred origin (Heyden 1983). Different parts of the body of Cipactli (the earth monster or mother earth) gave rise to the various earthly elements; for instance, from the skin came flowers. World order is maintained by four trees of the earth according to the *Códice Fejérváry-Mayer* (possibly of Mixtec origin) (Anders et al. 1994): kapok (*Ceiba pentandra*) in the north, acacia (*Acacia* sp.) in the west, cacao (*Theobroma cacao*) in the south, and shaving-brush (*Pseudobombax ellipticum*) in the east. Hence, the biological diversity of Mexico has a consecrated creation and maintenance according to the indigenous Mexicans' ancestors. Sacred trees are still highly regarded, such as the Montezuma cypress (*Taxodium mucronatum*) of Chalma, Mexico, various kapoks in central plazas and church-yards from Morelos to Chiapas, the balsam-of-Peru (*Myroxylon balsamum* var. *pereirae*) of Oaxtepec, Morelos, and the cacao-flower (*Quararibea funebris*) of the Central Valley of Oaxaca. Some honored trees have disappeared: for example, the cacao-flower tree in the churchyard of Izucar de Matamoros, Puebla, was cut down in 1914 by the parish priest in order to end pagan rituals (Rivera 1942). Other historic trees are threatened due to environmental changes, such as "El Arbol de Santa María del Tule," a Montezuma cypress in Oaxaca (Jiménez 1990). Much of the concern expressed by indigenous Mexicans about the conservation of plants is focused more on respect for all forms of life than on worry about the loss of actual or potential economic plant resources.

MEXICAN PLANT DIVERSITY

Mexico is considered one of the "megadiversity" countries of the world. Recent publications have attempted to document the current state of knowledge (Cantú et al. 1991; Challenger 1998; Gío and López 1993; Ramamoorthy et al. 1993). CONABIO (Comisión Nacional para el Conocimiento y Uso de la Biodiversidad) was created recently to foster the systematic study of Mexico's biological diversity from the standpoint of inventories, protection, and utilization (Sarukhán and Dirzo 1992).

Mexico's vegetal richness has evolved from the two major floristic kingdoms that have converged there: their subordinate regions and provinces interdigitate along the length of the country (Rzedowski 1978). The Holarctic kingdom consists of two regions: the North American Pacific region in Baja California with two provinces and the Mesoamerican Mountain region of the higher elevations from Chihuahua to Chiapas with four provinces. The Neotropic kingdom contains two regions: the Mexican Desert region with five provinces from sea level to the Central Plateau and the Caribbean region, which runs along both the Atlantic and Pacific coasts and penetrates the adjacent lower inland drainage. In addition, ten basic vegetation types have been classified (Rzedowski 1978), and the flora is estimated to contain over 30,000 species (Rzedowski and Equihua 1987), 21,600 of which are vascular plants (Rzedowski 1993).

TABLE 2.1

Vascular Plant Richness and Endemism of Mexico

VEGETATION TYPE	% TERRITORY	VASCULAR PLANT SPECIES		
		RICHNESS		ENDEMICS
		#	%	%
Desert	50	6000	20	60
Conifer-oak forest	21	7000	24	70
Cloud forest	1	3000	10	30
Humid tropical forest	11	5000	17	5
Dry tropical forest	17	6000	20	40
Wetland	—	1000	3	15
Weed	—	2000	6	20

SOURCE: derived from Rzedowski 1993.

In addition to the geographic shifting of the Holarctic and Neotropical floras over geological time, the different ecological zones and the drastic topographic corridors and barriers promoted evolutionary explosions, resulting in a high degree of richness as well as endemism. Species richness and endemism of vascular plants are widespread but especially great in the deserts, the conifer-oak forests, and the dry tropical forests (see table 2.1). The Mega-Mexico of Rzedowski (1993), which curiously matches the Spanish colony of New Spain, has an overall vascular plant endemism of 5 families, 400 genera, and 12,900 species.

MEXICAN CULTURAL DIVERSITY

The integrity of Mexican cultures may be indexed by the number of native speakers. Language is important in the formulation and communication of indigenous concepts, perceptions, and actions. In less than a century after the Spanish Conquest, the indigenous population declined drastically from 22 million to less than 1 million

(Gerhard 1986). The number of languages decreased dramatically as well. Only 54 languages of the 120 spoken at the time of the conquest are currently in use in Mexico (Martínez 1986). Nonetheless, about 8 million individuals (or 7.5% of the 1980 Mexican population) speak an indigenous language, and the absolute number of native speakers has been on the increase since 1950 (Valdés and Menéndez 1987). Four patterns of numerical change in indigenous speakers since 1930 have been identified (Olivera et al. 1982). One pattern is the increase in the number of people who practice the Amuzgo, Chol, Mazatec, Tlapanec, Tzeltal, and Tzotzil languages; however, these ethnic groups are small in population. The second pattern consists of a population of speakers whose number has remained constant, exemplified by the Chinantec, Huastec, Huichol, Mixe, and Mixtec. The third case involves the decline in the number of native speakers. Unfortunately, this group includes the larger indigenous populations such as the Maya, Chontal, Mayo, Nahuatl, Otomí, Mazahua, Tarahumara, and Zapotec. The fourth group includes ethnic groups such as the Chatino, Popoluca, Tojolabal, Totonaca, and Zoque in which the change in the number of native speakers has been variable over the years.

The most important groups of native speakers are located in nine geographic regions. The five major areas are (1) the Central-East region in the high valleys (2,000 m) of Mexico, Toluca, and Mezquital; (2) the Huastec region of the warm, subhumid Sierra Madre Oriental; (3) the Southern region in the highly dissected southern Sierra Madre Oriental, Sierra Madre del Sur, and Trans-Mexican Neovolcanic Belt with a warm, subhumid to dry climate; (4) the Southeastern region in the warm, humid mountains of Chiapas; and (5) the Yucatán Peninsula on the warm, subhumid flats. Four minor regions are (6) the Northwest arid coastal plains; (7) the Sierra Tarahumara of northwestern Mexico; (8) the West-Central Sierra Madre Occidental; and (9) the Lake zone of the west-central Trans-Mexican Neovolcanic Belt.

Contemporary resident indigenous populations are distributed principally in the rural regions of Mexico, based upon the linguistic distribution (Olivera et al. 1982) and ecological zones (Toledo et al. 1989). The distribution is relative (rather than absolute) due to incompleteness of the census data, the passage of twenty-five years since the information was gathered, and the omission of the "municipios" (equivalent to counties), which did not readily fit into the established categories (see table 2.2). Of the forty-two linguistic groups in the 1970 census, twenty-seven dwell in the dry tropical forests, twenty-one in the conifer-oak forests, twenty in the humid tropical forests, fifteen in the deserts and dry grasslands, and twelve

TABLE 2.2

Estimation of Ecological Distribution of Contemporary Resident Indigenous Populations in Major Ecological Zones of Mexico with Respective Dominant Vegetation Types

LINGUISTIC GROUP	POPULATION IN ECOLOGICAL ZONES				
	1	2	3	4	5
Mixtec	798	72,514	3,376	122,299	2,700
Nahua	381,913	92,305	32,758	205,799	30,965
Otomí	13,829	1,629	2,206	105,496	32,520
Zapotec	38,798	84,361	17,899	109,334	120
Mazateco	42,529	801	1,687	44,665	
Mixe	18,682	244	17,676	9,245	
Tzeltal	42,214	1,894	2,527	29,831	
Tzotzil	2,993	926	17,227	85,157	
Chinanteco	13,937	1,560	12,310		
Totonaco	107,998	2,008	144		
Zoque	14,431	3	4,361		
Chol	60	28			
Chontal	9,856				
Motozintleco	2,088				
Quiché	17				

TABLE 2.2 (continued)

Linguistic Group	Population in Ecological Zones				
	1	2	3	4	5
Huastec	34,415	17,712			222
Mame-Quiché	3,402	1,006		986	78
Maya	46,261	392,799			18
Popolaca	17,184		1,488	5,172	
Tojolabal	11,054			637	
Amuzgo		9,474			
Cora		5,083			
Huave		4,835			
Pima		46			
Tepehuan		649			
Choco-Popoloca		451		203	
Mayo		5,451			20,429
Mazahua		217		93,780	
Huichol		522		3,405	
Tarahumara		3,457		19,509	
Tarasco		4,864		48,125	12
Tlapaneco		902		23,084	
Matlatzinca				1,027	
Ocuitleco				386	
Cuicatec				1,044	
Tepehuano				3,538	
Cucapá					105
Jonas					481
Pápago					116
Paipai-Kiliwa-Cucapa					566
Seri					165
Yaqui					4,915

Source: Olivera et al. 1982.

Note: The population numbers and ecological classification are relative and for comparison only, because not all "municipios" had complete data or concurrence; also, the census is based upon information derived in 1970. 1: humid tropical = humid tropical forests; 2: subhumid tropical = dry tropical forests; 3: humid temperate = cloud forests; 4: subhumid temperate = conifer-oak forests; 5: arid and semiarid = deserts and dry grasslands (Toledo et al. 1989).

in the cloud forests. Four groups (Mixtec, Nahua, Otomí, and Zapotec) live in all five major ecological zones, while another four (Mazateco, Mixe, Tzeltal, and Tzotzil) inhabit four of the five regions. The following ethnic groups are confined to the respective ecological zones: Chontal, Motozintleco, and Quiché in the humid tropics; Amuzgo, Cora, Huave, Pima, and Tepehuan in the sub-humid tropics; Matlatzinca, Ocuitleco, Cuicatec, and Tepehuano in the subhumid temperate regions; and Cucapá, Jonas, Pápago, Paipai-Kiliwa-Cucapa, Seri, and Yaqui in the arid zones.

ETHNOBOTANICAL DIVERSITY

The diversity of plant-human interactions may be explored conceptually through the correlation of botanical richness and cultural richness with a complex ethnobotanical interaction. Mexico is an appropriate place to examine the plant-human richness relationships because of the great degree of diversification of cultures and biota in comparison to the rest of the Americas and the world (Robles and Toledo 1995). An estimation of Mexico's baseline plant-human richness relative to that of Latin America has been made by V. M. Toledo (1987) and J. Caballero (1987). In terms of absolute number of indigenous individuals, Mexico ranks first, with over 8 million people. It has fewer linguistic groups than the countries of Brazil, Colombia, and Peru, however. In terms of number of vascular plant species, Mexico stands second, after Brazil. About one-fifth of Mexico's indigenous societies have recorded ethnobotanical information.

Although no ethnobotanical inventory is available for the country, many projects are underway to compile and analyze useful plants in general (e.g., Instituto de Biología, Universidad Nacional Autónoma de México; Instituto de Ecología, A.C.) as well as according to specific anthropocentric uses such as medicinal purposes (Bye, Linares, and Estrada 1995). Ethnobotanical studies in Mexico have increased exponentially since 1963, as seen in the number of contributions in the National Botanical Congress (Martínez 1993, 1994). Examples of contemporary ethnobotanical inventories of indigenous groups in Mexico include the Seri of the coastal desert of Sonora (Felger and Moser 1985), Huave of coastal Oaxaca (Zizumbo and Colunga 1982), Mixtec of the mountains of Guerrero (Casas et al. 1994), and Nahua, Totonaco, Otomí, and Tepehua of the Sierra Norte de Puebla (Martínez et al. 1995). The utilization and management of biological resources of Mexico by indigenous peoples and *campesinos* have been of recent interest (Challenger 1998; Lara 1995; Leff et al. 1990; Toledo et al. 1989).

In Mexico, the mutual dependence between humans and plants has developed intricately over time and space. Mexico's cultural richness, combined with its floristic wealth, has diversified plant-human interactions. The derivation of an ethnobotanical diversity from the correlation of ethnic and biological richness is a useful exercise but may be less practical than considering the richness of plant species employed by Mexicans. The recognition and utility of plants as registered in ethnobotanical inventories approximate richness. Archaeological and historical records demonstrate the dynamics of vegetal taxa utilized throughout human history. The intensification by humans of certain ecological and evolutionary processes, such as erosion and selective elimination, has a negative impact upon plants. However, other actions tend to favor biological diversity.

Human actions influence the diversity of plants at the evolutionary, morphophysiological, and ecological levels (Bye 1993; Caballero 1990). Human interactions with plants have tended to span an evolutionary continuum and involve special activities in which human behavior (conscious of expected results or not) affects the survival and reproduction of the plant population and modifies its natural genetic composition and ecological behavior. With emphasis on the plant, three evolutionary phases (wild, weed, and domesticate) are generally recognized even though they do not form mutually exclusive categories. The path of plants evolving along this continuum is not necessarily unidirectional but may be reversible under certain circumstances. Wild plants survive and reproduce naturally without the necessity of human intervention. Weeds survive in habitats perturbed periodically by human activities, but their reproduction cycle is successfully completed without humans. They have evolved in human-made habitats from natural colonizers, hybrid derivatives of wild and domesticated species, and feral plants originating from abandoned domesticates that reestablished seed dispersal (de Wet and Harlan 1975). Subdivisions of weeds can be distinguished by their habitat preference (such as agrestals in cultivated fields, ruderals along routes of travel and near dwellings, etc.). Finally, domesticated plants' survival and reproduction cycle depends upon direct human intervention. Distinctive adaptation syndromes are products of various avenues that domestication processes have taken (Harlan 1975; Hawkes 1983). This continuum is based upon a coevolutionary process in which plants undergo morphological and autecological changes (which eventually may be genetically maintained) and humans modify their behavior. Because of this process, the plants are undergoing unnaturally rapid change and most likely are not fixed end products. Hence, this continuum reflects a dynamic component of biological diversity.

Human activities exert variable selection pressures that propel plants along this continuum and fall into three major categories that are not restricted to any particular phase of the continuum. Gathering products from plants that grow naturally or are concentrated in response to habitat modification may favor or diminish the population and possibly alter its genetic composition. Incipient management results from intensifying human actions whereby certain plants may be tolerated (e.g., selected plants are allowed to survive and reproduce rather than be eliminated), encouraged (e.g., people's efforts promote increased dispersal and distribution of sexual or vegetative propagules within the site or to a new site), and protected (e.g., plants have an advantage gained by removal of competitors, special supports, exclusion of predators, and other special care). The third interaction is cultivation, where people's special actions modify environmental conditions to promote optimal production and reproduction.

Mexico has been recognized as one of the major regions of domestication (Hernández 1993). Recent evidence indicates that the contemporary Mesoamerican crop triad (maize-bean-squash) is derived from relatives that grow in the dry tropical forest (Bretting 1990). The domestication process generating infraspecific taxa continues not only with these well-recognized crops but also with semidomesticated plants. The domesticated *frijol gordo* (*xoyamet* or *Phaseolus polyanthus*) of the Sierra Norte de Puebla has been traditionally grown as a vine on maize plants in multiple-cropping milpas of the Nahua, who gather the late-ripening pods after the maize harvest at the end of the growing season. With an increased demand for beans in the early growing season, precocious forms have been selected recently to provide green pods prior to the maize harvest. Normally edible greens or *quelites* are collected as weedy seedlings by the Nahua in their milpas in the Sierra Norte de Puebla at the start of the growing season. In order to prolong the availability of these greens as well as to favor colorful, tasty forms, certain *chichiquelites* (*Amaranthus hybridus*, *A. hypochondriacus*, and their hybrids) are being selected to produce in the cultivated fields, where the maize often grows 3 m tall (Mapes et al. 1996). The selection of *papaloquelite* (*Porophyllum ruderale* ssp. *macrocephalum*) in various communities of central Mexico has given rise to genetically different, flavorful leafy forms (Vázquez 1991). Such selection takes place not only in cultivated fields but also in the natural habitats. The variability and diversification of tropical genera such as *Acalypha, Croton, Euphorbia, Miconia, Paspalum, Piper,* and *Psychotria* may be the consequences of human activities in the recent past (Gómez-Pompa 1971). Tropical secondary vegetation created by humans provides greater niche diversity. The secondary vegetation behaves as a selective factor as well as an indirect ecological barrier and promotes speciation. Trees producing the edible seeds of *guajes* (*Leucaena esculenta*) with desirable flavor are spared in the clearing of the dry tropical forests, thus altering the genetic composition of the native population (Casas and Caballero 1996).

Human interaction can also favor productive plants without necessarily provoking genetic changes. The morphophysiological responses may reflect the phenotypic plasticity of the plants. For instance, the Tarahumara plant the introduced mustard (*Brassica rapa*) during the shorter days of fall to promote the growth of edible leaves and hypocotyl rather than seeding it during the longer days of the normal growing season when the plant would readily flower and produce little vegetal growth (Bye 1979b). The Zapotec of the Valley of Oaxaca continually harvest the aromatic flowers of *rosita de cacao* (*Quararibea funebris*) to assure continual production of the highly valued additive to *tejate*, the local maize drink; the cessation of flower harvest causes a decline in flower yield. The coppicing of oak trees (*Quercus rugosa*, *Q. laurifolia*) by the Nahua in the southern Valley of Mexico ensures that ancient trees maintain a physiologically young state, with the production of poles and wood for firewood and charcoal production. The need for fast-igniting kindling for fires as well as illumination at night has favored the management of pine trees (*Pinus* spp.) for *ocote*. The Nahua of central Mexico as well as the Tarahumara of the northern Sierra Madre Occidental, among other ethnic groups, provoke resin deposits in the scars of the tree trunks with fire and wounding to carve out pinepitch splinters periodically. The mature trees are said to be harvested for over a century in this condition before they are cut for timber purposes. The rescheduling of mushroom fruitbody production is another morphophysiological practice. Fruiting bodies of over ninety fungi are highly valued for home consumption as well as for the markets (Guzmán 1980). In the mountains of the southeastern Valley of Mexico, Nahua descendants keep dead trunks of the morning-glory tree (*Ipomoea murucoides*) in their gardens and periodically water them during the dry season to produce the delicious *oreja de cazahuate* mushroom (*Pleurotus ostreatus*). They do this not only to provide edible mushrooms "out of season" but also to conserve the food mushrooms (many of which have a mycorrhizal relationship with the forest trees), which are disappearing with the increased deforestation in the area.

The ecology of plants also changes with human intervention. The primary and secondary tropical forests of southeastern San Luis Potosí and adjacent Veracruz have experienced directional alteration by humans. The Huastec Indians constantly manage the *te'lom* or "group of trees," in which certain plants are removed, others are protected, and certain ones are favored (Alcorn 1984). Since prehispanic times, indigenous peoples of Mexico have altered the geographical ecology of plants by favoring their movement from their native habitats to new sites. The transport of such plants as cacao and tomato (*Lycopersicon esculentum*) permitted their transdomestication in Mexico—domestication outside of the natural area of distribution of their wild relatives (e.g., South America) (Harlan 1975). Isolated cultivated trees such as the hand-flower tree (*Chiranthodendron pentadactylon*) and kapok probably date back to prehispanic times when the trees were considered sacred and moved along with local gardeners from the cloud and tropical forests to the center of the Aztec Empire, where they continue to grow today. The Aztec Empire had a series of botanical gardens for maintaining and acclimating plants that were transferred to the capital of Tenochtitlán (Linares and Bye 1993). Change in the composition of a local flora is an ecological response to human alteration of the vegetation. Expansion of the agricultural activities creates new habitats for the establishment of plants that migrate into the area. J. Rzedowski (1986) explains the presence of twelve calcicolous herbs in the Valley of Mexico by their establishment on soil accumulated from erosion associated with the introduction of agriculture about 4,000 years ago. The plants were probably derived from populations growing on the dominant limestone soil to the north in the state of Hidalgo and entered through the Huehuetoca region.

The movement of humans into new sites influences their perception and utilization of plant resources. The mestizo population has expanded into the dry tropical forests of Mexico that have been abandoned by indigenous peoples over the centuries. Not only do the mestizos use fewer plants, but they also employ a smaller percentage of the edible species than indigenous peoples. For instance, 58% of the 305 useful plant taxa of the Tarahumara who live in the barrancas of Chihuahua are eaten, while mestizos who have inhabited similar vegetation areas in Tamaulipas, Jalisco, Guerrero, and Morelos consume 18 to 34% of fewer than 260 plants (Bye 1995a). Although there appears to be a reluctance on the part of mestizos to accept local plants in their diet (they usually prefer to rely on cultivated plants), they adopt indigenous medicinal plants to treat local diseases.

Agriculture has been the most impressive form of transforming Mexico's biodiversity. The diversity of ecological sites also presents challenges to increase productivity. Mexico is located on the global gene belt where the three major centers of agriculture originated along with many domesticated plants (Harlan 1975; Ramamoorthy et al. 1993). Native Mexicans employing traditional agricultural techniques have overcome many obstacles during the last 10,000 years. Thin tropical soils, some on calcareous or volcanic bedrocks, have been improved through swidden practices (*roza-tumba-quema*), which periodically incorporate organic material and minerals, as studies of the Mayan milpas have demonstrated (Hernández et al. 1995). Honeycomb cultivated parcels on open volcanic rock (*huamil*) continue to provide agricultural productivity in an otherwise hostile environment in southwestern El Bajío (Bye et al. 1989). Runoff agriculture traps the infrequent precipitation of the desert of northern Sonora, where the Sand Papago harness the precious liquid to cultivate drought-adapted crops (Nabhan 1985). The swampy margins of the lakes of the Valley of Mexico were transformed into food and ornamental plant production with chinampa systems (Rojas 1993). Home gardens (*solares*) are a means of maintaining a diversity of useful plants close to dwellings and efficiently using the limiting resources such as water in dry tropical zones (Caballero 1992). From these systems people harvest not only domesticated crops but also other edible plants such as associated weeds (e.g., *quelites*; Bye 1981) and border plants (e.g., prickly-pear pads and fruits [*Opuntia* spp.]; Colunga et al. 1986).

Agriculture in Mexico has always been changing. Industrialized agriculture has tended to decrease the diversity of Mexican crops as well as the varieties within the crops. The colonization of Mexican agriculture prior to the Mexican Revolution favored few landowners with large tracts of land (Gutelman 1984; Kaerger 1986), who greatly influenced the native crops. For example, five of the eight hard-fiber forms of *Agave fourcroydes* have become extinct after international demand for natural fiber promoted the large henequen plantations on the Yucatán Peninsula after the turn of the century (Colunga and May 1993). The post-Revolution agricultural reforms distributed the land among the rural population and resulted in *ejidos* and communal pastures and forests; these post-Revolution changes are now being modified by the North American Free Trade Agreement and the modification of Chapter 27 of the Mexican Constitution to privatize the land (Martínez et al. 1994).

Also, the changing land use practices, including nonarable lands, have altered the exploitation of plant resources. On one hand, deforestation for forest products and livestock grazing has destroyed traditional native plant resources (Bassol 1991). From the remaining deserts and forests rural people (*campesinos*), including indigenous peoples, attempt to generate additional income through the collection of resins, fibers, edible plants, and medicinal plants for sale in the local, regional, and national markets. However, the collectors' benefit in terms of percent of consumer price is less for wild collected plants than for their agricultural products (Hersch 1996). For example, Tarahumara receive US$0.33 per kilo for the dried root of

Porter's lovage or *chuchupate* (*Ligusticum porteri*) of the pine-oak forests of Chihuahua, while it retails for almost US$18 in the major medicinal plant market in Mexico City (Bye 1995b). Overexploitation of the natural resources as well as of the people who live off the land for foreign profit is part of the same destabilizing process in Mexico (Toledo 1983). The main objectives of the just participation of indigenous peoples in the benefits of bioprospecting and the recognition of their intellectual property rights are the conservation of the plants in their natural habitats and the well-being of the local inhabitants. An example of the application of this philosophy is the International Cooperative Biodiversity Group's project "Bioactive Agents from Dryland Plants of Latin America" (Grifo 1996): the Universidad Nacional Autónoma de México in collaboration with the University of Arizona is analyzing medicinal plants from the deserts and dry tropical forest of Mexico phytochemically and with forty-five bioassays and promoting local conservation efforts in the areas of study (Bye et al. 1997).

The gathering of wild plants by indigenous peoples may promote the abundance of wild plants, and, in some cases, the cessation of such practices may trigger their disappearance. Today sandfood (*Pholisma sonorae*), a root parasite on desert shrubs, is considered an endangered species, while a century ago it was an abundant wild food of the Sand Papago Indians of northern Sonora. The excavation to extract the buried edible stems promoted its propagation by permitting the seeds to fall into holes and come into contact with host roots (Nabhan 1985). Normally, the seeds would be released on the sandy surface and would not come into direct contact with the subterranean roots. Hence the Indians inadvertently dispersed the seeds to favorable germination sites while digging and promoted an increase in the plants. The collection of wild onions (*Allium* spp.) by the Tarahumara Indians of Chihuahua increases local populations because of the loosening of the normally compact soil, the reduction of competitive perennials, and the dispersal of the daughter bulbs upon cleaning of the central bulb (Bye

1985). The impact of tourism in once isolated regions of indigenous peoples has put new pressures on gathered wild resources. For the most part, the Tarahumara have continued traditional harvesting practices for beargrass leaves (*Dasylirion* spp. and *Nolina* spp.) (Bye, García, et al. 1995). They periodically harvest the intermediate-aged leaves of these woody perennials to assure the healthy state of the plant, often suppressing sexual reproduction in favor of vegetative propagation. Also, their creativity is seen in combining or replacing these hard-fiber leaves with the needles of the long-leaved Apache pine (*Pinus engelmannii*). Such strategies are similar to those for harvesting palm leaves (e.g., *Sabal uresana*: Joyal 1996; *S. yapa, S. mexicana, S. mauritiiformis*: Caballero 1993).

A Mexican example of a relationship between biological and cultural richness is based upon the "man-agave symbiosis" (Gentry 1982). The genus *Agave* has its natural range from the southern United States to South America. The major concentration of taxa is found in Mexico, which has 136 species according to Gentry's (1982) taxonomic treatment that reduced the plethora of named unnatural species. Magueys, as the various taxa of *Agave* are called by Mexicans, have been an important food, beverage, and fiber source for humans since prehistoric times. These drought-tolerant plants concentrate liquid, carbohydrates, and fiber, which can be exploited by people living in environments where sustenance is seasonal or unreliable. Based upon the relative occurrence of plant remains recovered from archaeological sites in northeastern and south-central Mexico, magueys have been consistently used throughout time, with a maximum representation at about 4,000 years ago (Callen 1965; Parsons and Parsons 1990; Smith 1967). With such prolonged contact and dependence upon magueys, one might assume that the greatest ethnobotanical diversification would be found where the highest *Agave* species richness and/or the greatest cultural richness occurs.

The production of pulque, the alcoholic beverage produced by fermenting the liquid extracted from maturing magueys, is one of the most advanced coevolutionary relationship between *Agave* and humans. The propagation of the maguey plants, the timely collection of the sweet juice (*aguamiel*), and the batch fermentation technology with its associated microorganisms depend upon direct human intervention. The people of central Mexico relied upon this uncontaminated beverage to alleviate thirst and hunger during stressful periods of the year. The antiquity of the critical importance of *Agave* is confirmed by the fact that many Aztec ceremonies included pulque along with human sacrifices and a major deity was the pulque goddess, Mayahuel (Gonçalves 1956). The human dependence upon fermented *Agave* juice ended only in the early twentieth century. After the Mexican Revolution, the economic and social importance of pulque in urban areas declined due to the abandonment of the maguey-producing haciendas and the greater availability of drinking water and industrialized beverages (Zorrilla 1988).

The dimensions of the maguey-human interaction are still present in rural areas, where older people rely upon pulque as daily beverages providing a dietary complement of calories, vitamin B complex, and protein (Ulloa et al. 1987). The farmers manipulate the maguey populations by conscious selection of different races and by transplanting vegetative propagules as part of traditional agroecosystems (Ruvalcaba 1983). The selective transplant and the hybridization between different species brought into close proximity (Gentry 1982) have resulted in the diversification of folk cultivars (Marino 1966), which are readily recognized by *pulqueros* but which defy scientific classification (Gentry 1982). The maintenance of maguey populations is dependent upon humans because the central bud (which contains the inflorescence) is destroyed in the collection process and the basal offshoots are too dense and close to the mother plant to guarantee survival and dispersal. The maguey's sweet water, which rapidly decomposes, is transformed to nutritionally enriched pulque through traditional manipulation of a micro-ecosystem involving ten species of bacteria and eight taxa of yeasts (Ulloa et al. 1987). Human behavior has adapted to pulque production due to the requirements of maintaining permanent row cultivation of magueys as an integral part of the agroecosystem and of daily harvesting and fermenting routines.

The antiquity of the pulque process is unknown, even though many cultures of central Mexico have their own myths. Analyses of these legends suggest that it originated about A.D. 900 (Lobato 1884; Zorrilla 1988), but undoubtedly it is much older. Today mestizos as well as Indians such as the Huastec, Matlatzinca, Mazahua, Nahua, Otomí, Purépecha, and Zapotec maintain this intensive *Agave*-human symbiosis (Ulloa et al. 1987; Zorrilla 1988). Given the broad distribution of the 136 species of *Agave* in Mexico, one would expect that this ethnobotanical process would be (1) confined to a related group of species or (2) correlated with centers of species richness. According to H. S. Gentry (1982), only five species distributed in four sections are the major pulque producers (see table 2.3); consequently, there is no taxonomic restriction. These pulque magueys originated and are cultivated in the southern Central Plateau (Gentry 1982), which is relatively poor in *Agave* species, and outside of the three regions of highest species concentration: the Sierra Madre Occidental, central-southern Sierra Madre Oriental, and southern Tehuacán Valley of Puebla (and adjacent northeastern Oaxaca) (Reichenbacher 1985). Hence, this plant-human interaction is not correlated with taxonomic affinity and assumed phylogeny, nor with centers of species richness. Another expected association would be the concurrence of the centers of both *Agave* and cultural richness. The state of Oaxaca has the greatest number of ethnic groups as well as the largest population of native speakers (Valdés and Menéndez 1987). Nonetheless, the nearest *Agave* richness center is located to the northeast of the populated areas. Also, the pulque process is recorded for one ethnic group in the region. The relationship between biological and cultural diversity is unclear and requires detailed analysis.

TABLE 2.3

Species of Agave that Produce Pulque

SECTION	NUMBER OF SPECIES PER SECTION	SPECIES USED FOR PULQUE
Americanae	6	*Agave americana*
Crenatae	6	*Agave hookeri*
Hiemiflorae	12	*Agave atrovirens*
Salmianae	4	*Agave salmiana*
		Agave mapisaga
Total species	28	5

SOURCE: Gentry 1982.

Ethnotaxonomy entails the description, classification, and nomenclature of indigenous peoples' view of the various plants of their world. Studies of the Maya Indians of Mexico have shown parallels of the major life forms (e.g., tree, herb, grass, vine, etc.) with those of the European tradition (Berlin et al. 1974; Brown 1979). Even though this universal concept appears to be well documented, it is possible that ethnotaxonomies may have other dimensions that reflect such characters as utility and ecology (Hunn 1982) as well as organoleptic features that have not been fully understood. For instance, the earliest ethnotaxonomic study in Mexico, which was written between 1558 and 1582 by Bernardino de Sahagún (1979), indicated that major taxonomic groups of the Mexica (Aztec) such as *quilitl* (edible greens) and *patli* (medicinal plants) were just as important as other higher taxa such as tree or herb (Ortiz 1990). These utilitarian classification units (parallel and nonexclusive) are still recognized by indigenous peoples today; for instance, the edible green category is known as *i:waki* by the O'odham (*O'odham I:waki* 1980), *guiribá* by the Tarahumara (Bye 1981), *quilitl* by Nahuatl speakers (Bye 1981), and *yuve* by Mixteco (Katz 1992). Biologically distinct plants with similar use and organoleptic properties are named and classified the same; the thirst-quenching leaves of sorrel

(*Oxalis*, Oxalidaceae) and the stems of begonia (*Begonia*, Begoniaceae) with the same use are both considered *chokobarí* by the Tarahumara and *xoxocoyol* by the Nahua.

Ethnotaxonomic studies need to incorporate the symbolic nature of the plants. Confusion over the identity of "true" and "false" ceremonial plants by Western researchers may be clarified by placing the plants in the cosmovision of each ethnic group. The "true peyote" (*Lophophora williamsii*) and "false peyote" (*Ariocarpus fissuratus*) of the Huichol and the Tarahumara, the "true *kiéri*" (*Solandra* spp.) and "false *kiéri*" (*Datura* spp.) of the Huichol deer-wind mythology, and the sierran and barrancan *bakanawi* (*Scirpus* sp., Cyperaceae; unidentified vine of Convolvulaceae) of the Tarahumara may appear to be contradictions or inconsistencies to Western taxonomists but are vital elements in the balance of the symbolic world of indigenous peoples of Mexico (Bye 1979a; Furst 1989; Levi 1993).

Ethnotaxonomy is a dynamic process that includes deletions and additions over time. Over the last 450 years, the knowledge of the majority of the plants known to Aztec and their neighbors shortly after the Spanish Conquest has been lost to contemporary Native speakers and Western social and natural scientists. Such is the case of the plants in such early colonial documents as *Libellus de Medicinalibus Indorum Herbis* of M. de la Cruz and J. Badiano (Valdés et al. 1992; 102 of 185 of the medicinal plants, or 55%, still unidentified), *Florentine Codex* of Bernardino de Sahagún (Estrada et al. 1988; 342 of 724 reported plants, or 47% percent, still unknown) and the *Historia Natural de Nueva España* of Francisco Hernández (Valdés and Flores 1985; 2,062 of 3,076 plant taxa, or 67% percent, undetermined). The rate of loss has continued since the 1800s. For instance, of the 113 useful plants of the Tarahumara documented botanically by Dr. Edward Palmer in 1885, only 71 species are still documentable among this indigenous group today; about 37% of the knowledge of utilitarian plants has been lost by the Rarámuri people in the last 100 years (Bye et al. 1999). Conversely, plants introduced by European colonists became incorporated into the ethnic classification, such as the African aloe (*Aloe barbadensis*, Liliaceae), which became part of the maguey ethnotaxon (*Agave*, Agavaceae) of the Tarahumara (*imé*), the Nahua (*metl*), and others. The name of a restricted class of Tarahumara cruciferous edible greens, *mekwásare* (*Thelypodiopsis byei*), was transferred to a widespread European mustard (*Brassica rapa*). Sometimes the introduction is linguistically marked, as in the case of cowpeas (*Vigna unguiculata*), known to the Tarahumara as *yorimuni* ('foreigner's bean'; *yori*, 'stranger'; *muni*, 'bean').

The availability of plant resources may be limited if they are not grown, gathered, or stored locally. From prehispanic times to the present, indigenous peoples have resolved this problem in ways other than transplanting and cultivating the plants. Some groups occupy the ecological gradient from the cool temperate forests to the hot, dry tropical forests. The Nahua, Totonaco, Otomí, and Tepehua of the Sierra Norte de Puebla exploit these ecological zones with cultivated fields and collecting in the forest through ecological complementarity (Martínez et al. 1995). The Tarahumara of the cool sierras and warm barrancas migrate seasonally to exploit the cultivated and wild resources in these contrasting ecological zones as well as trade plant products between the zones (Bennett and Zingg 1935; Pennington 1963).

The influence of the Aztec Empire covered most of Mega-Mexico, and the rulers and citizens of the central capital took advantage of vegetal riches of the land. The elite socioeconomic class of traders known as *pochtecas*, the tribute systems, and the web of markets assured the availability of plant products from the wide variety of ecological zones. With the collapse of the Triple Alliance caused by the conquest, some plants such as the sacred ear-flower (*Cymbopetalum penduliflorum*) disappeared, while others are still present today, such as the *nanche* fruits (*Byrsonima crassifolia*) (Bye and Linares 1990). The Mexican markets are still a productive laboratory for the study of ethnobotanical processes (Bye and Linares 1983).

Should a market plant species become rare or expensive, a back-up strategy that has been called a medicinal plant complex comes into play. This complex consists of different species and genera of plants that share vernacular names, curative uses, morphological features, and organoleptic properties (Linares and Bye 1987). The dominant species is preferred due to its efficacy and is marketed beyond its natural phytogeographic range, while the subordinate species are sold only within their natural extension. For example, *Psacalium decompositum* is the dominant species in the *matarique* complex. Recently, the short supply due to declining natural populations in Chihuahua prompted increasing demand for *P. peltatum* from México and Morelos.

CONCLUSIONS

Mexico continues to be a living laboratory for the evolution of plant-human interactions and relationships. Despite the initial decline of Mexican Indians after the Spanish Conquest and the accelerated habitat destruction in recent years, native Mexicans continue to promote, utilize, and conserve the plant richness in this megadiversity country. Ethnobotanical studies, though the most active in Latin America, are still in the initial phase of inventory and theory development. Ethnobotanical projects recognize the benefits and intellectual property rights of the Native peoples who generate and safeguard the cultural and biological diversity of one of the most diverse areas of the Western Hemisphere.

ACKNOWLEDGMENTS

The authors gratefully acknowledge the hospitality and knowledge shared by many Mexican Indians and mestizos during our studies throughout the country. Francisco Basurto, Myrna Mendoza,

Gustavo Morales, and Guadalupe Toledo assisted in the preparation of the manuscript; Javier Caballero, Miguel Angel Martínez,
and Cristina Mapes provided useful opinions and references.
Thank you to T. P. Ramamoorthy for his constant encouragement.
The projects that have generated our data and insights have been
supported by the Palmer Study Fund, National Geographic Society,
U.S. National Science Foundation, U.S. Agency for International
Development, U.S. Biodiversity Support Program (US AID), Inter-
national Cooperative Biodiversity Group (USA), Programa para el
Estudio de la Etnobotánica en Latinoamérica y Caribe (New York
Botanical Garden), Universidad Nacional Autónoma de México
(Instituto de Biología; Programa de Apoyo a Proyectos de Investi-
gación e Innovación Tecnológica), Consejo Nacional de Ciencia y
Tecnología, Consejo Nacional para el Conocimiento y Uso de la
Biodiversidad, McKnight Foundation, Harvard University, and
University of Colorado (Boulder).

REFERENCES CITED

Alcorn, J. B. 1984. Development Policy, Forests, and Peasant Farms:
    Reflections on Huastec-Managed Forests' Contributions to Commercial
    Production and Resource Conservation. *Economic Botany* 38:389–406.
Anders, F., M. Jansen, and L. Reyes García. 1994. *El libro de Tezcatlipoca,
    señor del tiempo (libro explicativo del llamado Códice Fejérváry-Mayer).*
    Mexico City: Fondo de Cultura Económica.
Bassol Batalla, A. 1991. *Recursos naturales de México—Teoría, conocimiento y
    uso.* Mexico City: Editorial Nuestro Tiempo.
Bennett, W. C., and R. M. Zingg. 1935. *The Tarahumara—An Indian Tribe of
    Northern Mexico.* Chicago: University of Chicago Press.
Berlin, B., D. E. Breedlove, and P. H. Raven. 1974. *Principles of Tzeltal Plant
    Classification.* New York: Academic Press.
Bretting, P. K. (ed.). 1990. New Perspectives on the Origin and Evolution
    of New World Domesticated Plants. *Economic Botany* 44(3S):1–116.
Brown, C. H. 1979. Growth and Development of Folk Botanical Life Forms
    in the Mayan Language Family. *American Ethnologist* 6:366–85.

Bye, R. 1979a. Hallucinogenic Plants of the Tarahumara. *Journal of Ethnopharmacology* 1:23–48.

———. 1979b. Incipient Domestication of Mustards in Northwest Mexico. *Kiva* 44:237–56.

———. 1981. Quelites—Ethnoecology of Edible Greens—Past, Present and Future. *Journal of Ethnobiology* 1:109–23.

———. 1985. Botanical Perspectives of Ethnobotany of the Greater Southwest. *Economic Botany* 39:375–85.

———. 1993. The Role of Humans in the Diversification of Plants in Mexico. In *Biological Diversity in Mexico: Origins and Distribution*, edited by T. P. Ramamoorthy, R. Bye, A. Lot, and J. Fa, pp. 707–31. New York: Oxford University Press.

———. 1995a. Ethnobotany of the Mexican Dry Tropical Forest. In *Seasonally Dry Tropical Forests*, edited by S. H. Bullock, H. A. Mooney, and E. Medina, pp. 423–38. Cambridge: Cambridge University Press.

———. 1995b. Prominence of the Sierra Madre Occidental in the Biological Diversity of Mexico. In *Biodiversity and Management of the Madrean Archipelago: The Sky Islands of Southwestern United States and Northwestern Mexico*, coordinated by L. F. DeBano, G. J. Gottried, R. H. Hamre, C. B. Edminster, P. F. Ffolliot, and A. Ortega-Rubio, pp. 19–27. General Technical Report RM-GTR-265. Fort Collins, Colo.: USDA, Forest Service.

Bye, R., A. García, E. Herrera, J. Reyes, K. Orpiwel, F. Mancera. 1995. Arts/Crafts Exploitation of Beargrass and Sotol. In *Proyecto de Recursos Tarahumara*, pp. 36–55. Technical Report, Phase Two, World Wildlife Fund and Biodiversity Support Program (US AID). Tucson, Ariz.: Native Seeds SEARCH and Sonoran Institute.

Bye, R., and E. Linares. 1983. The Role of Plants Found in the Mexican Markets and Their Importance in Ethnobotanical Studies. *Journal of Ethnobiology* 3:1–13.

———. 1990. Mexican Market Plants of the Sixteenth Century. I. Plants Recorded in Historia Natural de Nueva España. *Journal of Ethnobiology* 10:151–68.

Bye, R., E. Linares, and C. Bonfil. 1989. Ethnobotany and Markets. In *Field Trip Guide, 1989—Conference of Latin Americanist Geographers*, compiled by W. E. Doolittle, edited by B. Beaty-Benadom and C. R. Vernon, pp. 59–87. Austin: Department of Geography, University of Texas.

Bye, R., E. Linares, and E. Estrada. 1995. Biological Diversity of Medicinal Plants in Mexico. *Recent Advances in Phytochemistry* 29:65–82.

Bye, R., R. Mata, and R. Pereda-Miranda. 1997. Avance en el programa del International Cooperative Biodiversity Group en México. *Noticiero de Biología* (Chile) 5(2):41–45.

Bye Boettler, R., M. Mendoza Cruz, and V. Evangelista. 1999. Plantas medicinales del norte de México: Archivo etnohistórico del Dr. Edward Palmer (1869–1910). In *La medicina tradicional del norte de México*, coordinated by M. S. Ortiz Enchaniz, pp. 95–108. Mexico City: Instituto Nacional de Antropología e Historia.

Caballero, J. 1987. Etnobotánica y desarrollo: La búsqueda de nuevos recursos vegetales. In *Memorias: IV Congreso Latinoamericano de Botánica, Simposio de Etnobotánica*, pp. 79–96. Bogotá, Colombia: Instituto Colombiano para el Fomento de la Educación Superior.

———. 1990. El uso de la diversidad vegetal en México: Tendencias y perspectivas. In *Medio ambiente y desarrollo en México*, coordinated by E. Leff, pp. 257–96. Mexico City: Miguel Angel Porrua.

———. 1992. Maya Homegardens: Past, Present and Future. *Etnoecología* 1:35–54.

———. 1993. El caso del uso y manejo del la palma de guano (*Sabal* spp.) entre los Mayas de Yucatán, México. In *Cultura y manejo sustentable de los recursos naturales*, coordinated by E. Leff and J. Carabias, 1:203–48. 2 vols. Mexico City: Miguel Angel Porrua.

Callen, E. O. 1965. Food Habits of Some Pre-Columbian Mexican Indians. *Economic Botany* 19:335–43.

Cantú Díaz Barriga, Antonio, Fulvio Eccardi Ambrosi, Enrique Lira Fernández, Jesús Ramírez Ruiz, Manuel Serrato Tejeda, and Alfredo Zavala González. 1991. *México diverso—Un encuentro con su naturaleza*. Mexico City: Instituto de Seguridad y Servicios Sociales de los Trabajadores del Estado.

Casas, A., and J. Caballero. 1996. Traditional Management and Morphological Variation in *Leucaena esculenta* (Fabaceae: Mimosoideae) in the Mixtec Region of Guerrero, Mexico. *Economic Botany* 50:167–81.

Casas, A., J. L. Viveros, and J. Caballero. 1994. Etnobotánica mixteca—Sociedad, cultura y recursos naturales en la Montaña de Guerrero. Mexico City: Instituto Nacional Indigenista.

Challenger, A. 1998. *Utilización y conservación de los ecosistemas terrestres de México: Pasado, presente y futuro*. Mexico City: Comisión Nacional para el Conocimiento y Uso de la Biodiversidad; Instituto de Biología, Universidad Nacional Autónoma de México; Agrupación Sierra Madre, A.C.

Colunga-GarcíaMarín, P., and F. May-Pat. 1993. Agave Studies in Yucatán, Mexico. I. Past and Present Germplasm Diversity and Uses. *Economic Botany* 47:312–27.

Colunga G-M., P., E. Hernández X., and A. Castillo M. 1986. Variación morfológica, manejo agrícola tradicional y grado de domesticación de *Opuntia* spp. en El Bajío Guanajuatense. *Agrociencia* 65:7–49.

de Wet, J. M. J., and J. R. Harlan. 1975. Weeds and Domesticates: Evolution in the Man-made Habitat. *Economic Botany* 29:99–107.

Estrada Lugo, E. I. J., E. Hernández Xolocotzi, T. Rojas Rabiela, E. M. Engleman, and M. A. Casián Márquez. 1988. Códice Florentino: Su información etnobotánica. *Agrociencia* 71:275–86.

Felger, R. S., and M. B. Moser. 1985. *People of the Desert and Sea: Ethnobotany of the Seri Indians.* Tucson: University of Arizona Press.

Furst, P. T. 1989. The Life and Death of the Crazy Kiéri: Natural and Cultural History of a Huichol Myth. *Journal of Latin American Lore* 15:155–77.

Gentry, H. S. 1982. *Agaves of Continental North America.* Tucson: University of Arizona Press.

Gerhard, P. 1986. *Geografía histórica de la Nueva España 1519–1821.* Mexico City: Universidad Nacional Autónoma de México.

Gío-Argáez, Raúl, and Eucario López-Ochoterena. 1993. Diversidad biológica en México. *Revista de la Sociedad Mexicana de Historia Natural* 44:1–427.

Gómez-Pompa, A. 1971. Posible papel de la vegetación secundaria en la evolución de la flora tropical. *Biotropica* 3:125–35.

Gonçalves de Lima, O. 1956. *El maguey y el pulque en los códices mexicanos.* Mexico City: Fondo de Cultura Económica.

Grifo, F. T. 1996. Chemical Prospecting: An Overview of the International Cooperative Biodiversity Groups Program. In *Biodiversity, Biotechnology, and Sustainable Development in Health and Agriculture: Emerging Connections,* edited by J. Feinsilver, pp. 12–28. Washington, D.C.: Pan American Health Organization.

Gutelman, M. 1984. *Capitalismo y reforma agraria en México.* Mexico City: Ediciones Era.

Guzmán, G. 1980. *Identificación de los hongos comestibles, venenosos y alucinantes.* Mexico City: Editorial Limusa.

Harlan, J. R. 1975. *Crops and Man.* Madison, Wis.: American Society of Agronomy.

Hawkes, J. G. 1983. *The Diversity of Crop Plants.* Cambridge, Mass.: Harvard University Press.

Hernández Xolocotzi, E. 1993. Aspects of Plant Domestication in Mexico: A Personal View. In *Biological Diversity in Mexico: Origins and Distribution*, edited by T. P. Ramamoorthy, R. Bye, A. Lot, and J. Fa, pp. 733–53. New York: Oxford University Press.

Hernández Xolocotzi, E., E. Bello Baltazar, and S. Levy Tacher (comps.). 1995. *La milpa en Yucatán—Un sistema de producción agrícola tradicional.* Montecillos, Mexico: Colegio de Postgraduados.

Hersch, P. 1996. *Destino común: Los recolectores y su flora medicinal.* Mexico City: Instituto Nacional de Antropología e Historia.

Heyden, D. 1983. *Mitología y simbolismo de la flora en el México prehispánico.* Mexico City: Universidad Nacional Autónoma de México.

Hunn, E. S. 1982. The Utilitarian Factor in Folk Biological Classification. *American Anthropologist* 84:830–47.

Jiménez, V. 1990. *El Arbol de El Tule en la historia.* Mexico City: Codex Editores.

Joyal, E. 1996. The Palm Has Its Time: An Ethnoecology of *Sabal uresana* in Sonora, Mexico. *Economic Botany* 50:446–62.

Kaerger, K. 1986. *Agricultura y colonización en México en 1900.* Chapingo, Mexico: Universidad Autónoma Chapingo.

Katz, E. 1992. La cueillette des adventices comestibles au Mexique. *Ecologie Humaine* 10:25–41.

Lara Plata, L. (coord.). 1995. Manejo y conocimiento de la biodiversidad entre los indígenas de México. Mexico City: Instituto Nacional Indigenista.

Leff, E., J. Carabias, and A. I. Batis (coords.). 1990. *Recursos naturales, técnica y cultura: Estudio y experiencias para un desarrollo alternativo.* Cuadernos del Centro de Investigaciones Interdisciplinarias en Humanidades, Universidad Nacional Autónoma de México. Serie Seminarios 1. Mexico City: Universidad Nacional Autónoma de México.

Levi, J. M. 1993. Pillars of the Sky—The Genealogy of Ethnic Identity among the Rarámuri-Simaroni (Tarahumara-Gentiles) of Northwest Mexico. Ph.D. dissertation. Harvard University, Cambridge, Mass.

Linares, E., and R. Bye. 1987. A Study of Four Medicinal Plant Complexes of Mexico and Adjacent United States. *Journal of Ethnopharmacology* 19:153–83.

———. 1993. Los jardines botánicos y las plantas medicinales. In *La investigación científica de la herbolaria medicinal mexicana*, coordinated by M. Juan, A. Bondani, J. Sanfilippo B., and E. Berumen, pp. 75–83. Mexico City: Secretaría de Salud.

Lobato, J. G. 1884. *Estudio químico-industrial de varios productos del maguey mexicano y análisis químico del aguamiel y el pulque.* Mexico City: Secretaría de Fomento de México.

Mapes, C., J. Caballero, E. Espitia, and R. Bye. 1996. Morphological Variation in Some Mexican Species of Vegetable *Amaranthus*: Evolutionary Tendencies under Domestication. *Genetic Resources and Crop Evolution* 43:283–90.

Marino Ambrosio, A. 1966. The Pulque Agaves of Mexico. Ph.D. dissertation. Harvard University, Cambridge, Mass.

Martínez Alfaro, M. A. 1993. Etnobotánica. In *Logros y perspectivas del conocimiento de los recursos vegetales de México en vísperas del siglo XXI*, compiled by S. Guevara, P. Moreno-Casasola, and J. Rzedowski, pp. 39–55. Xalapa, Veracruz: Instituto de Ecología, A.C.

———. 1994. Estado actual de las investigaciones etnobotánicas en México. *Boletín de la Sociedad Botánica de México* 55:65–74.

Martínez Alfaro, M. A., V. Evangelista Oliva, M. Mendoza Cruz, G. Morales García, G. Toledo Olazcoaga, and A. Wong León. 1995. *Catálogo de plantas útiles de la Sierra Norte de Puebla, México.* Mexico City: Instituto de Biología, Universidad Nacional Autónoma de México.

Martínez R., J. 1986. *Diversidad monolingüe de México en 1970.* Mexico City: Universidad Nacional Autónoma de México.

Martínez S., T., J. Trujillo A., and F. Bejarano G. (comps.). 1994. *Agricultura campesina—Orientaciones agrobiológicas y agronómicas sobre bases sociales tradicionales vs. trato de libre comercio.* Montecillos, Mexico: Colegio de Postgraduados.

Nabhan, G. P. 1985. *Gathering the Desert.* Tucson: University of Arizona Press.

Olivera, M., M. I. Ortiz, and C. Valverde. 1982. *La población y las lenguas indígenas de México en 1970.* Mexico City: Universidad Nacional Autónoma de México.

O'odham I:waki/Wild Greens of the Desert People. 1980. Tucson, Ariz.: Meals for Millions Foundation.

Ortiz de Montellano, B. R. 1990. *Aztec Medicine, Health and Nutrition.* New Brunswick, N.J.: Rutgers University Press.

Parsons, J. R., and M. H. Parsons. 1990. *Maguey Utilization in Highland Central Mexico: An Archaeological Ethnography.* Anthropological Papers. Ann Arbor: University of Michigan.

Pennington, C. W. 1963. *The Tarahumar of Mexico—Their Environment and Material Culture.* Salt Lake City: University of Utah Press.

Ramamoorthy, T. P., R. Bye, A. Lot, and J. Fa (eds.). 1993. *Biological Diversity in Mexico: Origins and Distribution*. New York: Oxford University Press.

Reichenbacher, F. W. 1985. Conservation of Southwestern Agaves. *Desert Plants* 7:103–6, 88.

Rivera M., I. 1942. Estudio botánico e histórico acerca del "palo copado," *Quararibea funebris* (Llave). *Standl. Anales del Instituto de Biología (UNAM, México)* 13:499–502.

Robles Gil, P., and V. M. Toledo. 1995. *México: Diversidad de culturas*. Mexico City: Agrupación Sierra Madre, A.C.; CEMEX.

Rojas Rabiela, T. 1993. *La agricultura chinampera*. Chapingo, Mexico: Universidad Autónoma Chapingo.

Ruvalcaba M., J. 1983. El maguey manso: Historia y presente de Epazoyucán, Hidalgo. Chapingo, Mexico: Universidad Autónoma Chapingo.

Rzedowski, J. 1978. *Vegetación de México*. Mexico City: Editorial Limusa.

———. 1986. Las plantas calcicolas (incluyendo una gipsófita) del Valle de México y sus ligas con la erosión edáfica. *Biotropica* 18:12–15.

———. 1993. Diversity and Origins of the Phanerogamic Flora of Mexico. In *Biological Diversity in Mexico: Origins and Distribution*, edited by T. P. Ramamoorthy, R. Bye, A. Lot, and J. Fa, pp. 129–44. New York: Oxford University Press.

Rzedowski, J., and M. Equihua. 1987. *Atlas cultural de México: Flora*. Mexico City: Secretaría de Educación Pública.

Sahagún, Fray Bernardino de. 1979. *Códice Florentino* (fascimile). 3 vols. Mexico City: Archivo General de la Nación.

Sarukhán, J., and R. Dirzo (comps.). 1992. *México ante los retos de la biodiversidad*. Mexico City: Comisión Nacional para el Conocimiento y Uso de la Biodiversidad.

Smith, C. E. 1967. Plant Remains. In *The Prehistory of the Tehuacán Valley, Vol. 1: Environment and Subsistence*, edited by D. W. Byers, pp. 220–55. Austin: University of Texas Press.

Toledo, V. M. 1983. Ecologismo y ecología—La otra guerra florida. *Nexos* 69:15–24.

———. 1987. La etnobotánica en Latinoamérica: Vicisitudes, contextos, disafíos. In *Memorias: IV Congreso Latinoamericano de Botánica, Simposio de Etnobotánica*. Bogotá, Colombia: Instituto Colombiano para el Fomento de la Educación Superior.

Toledo, V. M., J. Carabias, C. Toledo, and C. González-Pacheco. 1989. *La producción rural en México: Alternativas ecológicas*. Mexico City: Fundación Universo Veintiuno.

Ulloa, M., T. Herrera, and P. Lappe. 1987. *Fermentaciones tradicionales indígenas de México*. Mexico City: Instituto Nacional Indigenista.

Valdés, J., and H. Flores. 1985. Historia de las plantas de Nueva España. In Comisión editora de las obras de Francisco Hernández, *Comentarios a la obra de Francisco Hernández, Obras completas*, 7:7–222. 7 vols. Mexico City: Universidad Nacional Autónoma de México.

Valdés, L. M., and M. T. Menéndez. 1987. *Dinámica de la población de habla indígena (1900–1980)*. Mexico City: Instituto Nacional de Antropología e Historia.

Valdés Gutiérrez, J., H. Flores Olvera, and H. Ochoterena-Booth. 1992. La botánica en el Códice de la Cruz. In *Estudios actuales sobre el Libellus de Medicinalibus Indorum Herbis*, pp. 129–80. Mexico City: Secretaría de Salud.

Vázquez Rojas, M. C. 1991. Tendencias en el proceso de domesticación en papaloquelite (*Porophyllum ruderale* (Jacq.) Cass. subsp. *macrocephalum* (DC.) R.R. Johnson, ASTERACEAE). Master's thesis. Facultad de Ciencias, Universidad Nacional Autónoma de México, Mexico City.

Zizumbo Villarreal, D., and P. Colunga García-Marín. 1982. Los Huaves— La apropiación de los recursos naturales. Chapingo, Mexico: Universidad Autónoma Chapingo.

Zorrilla, L. 1988. *El maguey: "Arbol de las Maravillas."* Mexico City: Museo Nacional de Culturas Populares.

CHAPTER THREE

ETHNOPHARMACOLOGY AND THE SEARCH FOR NEW THERAPEUTICS

WALTER H. LEWIS

INTRODUCTION

There is a worldwide need to consider the use of ethnopharmaceutical data obtained from indigenous and other peoples in the discovery process leading to the development of new pharmaceuticals to improve human health. Given this exigency, it behooves the researchers and their organizers and administrators to provide a collaborative program among all parties so that their rights and benefits will be adequate and fair. To address these aspects of therapeutic discoveries, focusing on North America, this chapter is divided into four parts: targeted versus random collecting; collaborative agreements; ethnopharmacology of two North American plants; and future ethnopharmacological discoveries in North America: a model of procedure. North America is defined as "north of Mexico" following the *Flora of North America* project definitions (1993).

TARGETED VERSUS RANDOM COLLECTING

There is great promise for new drug discoveries based on traditional medicinal plant uses throughout the world (Lewis and

Elvin-Lewis 1995). As two-fifths of all modern U.S. pharmaceutical products contain one or more naturally derived ingredients (Oldfield 1984), a frequency that would double if synthetic compounds modeled on natural products and semisynthetic compounds derived from such products were added, an exceptional opportunity exists to optimize the search for novel pharmaceuticals.

In this search for therapeutic natural products, collections can be made using a number of distinct strategies. Random collecting is the most obvious, simply collecting all plants on a strictly random basis, but this approach is rarely used by biologists or anthropologists. Their training dictates some degree of selectivity, whether based on taxonomic, chemical, ecologic, or other disciplines. Although several of these approaches may be important features of what was called "modified random" collecting (Lewis and Elvin-Lewis 1995), they do not as a rule provide targeted evidence needed to test the material for activity. We know the structures of over one hundred thousand natural products, yet why have so few among them become useful pharmaceuticals? To answer this question, G. Albers-Schönberg (1996) wrote: "I propose that it is precisely because we have spent our efforts on random approaches and have completely neglected ecological points of view." He further added that we should not be interested in natural products as a random collection of diverse structures, for nature optimizes structures for specific biochemical functions within organisms. We should, therefore, search for compounds for which our intended applications correlate with their biochemical functions as intended by nature.

Speculating about this question with regard to microorganisms, Albers-Schönberg provided an interesting example. There are an incredible number of toxic terpenoid natural products. Could it be, he suggested, that the ability to prevent the formation of such compounds confers a distinct advantage on organisms that can block the synthesis of these toxins? The fungi *Aspergillus terreus* and *Monascus ruber* produce the potent and effective cholesterol-lowering compound lovastatin (Mevacor[R]), from which the even more effective semisynthetic simvastatin was formed. Lovastatin

specifically inhibits the synthesis of mevalonic acid, a key intermediate in the synthesis of cholesterol, as well as of the toxic
terpenes. Even though this postulated function did not play a role
in the discovery of the anticholesterol lovastatin, in hindsight, the
high potencies of the compound, the targeted specificity, and the
compound structure all insinuate that it is not a random product in
these fungi. Albers-Schönberg concluded that the search for functional relationships may well be the key to new discoveries of extra-
ordinary natural products and may become far more successful
than massive random screening.

Unlike many microorganisms and animals, and much marine
life, large numbers of terrestrial plants have already provided us
with insights into important functional targets. They do so, not
because we necessarily understand their functions in plants, but
because of what humans have been doing for centuries, and indeed
millennia, in selecting, testing, and using plants for particular
purposes. Thus, humans have been sampling biochemical pathways and their chemical products during the process of learning
which plants function well, and which do not, in relation to disease
states and syndromes. Clearly, such functional assay experiments
by us have been underway for a very long time, and they continue
today in many areas of the world (see fig. 3.1). Good ethnomedicinal data, therefore, provide the functional relationships needed to
catapult researchers into targeted screening with an early insight
toward discovering new natural products and therapeutics.

A recent example provides support for human selections of
plants targeted for particular uses (Lewis and Elvin-Lewis 1995).
Fifty crude extracts of twenty-five vascular plant collections were
submitted to the primary Acquired Immune Deficiency Syndrome
(AIDS) anti–Human Immunodeficiency Virus (HIV) screening
program of the U.S. National Cancer Institute (NCI). Collections
representing twenty-three genera in nineteen families from four
continents had been functionally targeted based on their traditional
medicinal use for anti-infective activity. Results of such testing were

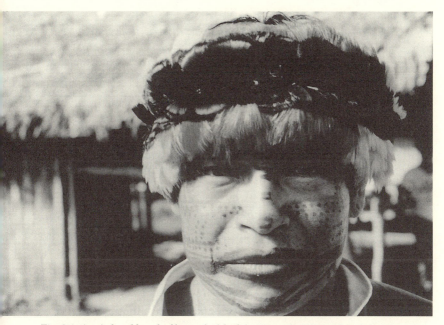

Fig. 3.1. An Achual head of household of the Jívaro linguistic family, which consists of four tribes in Peru and Ecuador: Achual, Aguaruna, Huambisa, and Shuar.

then compared with extracts of terrestrial plants obtained randomly throughout the world and tested by NCI in the same anti-HIV screening program.

Of the fifty samples tested, without regard to type of ethno-medicinal infection, extract procedure, or source of information, fifteen samples or 30% proved weakly to strongly active against HIV in vitro. When these results were compared with the 1,429 or 8.5% of the 16,886 total extracts of terrestrial plants obtained randomly by the NCI that proved active in their primary anti-HIV screens, anti-infective, functionally pretargeted samples proved significantly different (P <0.001) (see table 3.1). Included in these data were anti-infective plants traditionally used to treat a virus considered ancestrally related to HIV (Elvin-Lewis, unpublished

TABLE 3.1

Ethnomedicinially Targeted Anti-infective Plants Tested in the NCI Primary Anti-HIV Screen

	SCREENS	ACTIVE (NO./%)	SIGNIFICANCE
NCI modified random	16,886	1,429/8.5%	
Anti-infective targeted	50	15/30%	$P < 0.001$
Related antiviral subset	14	10/71.4%	$P < 0.001$

data). When this subset of extracts, which presumably was functionally more associated with the assay than were the general anti-infectively targeted extracts, was examined using the primary anti-HIV assay, 10 of 14 samples or 71.4% proved active compared to 30% of anti-infectively targeted plants in general and only 8.5% activity among random plant collections. These highly significant differences between targeted ethnomedicinal and random collections show that for anti-infectives, at least, an ethnomedicinal strategy should be widely adopted in targeting functional relationships and the search for new therapeutics.

In another case, a liver cancer cell line was used to screen 1,000 Chinese medicinal plants for specific bioreactivity. The activity rate was about 13%, a somewhat higher frequency than would normally be found in general random screens. When this subset of active plants was compared with their ethnomedicinal uses, however, it was found that 93% were already known for treating malignancies (John Babish, personal communication, 1994).

In areas of disease poorly recognized in traditional medical practices, such as certain cancers, the "modified random" strategy used by the NCI is perhaps appropriate. For instance, the NCI discovery in the early 1970s of the antineoplastic compound taxol from *Taxus brevifolia* (Taxaceae) in a broad collection program in the Pacific Northwest of the United States and Canada is presumably an example of randomness and therefore pure serendipity. It is unlikely that the collectors knew that an allied species, *T. baccata*, which is now known to possess frequencies of taxol even higher than those of *T. brevifolia* (Elias and Korzenevsky 1992), had long been used in Asian Indian traditional medicine to treat cancer. In retrospect, based on this use in Asia, it would not be unusual to find an American species in the same genus having a similar compound and efficacy (Lewis and Elvin-Lewis 1995). Clearly, then, inter-specific considerations and certain intergeneric relationships should be routine strategies in targeting potential candidates for screening. This would be reason enough for taxonomists with ethnobotanical training, or vice versa, to be involved in searching for novel natural products, for one species of a cluster that had been ethnofunc-tionally targeted might lead rapidly to the discovery of biochemical diversity and allied but different compounds with similar functions. Likewise, small, closely related genera would also be valuable sources of genetic material if a species of one genus were already targeted ethnomedicinally. Such approaches to bioprospecting are important and perhaps most relevant when biodiversity is greatest.

COLLABORATIVE AGREEMENTS

As I have described, an extremely important and too often neglected strategy is to obtain detailed primary ethnomedicinal information regarding all aspects of the use of biological materials, including when possible field confirmation of efficacy by others. This confirmation may include the same use in the same way among different peoples or the opinion of physicians, healers, and others who have observed the healing process. Such data, together with biological materials used for treatment and for preparing museum vouchers, are fundamental to the whole strategy asso-ciated with ethnomedicinal information.

We must recognize, therefore, that both intangible resources, or knowledge, and tangible resources, or biological material, are being provided directly or indirectly by individuals contributing information. But whose knowledge is being given? Is it simply that of the individual informant who is providing the unique data, is it information that is considered common knowledge in the community, region, tribe, or even beyond, or is it somewhere in between, perhaps restricted to the informant's family or to like-trained individuals? And what of the biological material: does it belong to individual landowners, is it community or tribal property, or is it solely the genetic resource of the state? These and other important questions need examination before appropriate agreements can be forthcoming and before ethnobotanical research should commence.

We recently concluded a set of agreements as part of the International Cooperative Biodiversity Group (ICBG) program "Peruvian Medicinal Plant Sources of New Pharmaceuticals." I shall describe the main points of these agreements, which may serve in part as models for future negotiations elsewhere. The agreements are between Washington University in St. Louis, recipient of the five-year ICBG grant administered by the Fogerty International Center, National Institutes of Health (NIH), and three types of institutions or organizations: two universities in Lima, Peru, clan organizations of certain Aguaruna indigenous people in northern Peru, and an American corporation, Monsanto/Searle & Co. of St. Louis. They include five interconnected agreements (see fig. 3.2):

1. License Option and License Option Amendment Agreements—establish royalty rates for pharmaceutical products and how these rates will be shared.
2. Biological Collecting Agreement—outlines who will be involved in the collection program, where collecting can occur and under what circumstances, and what annual collecting fees will be provided to the collaborating Aguaruna clans by the corporate partner.
3. Know-how License Agreement—describes annual license fees to be paid by the corporate partner to the collaborating Aguaruna clans while their knowledge is being used in

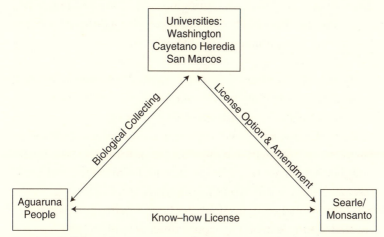

Fig. 3.2. Collaborative agreements between parties of the International Cooperative Biodiversity Group–Peru program.

extraction and screening programs; it also establishes milestone payments to be paid by the corporate partner.

4. Museo de Historia Natural, Universidad Nacional Mayor de San Marcos Agreement—outlines collaboration in the field program, inventory, conservation, and ecologic research, and curating and housing of specimens, funded through Washington University.

5. Universidad Peruana Cayetano Heredia Agreement— describes the crude plant extraction program and functional assays of specific disease states, funded through Washington University.

A few general highlights of these agreements are of particular note. With regard to indigenous rights, the parties clearly recognize ownership of the medicinal plant knowledge by the Aguaruna people: their knowledge represents a cultural legacy that needs to be wisely and responsibly used for the benefit of their people now and in the future. Information about their medicinal plants is received voluntarily through prior informed consent and retained in confidence. Should such data prove valuable following biological and chemical experimentation, the original intellectual property and subsequent research will be protected largely through the filing of appropriate patents. These patents will involve individual Aguaruna as inventors or at a minimum the recognition of the Aguaruna people as contributors to the inventions.

As part of the agreements the Aguaruna people recognize the Peruvian government's ownership and patrimony over certain tangible resources (i.e., the genetic material collected by the researchers in Peru for scientific purposes). They acknowledge the need for voucher collections to be permanently deposited, curated, and researched for noncommercial purposes at national and international repositories. Biological collections obtained for the intended purpose of extracting compounds for commercial purposes remain the property of the Aguaruna, however, unless released from their ownership.

Collection activities in designated regions guarantee that populations of medicinal plant species and the supply or accessibility of such plants required by the indigenous people will not be endangered. In addition, a program of reforestation has been initiated to conserve medicinal plants already overexploited and to provide a sustainable resource for the people.

Specific types of compensation were agreed to by collaborating researchers, institutions, and the participating Aguaruna clans during collection, research, development, and commercial stages of the program. Currently, annual payments of collection and know-how fees are being provided to the Aguaruna by the corporate partner, and these will continue for the duration of the NIH grant. Recollection payments will be negotiated on a collection-as-needed basis. Furthermore, know-how fees will continue to be paid to the Aguaruna even after the completion of the ICBG grant as long as extracts or their fractions are being researched. Milestone payments will be made to the Aguaruna people for each potential commercial product during specified research and development phases. When a commercial product is released for public use, royalties based on net sales will be paid by the corporate partner, with provisions made for increased royalty rates when activities and discoveries by the universities prove relevant. Royalty rates will usually be divided equally between the three universities and the collaborating Aguaruna clans, with no less than 75% of the royalty income returning to Peru.

Legal representation is an essential component of negotiations leading to these agreements. All parties involved ought to be well represented and ultimately be satisfied with the negotiations and agree to conclusions regarding informed consent, intellectual property, compensation, recognition, and numerous other aspects.

ETHNOPHARMACOLOGY OF TWO NORTH AMERICAN PLANTS

There are, unfortunately, few examples of plants native to Canada and the United States having been selected as targeted ethnomedicinal candidates that have proved important in the development of new pharmaceuticals or other drugs. Two of the best examples provide valuable insights into what could be discovered in the future using ethnotargeting of plants.

PODOPHYLLUM PELTATUM
(MAY APPLE, AMERICAN MANDRAKE) (BERBERIDACEAE)

Long used by American Indians as a drastic purgative, extracts from May apple (see fig. 3.3) rhizomes and roots became widely available as podophyllin in the nineteenth century, not only as a laxative, but also to treat hepatic diseases including hepatitis, edema, venereal diseases, and other conditions. Early in the last century, white "Indian Doctors" in the eastern United States also used podophyllin to treat cancerous tumors and skin ulcers, a practice perhaps learned from the American Indians, although the early destruction of information from the eastern tribes makes this suggestion difficult to confirm. More likely their use of podophyllin as a superficial corrosive stemmed from its known toxicity, irritating quality, or drastic purgative property. In materia medicas of P. P. Good (1845) and J. Kost (1858), podophyllin was recommended for the treatment of cancerous tumors, polyps, and unhealthy granulations. By the end of the century, extracts were being used in Louisiana, Mississippi, and Missouri to treat venereal warts (condyloma acuminata) and other papillomas; and in the twentieth century, podophyllin became the drug of choice for this purpose. Its use in the 1930s by the Penobscot of Maine was probably an adoption from earlier white uses rather than from traditional Indian medicine.

Fig. 3.3. (a) *Podophyllum peltatum* (May apple) near St. Louis in May: typical deciduous forest habitat and growth of the herbaceous perennial in colonies and/or clones; and (b) an aerial stem with lobed, umbrella-like leaves and flower.

b

May apple rhizomes and roots contain 3.5 to 6% of a resin whose active principles are lignans, mainly podophyllotoxin (see fig. 3.4), alpha-peltatin, and beta-peltatin. The purgative properties are due to the peltatins present, while the antitumor effects are attributed to both podophyllotoxin and the peltatins. Podophyllotoxin is a mitotic poison, inhibiting cell division during metaphase by binding to the protein fibers, which constitutes the mitotic spindle that holds the chromosomes during this phase of cell division. In clinical trials, however, podophyllotoxin proved too toxic for use as a cancer chemotherapeutic agent.

Attempts to find safer compounds of podophyllotoxin resulted in further isolations and the synthesis of hundreds of analogs by Sandoz Laboratories. One, 4'-demethylepipodophyllotoxin benzylidene glucoside, proved a highly potent antileukemic factor, and one of its many analogs, the semisynthetic teniposide, was introduced into the clinic in 1967 on an experimental basis. After it had been shown to be effective in treating reticulosarcoma, Hodgkin's disease, and bladder carcinoma, teniposide was marketed by Sandoz in 1976 in some European countries. Only recently has it been approved for treating certain cancers in the United States.

A second semisynthetic compound, etoposide (see fig. 3.4), proved superior to teniposide in its ability to prolong the life-span of mice inoculated with L-1210 leukemia; further, it was orally active while teniposide required injection. Etoposide was first tested clinically in 1971; it was found most valuable in the treatment of non–small cell lung cancer, testicular cancer, and lymphomas, and it was the first drug found effective against acute monocytic leukemias by preventing target cells from entering mitosis. Sandoz licensed both teniposide and etoposide to Bristol-Myers Squibb (BMS) in 1978, because of that company's greater expertise in cancer chemotherapy, and in 1983 etoposide was approved for use in the United States.

For fifteen years, therefore, the semisynthetic etoposide derived from podophyllotoxin found in May apple rhizomes and roots has

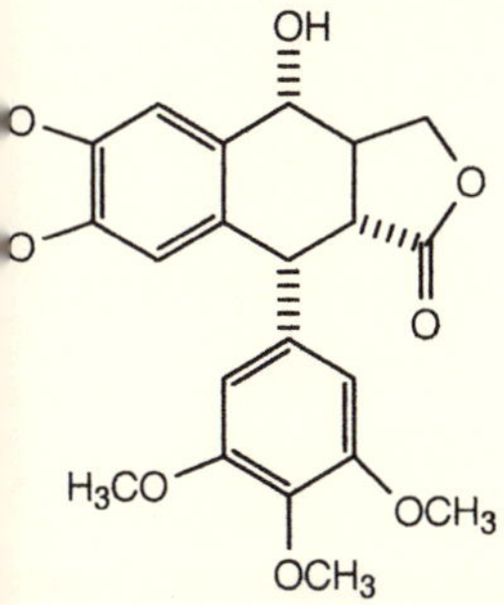

PODOPHYLLOTOXIN

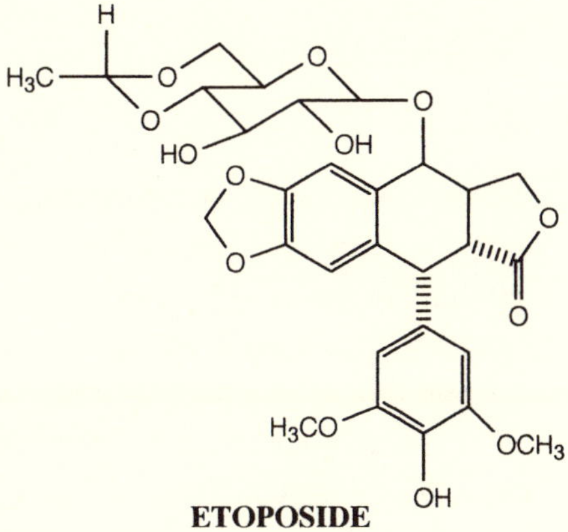

ETOPOSIDE

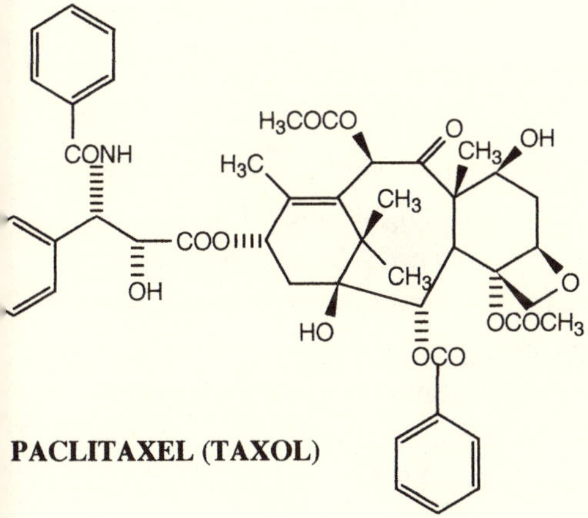

PACLITAXEL (TAXOL)

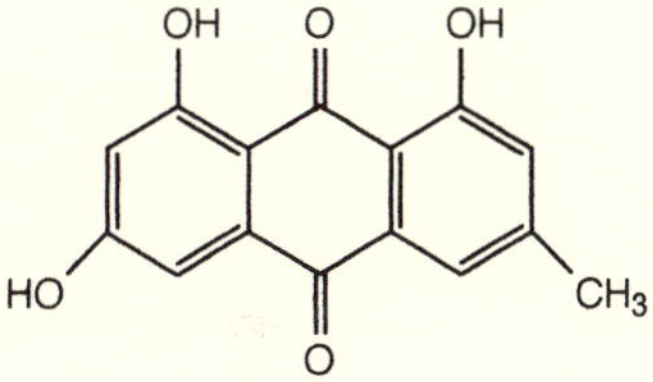

EMODIN

Fig. 3.4. Chemical structures of podophyllotoxin, etoposide, taxol, and emodin.

been used in chemotherapy to treat at least four major types of cancer, either singly or in combination. Peak annual sales of the compound reached approximately $300 million in the late 1980s and early 1990s, though sales and income are now much reduced. Costs for research and development by both BMS and Sandoz were

about $10 million. (This contrasts with BMS's recent research and
development costs of over $100 million to commercialize the anti-
neoplastic taxol [see fig. 3.4], a far more complex situation than that
of developing etoposide, requiring more extensive chemical, clinical, and field supply studies at a more expensive time.)

No contribution is being paid by BMS to original sources because
intangible resource information regarding podophyllin in the
treatment of topical cancers, tumors, and papillomas has been in
the public domain since the nineteenth century. No indigenous use
to treat cancer can be established prior to this time, but even if it
were, there is probably no retroactive legal recourse for claiming
compensation.

RHAMNUS PURSHIANA
(CASCARA SAGRADA, SACRED BARK) (RHAMNACEAE)

Many plants in the Rhamnaceae have long histories of use as
purgatives, such as *Rhamnus frangula* (frangula, alder buckthorn),
which grows throughout Europe, northern Africa, and northern
Asia. Since ancient times, it was the popular laxative in these areas
until superseded by the American *R. purshiana* (see fig. 3.5), native
from northern California to British Columbia and east to Montana.
The wide use of this species came into medical prominence in the
nineteenth century through the efforts of Dr. J. H. Bundy of Colusa,
California, and Park, Davis & Co. of Detroit, which commercialized
the product in 1877. There was never a dispute regarding the bark's
original use as a purgative by many indigenous peoples of the
Pacific Northwest (Vogel 1970).

Rhamnus purshiana bark contains the laxative glycosides frangulin
A and B, which are formed from their corresponding anthraquinols
during extraction (Sneader 1996). They pass unchanged through
the small intestine, but in the colon they are exposed to bacteria that
enzymatically hydrolyze the glycoside linkages to release the

Fig. 3.5. Flowering branches of the small tree *Rhamnus purshiana* (cascara sagrada), June 1997, Victoria, B.C. Courtesy of Robert Turner.

aglycone emodin (see fig. 3.4). Emodin is then responsible for increased intestinal motility, assisting defecation. The pure frangulins are not used in therapeutics, but extracts containing these, together with other ingredients, are available in over-the-counter (OTC) proprietary preparations. The laxative action of these is unpredictable because the anthraquinone content is not effectively standardized. These preparations and formulations are often trademarked and protected as trade secrets.

With the exception of fully characterizing the frangulins (which did not take place until 1972) and understanding their similar mode of action, minimal research was necessary to commercialize and continue to market this laxative after its introduction in 1877. This contrasts with major expenditures required to develop the antineoplastic pharmaceutical drugs teniposide and etoposide, described above, where net sales are much higher than for OTC products, but by comparison research and development costs involving cascara sagrada and many other OTC products are minuscule.

Because of the rapid destruction of wild *R. purshiana* by the 1920s, the U.S. Department of Agriculture (USDA) established tree plantations in the Pacific Northwest and certain eastern states. In the 1940s, bark from these sources was being used for commercial purpose (Osol and Farrar 1947), thus reducing the dangerous overexploitation of natural populations.

FUTURE ETHNOPHARMACOLOGICAL DISCOVERIES IN NORTH AMERICA: A MODEL OF PROCEDURE

Even though plant diversity and uniqueness is less in North America than in many other parts of the world, there still exist great opportunities for discovering new therapeutics in the continent. How should such research proceed? What obligations exist to the state and particularly to the custodians of traditional knowledge when commercialization is a goal? There are many possible scenarios, but let me propose a hypothetical situation using the South American Aguaruna model already outlined.

In the mountains of western Utah, researchers discovered and described a new, endemic species of *Veratrum* (false hellebore) (Liliaceae). Subsequent exploration in the region revealed that most populations of the new species were adjacent to or within reservation lands of the western Shoshoni Indians. Researchers noted then that members of several Shoshoni communities used the species medicinally, but no further data were obtained.

Since it was known that the allied *V. californicum* (corn lily) had been used to treat cancerous sores and tumors, researchers decided to conduct global ethnomedicinal and chemical dereplications of the twenty-five known species of *Veratrum*. They found as might be expected that not all species had been studied, but among those that had (fewer than half), cytotoxic effects and traditional medicinal uses associated with topical cancerous tumors predominated. Reports of chemical analyses were minimal.

Based on the above data, researchers decided that it could be significant to conduct an ethnopharmacological research program focusing on the new *Veratrum* and other medicinal species, if a collaborative effort with the Shoshoni could be organized on mutually agreed terms. These terms would include access, use, and sharing of benefits equitably where each party has the capacity and goodwill to ensure that the terms of an agreement are adhered to (Mugabe et al. 1996). Such efforts would include research, development, and commercialization of active leads in collaboration with other researchers and organizations, and those of the Shoshoni would involve sharing of ethnomedicinal data, while providing access to biological materials for analysis both initially and in the future. When warranted, growing of the species would be organized to prevent overexploitation of populations and thus retain the biodiversity of each species being studied in depth. Access to these genetic resources, as outlined by the Convention on Biological Diversity (hereafter Convention) in force in 1993, Article 15(4), must be on mutually agreed terms.

Access to genetic and know-how resources is subject to prior informed consent (PIC) of the party providing the resources (Convention, Article 15[5]). The PIC document should provide prior information regarding the collection of resources, who will be involved, what procedures will be followed, when the resources will be available for use, and what parties will be able to research the material. As a part of bioprospecting among the Shoshoni communities, the Convention, Articles 8(j) and 10(c), calls on the state to ensure that local and indigenous knowledge, practices, and innovations are protected and recognized by the parties (i.e., the traditional knowledge of the Shoshoni people).

Benefits for utilizing intangible traditional knowledge (know-how) and tangible genetic resources obtained for potential commercialization must be shared fairly, effectively, and equitably with the Shoshoni communities. As described in the South American agreements discussed above, collection fees, know-how fees, milestone payments, and royalty payments should be considered, negotiated, and agreed to as elaborated in Article 15 of the Convention. These payments, together with a supplier agreement (see below), could provide a substantial income to the people for community projects, education, health, and other purposes.

Traditional knowledge of the Shoshoni must be received voluntarily and kept in confidence until the parties involved agree to distribute the information publicly. This could occur following thorough testing of extract samples that proved inactive. When such information proves useful, the intellectual property of all parties must be protected through the filing of appropriate patents. As described for the South American Aguaruna, the Shoshoni should be involved as inventors whenever possible or at a minimum they can be recognized in the text of the patent for their contribution to the invention.

The discovery of an active compound from rhizomes of the new *Veratrum* species to treat tuberculosis, which researchers learned was used by the Shoshoni to treat this infection, requires protection by filing appropriate patents. The value of this confirmation of use and reduction to practice of the compound (novel or otherwise) is particularly important because no other species of *Veratrum* has been found as a treatment for this disease based on dereplication results. Protection is a concern for all parties involved in this project, but particularly for the corporate party, who will contribute large sums of money to cover research, development, and commercialization costs necessary to bring the natural products or their chemical derivatives to market.

Essential is a program of cultivation to provide a supply of rhizomes of the new *Veratrum* species for clinical research and testing and ultimately as the commercial source of material at least until (if ever) a synthetic compound is produced. This program should be developed as a collaborative effort by all parties, with the opportunity and resources provided to the Shoshoni people to develop the commercial production of the plant through a supplier agreement and so stimulate long-term employment and economic return to their communities while at the same time preventing the overexploitation of the species in their lands.

Modified for each unique circumstance, agreements such as those proposed in this hypothetical case and those already in existence through the ICBG project with the collaborating Aguaruna clans in Peru should be provided to all American Indian and other groups in North America and elsewhere who contribute to the discovery process of new pharmaceuticals. A truly collaborative effort that protects the rights of all parties involved and provides equitable compensations for all collaborators is essential. Such an action is particularly relevant in the United States since the 1993 Convention on Biological Diversity, though signed by President Bill Clinton in 1995, had not been ratified by the Senate by 1999.

CONCLUSIONS

1. Randomness in the selection and screening of organisms and compounds needs to be balanced and even replaced with efforts involving nonrandom strategies in the search for novel natural products of value in health.

2. For many microorganisms and other nonterrestrial organisms, new functionally oriented strategies to target biochemical pathways and compounds should include ecologic, taxonomic, and chemical insights.

3. For many terrestrial plants, ethnofunctional data target potentially unique biochemical pathways and compounds of immense medical value. Ethnomedicinal knowledge,

therefore, must become a paramount selective strategy in plant bioprospecting.

4. Interspecific and certain intergeneric relationships need consideration in developing targeted collecting strategies in order to optimize discoveries of biochemical diversity correlated with function among related species and genera.

5. Collaborative agreements among researchers, those peoples having ethnomedicinal knowledge, corporate and other partners, and perhaps the state need to address such issues as ownership of intellectual property and tangible biological materials; collecting area scope and conservation, including permits to collect, research, and commercialize biological materials; relationships and responsibilities of all partners; and compensation due parties during each stage of research, development, and commercialization.

6. Although there are few examples of ethnopharmacology contributing to the development of new pharmaceuticals in North America, two do illustrate the importance of targeting plants by either early settlers (*Podophyllum peltatum*) or indigenous peoples (*Rhamnus purshiana*) for research and future commercialization.

7. A model based on the ICBG program in Peru is provided for consideration in future ethnopharmacological research projects in North America. There exist great opportunities for discovery of new natural products and therapeutics in consort with indigenous and other peoples.

ACKNOWLEDGMENTS

This paper is based on research supported by Grant No. U01TW00331, International Cooperative Biodiversity Group (ICBG) program, funded by the National Institutes of Health (NIH), National Science Foundation, and U.S. Agency for International

Development. The grant was awarded to Washington University (Walter H. Lewis, PI) with the Museo de Historia Natural, Universidad Nacional Mayor de San Marcos, Lima (Gerardo Lamas), Universidad Peruana Cayetano Heredia, Lima (Abraham Vaisberg), and G. D. Searle & Co., St. Louis (David M. Corley). Special thanks are extended to the Aguaruna people for their interest and collaboration in the program, particularly to César Sarasara (CONAP), the clan leaders of OCCAAM, FAD, and FECONARIN, and their legal representatives (Brendan Tobin of SPDA and Mercedes Manriquez) involved in agreement negotiations. Finally, to all field and laboratory researchers and to administrators with the Fogarty International Center of NIH, Bethesda (Joshua Rosenthal in particular), I extend my appreciation for their time and effort given to the Peruvian ICBG.

REFERENCES CITED

Albers-Schönberg, G. 1996. Higher Plants versus Microorganisms: Their Future in Pharmaceutical Research. In *Medicinal Resources of the Tropical Rainforest: Biodiversity and its Importance to Human Health*, edited by M. J. Balick, E. Elisabetsky, and S. A. Laird, pp. 75–77. New York: Columbia University Press.

Elias, T. S., and V. V. Korzenevsky. 1992. The Presence of Taxol and Related Compounds in *Taxus baccata* Native to the Ukraine (Crimea), Georgia, and Southern Russia. Aliso 13:463–70.

Flora of North America Editorial Committee. 1993. *Flora of North America*. Vol. 1. New York: Oxford University Press.

Good, P. P. 1845. *The Family Flora and Materia Medica Botanica*. 2 vols. Elizabethtown, N.J.: Published by the author.

Kost, J. 1858. *The Elements of Materia Medica and Therapeutics*. 2nd ed. Cincinnati: Moore, Wilstach, Keys and Co.

Lewis, W. H., and M. P. Elvin-Lewis. 1995. Medicinal Plants as Sources of New Therapeutics. *Annals of the Missouri Botanical Garden* 82:16–24.

Mugabe, J., C. V. Barber, G. Henne, L. Glowka, and A. La Viña. 1996. *Managing Access to Genetic Resources: Towards Strategies for Benefit-Sharing*. Biopolicy International Series 17. Nairobi: Acts Press.

Oldfield, M. L. 1984. *The Value of Conserving Genetic Resources*. Washington, D.C.: U.S. Department of the Interior, National Park Service.

Osol, A., and G. E. Farrar, Jr. 1947. *The Dispensatory of the United States of America*. 24th ed. Philadelphia: J. B. Lippincott Co.

Sneader, W. 1996. *Drug Prototypes and Their Exploitation*. Chichester: Wiley and Sons.

Vogel, V. J. 1970. *American Indian Medicine*. Norman: University of Oklahoma Press.

Ethnographic Case Studies

"WE LIVE BY THEM"

Native Knowledge of Biodiversity in the Great Basin of Western North America

CATHERINE S. FOWLER

The phrase "we live by them," often repeated by elderly Numic-speaking Great Basin Indian people in the 1960s and 1970s while I was doing ethnobiological fieldwork, was, I believe, meant in two ways: (1) as an indication of the importance of plants and animals (but particularly plants) to the lives of the indigenous residents of the region in an economic or utilitarian sense ("we live *by means of* them"); and (2) as an additional indication of the perpetual and intimate association of humans with biotic species in the intellectualist's sense ("we live *surrounded by* them").[1] During these and subsequent years of field research, I have been continually impressed by both the deep sense of the practical with reference to discussions of plants and animals and the deeper sense of the overall importance of maintaining good relationships among humans and the land and its resources. Thus the dual meanings of "we live by them."

Indigenous peoples in the Great Basin of western North America were at one time broad-spectrum hunters and gatherers. Their interactions with the local biota included not only the collection of

certain products for foods, manufactures, and medicines, but also
the management of selected species, populations, and habitats. For
plants, management activities included pruning, clearing, burning,
coppicing, tilling, and transplanting, along with small-scale cultivation. Animals were less actively managed, although practices
involving some feeding, salting, selective harvesting, and culling
have been noted. Through time, much of this knowledge base and
many of these practices have been lost along with the general ability
to identify and talk about resources. Since the 1840s,[2] habitat
changes due to grazing, settlement, stream diversion, and the establishment of reserves and preserves have likewise affected changes
in indigenous knowledge systems. The materials and discussion
that follow are intended to assess something of indigenous Great
Basin knowledge of biodiversity and suggest some ways in which
that knowledge might still be usefully applied to some of the
problems in the region today. Because the Great Basin is a large
region (see map 4.1) with diverse peoples, and subject to varying
definitions (see d'Azevedo 1986), the focus is on selected examples
only. By general consensus, Great Basin indigenous groups include
communities of speakers of Numic languages of the Uto-Aztecan
family (Northern Paiute, Owens Valley Paiute, Southern Paiute,
Timbisha or Panamint, Shoshone, and Ute), as well as the Washoe,
speakers of a Hokan language (Jacobsen 1986; Miller 1986).

THE HISTORY OF GREAT BASIN
ETHNOBOTANICAL STUDIES

Data on the utilization of species of plants and animals by Great
Basin peoples have been supplied by a variety of individuals
through the years. Among the first to make observations were
explorers, such as the Franciscan father Silvestre Vélez de Escalante,
who in 1776 journeyed from Santa Fe, north through western
Colorado, northern and central Utah, and northern Arizona in

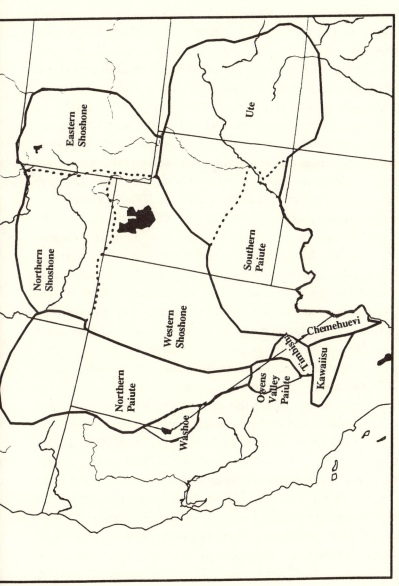

Map 4.1. The Great Basin of western North America, showing the territories of its principal ethnic/linguistic units.

search of a route of passage to California. Escalante, the party's diarist, made careful notes on the activities of the Indian peoples they encountered, describing berry harvesting among the Southern Ute, fishing with weirs among the Utah Lake Ute, netting hares and small garden farming among the Southern Paiute, and more (Bolton 1950; Euler 1966). John C. Frémont, one of the first of the military explorers to traverse the region, in 1844 described the richness of the Pyramid Lake trout fishery and Northern Paiute uses of the fish, as well as the collection of several plant species, and small-scale gardening procedures among the Southern Paiute (Frémont 1845). Another military explorer, J. H. Simpson (1876), who traversed the central Great Basin in 1858, provided data on the collection of what are probably wood rats among the Western Shoshone and fishing and decoy duck hunting among the Northern Paiute. Although often lacking in species identifications, these and other early accounts are invaluable for their information on techniques as well as resource availability. Most of the early explorers, as well as trappers and traders and early emigrants, also provided a wealth of data on the general condition of the country, as they were interested for practical purposes in the nature and distribution of forage, water, timber, and other resources.

Several biologists were also among those who took an interest in Native utilization of plants and animals in the region fairly early. Edward Palmer, noted plant explorer, collected valuable samples of seeds among the Southern Paiute in the 1870s, leaving Robert Bye (1972) to identify them a century later. Frederick Coville (1892), botanist on the 1891 Death Valley Expedition, made important observations among the Panamint or Timbisha Shoshone on the uses of native plants and offered the first technical identifications. Other members of that expedition, including C. Hart Merriam, Vernon Bailey, E. W. Nelson, and B. H. Dutcher, also made valuable observations of Native uses of plants, mammals, and birds while cataloguing and collecting the valley's biota. Some of these materials remain to be published (see, for example, Coville 1891). Merriam also went on to catalogue at least the names of plants and animals in several languages and communities in the Great Basin and California (Heizer 1979).

It is a botanist who is credited with the first attempt at a thorough treatment of the uses of plants by a single Great Basin group: Ralph Chamberlin with his study of Gosiute Shoshone ethnobotany in 1905 (Chamberlin 1911). In this work he catalogued the uses of over 300 plant species, along with providing some notes as to Native principles of nomenclature and an overall assessment of the role of plants in the lives of the people. Chamberlin followed this work with a list of some plant names in Ute (Chamberlin 1909), seemingly collected from a Ute speaker resident among the Gosiute. Unfortunately, there has been little follow-up among the Ute people since that time, so that, at best, scattered notes are all that contribute to a Ute ethnobotany.

Early ethnographers in the region made some valuable contributions, especially by collecting samples of food and medicinal plants for museums. Stephen Powers, who coined the term "aboriginal botany" (Powers 1873–75), made a valuable collection containing approximately 50 samples of "foods" and "medicines," all accompanied by Native names, among the Pyramid Lake and Walker River Northern Paiute in 1875. He was collecting for the Smithsonian's exhibition at the 1876 Centennial Exposition in Philadelphia. Robert H. Lowie, collecting for the American Museum of Natural History in 1914, made a smaller collection (40 samples, largely seeds) among the Fallon Northern Paiute and Moapa Southern Paiute. And Samuel Barrett, collecting for the Milwaukee Public Museum in 1916, gathered more than 150 samples from the Northern Paiute and Washoe peoples along with his more extensive ethnographic collections. None of these collections have associated voucher specimens, but the Native names provide additional clues as to their identification. The early field collectors did not gather samples of animal foods, although occasionally insect foods were taken (for example, the Mono Lake brine fly, *Ephedra hyens*).

Although monographic ethnographies of various Great Basin peoples began in the early 1900s with the work of Robert Lowie among the Northern Shoshone (1909), the period of the 1930s actually saw more field activities. By 1940, Isabel Kelly had worked among the Surprise Valley Northern Paiute and several Southern Paiute groups (Kelly 1932, 1964), Julian Steward had worked among the Owens Valley Paiute and Western Shoshone (Steward 1933, 1938), Lowie had done additional work among the Washoe and to a lesser extent the northern Nevada Northern Paiute and southern Nevada Southern Paiute (1924, 1939), Willard Park had spent several summers among the Northern Paiute (Fowler 1990b), and Omer Stewart (1941, 1944) and Demitri Shimkin (1947) had gotten started on long-term studies of the Washoe, Northern and Southern Paiute, and Ute (Stewart) and Wind River Shoshone (Shimkin). All of these studies contain data on plant and animal uses in greater or lesser amounts, usually with attempts at identification. These, as well as several other earlier sources, also contain names for biota in the Native languages, but evidence varying skills in transcription (see also, for example, Powers [Fowler and Fowler 1970] and John Wesley Powell [Fowler and Fowler 1971]). The 1930s and 1940s was also the period of A. L. Kroeber's Culture Element Distribution Surveys, which added some useful data to the study of Great Basin ethnobiology, but little actual identification (Driver 1937; Drucker 1937; Steward 1941, 1943; Stewart 1941, 1942). Additional field studies in the 1950s among the Washoe by Warren d'Azevedo (1986), James Downs (1961), and the linguist William Jacobsen (1955); in the 1960s through 1980s among the Northern and Southern Paiute by me (Fowler 1972, 1986, 1990a, 1990b, 1992; Fowler and Leland 1967); and in the 1970s and 1980s by Janet Smith (1972) among the Western Shoshone and Marilyn Couture among the Northern Paiute (Couture 1978; Couture, Ricks, and Housley 1986) have also added to the database. Maurice Zigmond, who in the 1930s worked among the Kawaiisu, a group linguistically related to the Southern Paiute, also completed his ethnobotany of that group (Zigmond 1981). More recently, plant utilization and management techniques of the Timbisha Shoshone of Death Valley have been explored by Fowler et al. (1994; see also Fowler 1996).

Thus, in overall assessment, even with the lack of specific ethno-biological studies among a number of Great Basin groups, a fair amount is known about plant and animal utilization in the region. Unfortunately, far more is known about the basic facts of utilization than about the quantitative or qualitative aspects. Most Great Basin ethnographers began their studies too late to capture more than remnant knowledge and were forced to focus their attention on reconstructive syntheses rather than actual participant activities. By the time of ethnographic work in the 1930s, Native communities were probably depending on native sources for 50% or less of their subsistence, although knowledge of traditional medicinal plants remained higher (see Train, Henrichs, and Archer 1941). But for certain food-producing species that had remained important to the people, information of good quality was collected and can still be gleaned in close cooperation with those people who have main-tained their vital linkages to the land.

INDIGENOUS UTILIZATION AND MEASURES OF BIODIVERSITY

The Great Basin is a large and biotically diverse region, with no single catalogue presently available as to its biodiversity (Glenn Clemmer, Nevada Natural Heritage Program, personal communi-cation, 1997). Nor is such an assessment likely, given that the cul-turally defined Great Basin (d'Azevedo 1986a) takes in the whole of the states of Nevada and Utah as well as portions of Colorado, Wyoming, Idaho, Oregon, California, and Arizona. Rather, the approach of most biodiversity programs is to work by state, recog-nizing that even lists of known species by state are probably not complete for vertebrates or plants and likely quite incomplete for

TABLE 4.1
Biodiversity in Nevada

	FAMILIES	SPECIES
Plants	130	2,700
Mammals	23	124
Birds	44	458
Amphibians	4	23
Reptiles	9	51
Fishes	5	44
Invertebrates		
Butterflies		181
Total:	215	3,581

Data supplied by the Nevada Natural Heritage Program, 1997.

invertebrates. The peculiar biogeographic character of the more tightly defined physiographic or hydrographic Great Basin, with its many mountain ranges having species that have been isolated for several thousand years (Grayson 1993), has also led to rather high speciation overall. For example, Nevada is ranked sixth in the nation in terms of known plant species (2,700), ninth in resident and colonist butterflies (181 species), and eighteenth for all vertebrates (730 species). Table 4.1 presents counts of species (and some families) for what is known of the state's biodiversity.

If these figures are roughly compared to what is known for indigenous utilization as foods and medicines for Nevada Native American groups (Northern Paiute, Southern Paiute, Western Shoshone, Washoe), we get at least one measure of indigenous knowledge of biodiversity (see table 4.2).[3] Given that large gaps probably exist in the database on Native utilization due to the late starting date for studies, plus the lack of in-depth studies for many groups, this measure should not be taken too seriously. In particular, given the lack of field collecting and thus proper identification,

TABLE 4.2
Known Utilization of Nevada Species by Native Americans

	FAMILIES	SPECIES
Plants	77	470
Mammals	15	52++
Birds	23	68+
Amphibians		1+
Reptiles		6+
Fish	4	29
Insects		10+
Total		636+

Figures based on Fowler 1986; Train, Henrichs, and Árcher 1941; and unpublished field data in Fowler's possession.

counts of small mammals are largely by genus, not species, as are those for amphibians, reptiles, and insects (hence the ++ and + in table 4.2). The counts also do not include plants used in manufacturing or ceremonially or plants or animals named but not utilized. It is doubtful, however, that these alone would raise the figures significantly.[4] Based on some rough comparisons of rates of retention vs. loss of ethnobotanical knowledge over the past 125 years, these figures may underrepresent knowledge and utilization by as much as 50% (see The Present State of Indigenous Knowledge of Biodiversity, below). However, they do suggest some points of interest.

On the conservative side, roughly one-sixth of Nevada's species were known or utilized by Native peoples. A more expansive estimate would be that one-third plus were the focus of enough attention to be named. This certainly does not mean that the other biotic forms were ignored or went unnoticed, however, as people cared deeply for all forms. As a Shoshone elder remarked, "Even that little *himbi* [thing, something] over there, we must take care of it."

Of the plant families, the most important for food (ten or more species utilized; see table 4.3) were the Umbel (Apiaceae), Aster (Asteraceae), Mustard (Brassicaceae), Goosefoot (Chenopodiaceae), Pulse (Fabaceae), Lily (Liliaceae), Grass (Poaceae), Rose (Rosaceae), and Saxifrage (Saxifragaceae) families. Significant families for medicinal uses (five or more species utilized; see table 4.3) were the Umbel (Apiaceae), Aster (Asteraceae), Pulse (Fabaceae), Mint (Lamiaceae), Lily (Liliaceae), Phlox (Polemoniaceae), Buckwheat (Polygonaceae), Rose (Rosaceae), Figwort (Scrophulariaceae), Nightshade (Solanaceae), and Valerian (Valerianaceae) families. Twenty plant families were used only medicinally, but only two of these, the Mint (Laminaceae) and the Figwort (Scrophulariaceae), had species counts above five (see table 4.4). Most of these families are also the largest and most diverse in Nevada, with the highest species counts (see table 4.5). They also appear to be the families whose members are most sought after for foods, medicines, and manufactures in the Great Basin region generally (King 1996:table 4). Daniel Moorman (1991), who has tried a statistical method of residuals to adjust between diversity within plant families and subclasses and Native uses as medicines for the whole of Native North America, also notes higher than predicted uses for the Aster, Rose, and Lily families as well as several other divisions that do not occur in Nevada (exception: Gymospermae; see his table 3). Although no such statistics were run here, it seems quite clear that these families are also key ones for Nevada Native peoples.

Interestingly, some plant families with small numbers of species did show utilization, including the Berberidaceae (3 species, 2 utilized), Equisetaceae (3 species, 2 utilized), Ericaceae (4 species, 1 utilized), Paeoniaceae (1 species, 1 utilized), and Cucurbitaceae (3 species, 1 utilized). Some are unique in appearance or common in distribution, but that does not explain all choices. More remains to be done in data comparisons such as these to assess Native knowledge of biodiversity.

TABLE 4.3

Key Nevada Plant Families Used for Foods and Medicines
(10+ species for foods, 5+ species for medicines)

	FOOD	MEDICINE
Umbel (Apiaceae)	16	16
Aster (Asteraceae)	33	32
Mustard (Brassicaceae)	14	0
Goosefoot (Chenopodiaceae)	19	2
Pulse (Fabaceae)	9	9
Mint (Lamiaceae)	0	6
Lily (Liliaceae)	24	5
Grass (Poaceae)	30	3
Phlox (Polemoniaceae)	1	6
Buckwheat (Polygonaceae)	6	7
Rose (Rosaceae)	18	9
Saxifrage (Saxifragaceae)	11	3
Figwort (Scrophulariaceae)	0	9
Nightshade (Solanaceae)	6	5
Valerian (Valerianaceae)	1	11

NOTE: Medicinal counts are *additional* species; species also used as food are not included in the figures (Fowler n.d.).

INDIGENOUS MANAGEMENT SYSTEMS

Ethnographers working in the region in the 1930s were the first to show specific interest in Native Great Basin concepts of environmental manipulation. After field studies in the Owens Valley, Steward (1930) raised the case of "irrigation without agriculture," based on data related to him describing the irrigation of wild seeds and tubers (*Eleocharis* spp.; *Dichelostemma pulchella*). This case generated considerable interest in the theoretical literature, with various papers through the years attempting to argue for the origins of the practice as independent invention, diffusion from the adjacent

TABLE 4.4

Nevada Plant Families Used Only for Food and Medicine

	FOOD	MEDICINE
Agave (Agavaceae)	+	
Amaranth (Amaranthacaceae)	+	
Cashew (Anacardiaceae)	+	
Milkweed (Asclepiadaceae)		+
Hazel (Betulaceae)	+	
Mursard (Brassicaceae)	+	
Cactus (Cactaceae)	+	
Caper (Capparaceae)	+	
Pink (Caryophyllaceae)		+
Convolvulus (Convolvulaceae)		+
Dodder (Cuscutaceae)		+
Sedge (Cyperaceae)	+	
Oleaster (Elaeagnaceae)	+	
Horse Tail (Equisetaceae)		+
Spurge (Euphorbiaceae)		+
Beech (Fagaceae)	+	
Gentian (Gentianaceae)		+
St. John's Wort (Hypericaceae)		+
Iris (Iridaceae)		+
Rush (Juncaceae)	+	
Mint (Lamiaceae)		+
Linen (Linaceae)		+
4-O'Clock (Nyctaginaceae)		+
Orchid (Orchidaceae)		+
Peony (Paeoniaceae)		+
Plantain (Plantaginaceae)		+
Crowfoot (Ranunculaceae)	+	
Willow (Salicaceae)		+
Lizard Tail (Saururaceae)		+
Figwort (Scrophulariaceae)		+
Cattail (Typhaceae)	+	
Nettle (Urticaceae)		+
Grape (Vitaceae)	+	
Caltrop (Zygophyllaceae)		+

SOURCE: Fowler n.d.

TABLE 4.5

Nevada Plant Families with the Highest Species Counts
(higher than 25 species)

Umbel (Apiaceae)	72
Aster (Asteraceae)	475
Borage (Boraginaceae)	103
Mustard (Brassicaceae)	191
Cactus (Cactaceae)	25
Pink (Caryophyllaceae)	59
Goosefoot (Chenopodiaceae)	79
Sedge (Cyperaceae)	129
Spurge (Euphorbiaceae)	28
Pulse (Fabaceae)	212
Waterleaf (Hydrophyllaceae)	81
Rush (Juncaceae)	36
Mint (Lamiaceae)	35
Lily (Liliaceae)	49
Loasa (Loasaceae)	29
Primrose (Onagraceae)	77
Phlox (Polemoniaceae)	84
Buckwheat (Polygonaceae)	121
Purslane (Portulacaceae)	26
Crowfoot (Ranunculaceae)	52
Rose (Rosaceae)	86
Willow (Salicaceae)	29
Saxifrage (Saxifragaceae)	26
Figwort (Scrophulariaceae)	140
Nightshade (Solinaceae)	30

SOURCE: Kartesz 1987.

Southwest, or diffusion from Spanish California (see Lawton et al. [1976] for a summary and reidentification of one of the plants involved as *Cyperus esculentus*). During the time of the Culture Element Distribution Surveys in the late 1930s and early 1940s, ethnographers asked not only about Native seed sowing and watering, but also about burning to increase the harvests of certain seeds and tobacco (Driver 1937; Drucker 1937; Steward 1938, 1941, 1943; Stewart 1941, 1942). Steward (1938), in his very influential monograph *Basin-Plateau Aboriginal Sociopolitical Groups*, itself an outgrowth of the CED work, devoted space in several sections to identification of the practices, finding at least sowing and burning for tobacco among most Western Shoshone groups. Stewart (1955) pulled together data from early historical sources for the region to show that in some cases burning was on a fairly large scale and probably was related to increasing fodder for game animals. In 1964, as part of his assignment to summarize data on subsistence and environmental relationships for the region, Downs (1966) discussed these materials in terms of the then emerging theoretical question as to whether hunters and gatherers, including the peoples of the Great Basin, were involved in forms of "proto-domestication."

Since then, Fowler (1986:93–95) has summarized additional cases of Great Basin environmental manipulation, adding data from the subsequent literature and field studies on pruning and coppicing willow (*Salix exigua*) for basketry, pruning tobacco (*Nicotiana biglovii*) plants to increase leaf size, burning lemonade berry (*Rhus trilobata*) for basketry, pinching the growth tips of pinyon (*Pinus monophylla*) branches to encourage additional cone development, spearing only male trout and salmon during runs and spawning, cutting browse for deer during the winter so that they would remain in an area longer, and so forth. More recently, Fowler (1996) has reported specifically on practices among the Timbisha Shoshone of Death Valley, California, where various ideas involving modifications for species are still recalled. Some of their practices and principles are briefly reviewed here.

Native Management in Death Valley

Death Valley is an interesting region, as it represents one of the most severe climatic regimes within the Great Basin. The temperature extremes within Death Valley, the deepest valley in the Mojave Desert, can range from +135° F (57.2° C) in the summer on the valley floor to 30° F (34.4° C) in the immediately adjacent mountains in the winter (Jaeger 1957). Annual precipitation rarely exceeds 3–5 inches (7.62–12.7 cm) on the valley floor, sometimes with as much as 20 inches (50.8 cm) annually in the mountains. The historic inhabitants of Death Valley, the Timbisha Shoshone, thus hunted and gathered under difficult conditions at best, developing a distinct pattern of seasonal transhumance (valley in winter, mountains in summer) to cope with the extremes. Flora and fauna were often sparsely distributed, calling for ingenious solutions to both locating and securing them (Fowler et al. 1994).

Today cases of Timbisha Shoshone management of plants are far clearer than for animals, probably because it has been the Timbisha women who have been able to continue some of their collecting activities. Hunting in any form (usually men's work) within the boundaries of Death Valley National Park was banned in the early 1940s, causing severe loss of traditional knowledge of practices. Although a few men continued to hunt outside of park boundaries, there was little incentive to do so because of the need to explain exactly where animals were secured to inquisitive park rangers. Women continued to take a few small mammals through the 1950s, and men occasionally poached a bighorn sheep or chuckwalla, but the era of subsistence hunting was clearly over.

Management of plants includes the use of fire, clearing, pruning, and coppicing, limited transplanting, and some cultivation (see Fowler 1996 for details on the last three). The use of fire on selected plants and habitats was the most common and continued well into the 1950s in areas outside the park. Clearing, pruning, and coppicing were also common and in many ways the most interesting. Timbisha people today recall using fire in the following ways:

1. To encourage growth of tobacco (*Nicotiana attenuata*) at specific sites immediately west of Death Valley. Usually about five-acre plots within areas dominated by big sagebrush (*Artemisia tridentata*) or sagebrush and juniper (*Juniperus* spp.) would be chosen for firing once during spring or fall.

2. To clear areas around springs and streams for planting cultigens (maize, squash, beans, introduced melons).[5] Willow (*Salix* spp.) was the particular target, as it often spread quickly in stream-side areas and ruined their potential for cultivation.

3. To open up marshes for waterfowl and other purposes by reducing the growth of cattail (*Typha latifolia*) and three-square (*Scirpus americanus*). Both of these invasives had to be controlled if the marshes were to be utilized for water-fowl hunting and collecting important basketry plants such as bulrush root (*Scirpus acutus*).

4. To encourage the growth of some seed plants such as white-stemmed blazing star (*Mentzelia albicaulis*). Areas were sometimes also fired to drive rabbits, but the following year they would be revisited for the harvest of seeds that would quite surely follow (see also Irwin 1980:15).

Documented for the larger Panamint Shoshone area (the Timbisha Shoshone are a subgroup of the Panamint) is the use of fire in deer drives as well as rabbit drives (Irwin 1980). Backfires were set on small hills or in linear arrangement to keep the animals moving toward other waiting hunters.

It is very difficult at this time to estimate the amount of Timbisha territory that was manipulated by fire. From extant accounts, fire was not used on a large scale, but rather in a patchy distribution and on targeted species or habitats. Tobacco burning, for example, was small-scale, as people burned different plots each year. Marshes and stream-side planting areas are also limited within the valley and surrounding canyons. Burning for seeds, especially as an adjunct to rabbit hunting, probably cleared larger areas—perhaps 50 to 100 acres at a time. The overall effect of this pattern may have been to create a mosaic of successional stages, likely increasing biodiversity at that time. Whether these were lasting effects is not known.

Clearing, pruning, and coppicing were another set of related management tools used in several ways by the Timbisha people. Most intriguing were Timbisha ideas about clearing and pruning pinyon (*Pinus monophylla*) and mesquite (*Prosopis glandulosa*), while the use of coppicing for renewing growth of willow follows other Great Basin practices.

For the management of both pinyon camps and collecting areas and mesquite groves, an ethic of keeping the land clean and litter-free prevailed. This was taught by the elders as part of the more general ethic of caring for the land and its resources. The use of fire was also part of this ethic, as fire was considered a cleansing force. Natural fires as well as human-made ones were viewed as beneficial.

Areas where people camped in the pinyon forests in the mountains or in the mesquite groves on the valley floors were always kept clean and free of underbrush and grass. Trees were trimmed of lower branches to provide fuel, but also to allow freer access for camping and food collecting. Clean areas prevented the spread of campfires to undesired areas, should the wind come up unexpectedly. Moreover, people used these practices with the specific aim that the land and the trees should look cared for.

These activities led to important benefits for the mesquites on the floor of Death Valley. Trimming and opening up the groves allowed the blowing sand to pass through the trees without forming hummocks that bury them and ultimately cause them to produce little fruit. Today a number of mesquites on the floor of Death Valley are being taken over by blowing dune sand so that they are almost completely engulfed. Although this is probably a natural process, Timbisha people feel that lack of management of the trees in former ways has increased this process and will eventually lead to the death of the trees. Today the groves also look unkempt with all of the dead wood and debris, which itself stops sand.

Another benefit of cleaning and clearing mesquite groves is more subtle and is suggested as an important ethnoecological principle relating people to mesquites. According to authorities (Mooney, Simpson, and Solbrig 1977), mesquite seedlings are not good competitors with grasses and other types of undergrowth. They require sunlight, which would have resulted from opening up the groves through trimming the trees. The seeds also germinate best if they enter the ground even slightly, which probably occurred as a by-product of people walking among the trees. When processing mesquite pods for food, a wooden mortar and a long stone pestle were used to reduce the spongy exocarp, mesocarp, and endocarp of the "bean" to meal. The hard seeds were normally discarded within the grove after the extensive pounding process. Pestle scarification might have given seeds the extra impetus to break dormancy, further solidifying the relationship of mesquite and people. These human processes seem to mimic the current effects of cattle grazing on mesquites in the Southwest, a factor attributed to their expansion in that region (Fisher 1977). The groves in Death Valley are contracting rather than expanding, due in part to changes in the water regime, but also perhaps due to lack of Native management.

Timbisha people pruned their pinyon pine trees by whipping them with the long harvesting poles at the end of the harvest season and by pinching the growth tips of the branches. And they pruned leafy plants such as prince's plume (*Stanleya pinnata, S. elata*) of old dead stems and leaves each spring as part of the harvest and routine maintenance (see fig. 4.1). They were also known to have transplanted willow used in basketry to desired locations.

Fig. 4.1. Collecting prince's plume (*Stanleya elata*) in Death Valley, California, by Timbisha Shoshone, 1993. Photograph by C. S. Fowler.

Waterholes, especially rock tanks and small springs, were routinely cleaned of debris to benefit animals as well as people. There were general taboos against killing bighorn sheep with lambs, deer with fawns, or rabbits known to be nesting. No one was able to recall specifically whether salt was set out or fodder cut to attract game animals. People did recall taking only one big game animal at a time and changing areas frequently to relieve pressure on the herds. There is also considerable knowledge of historic migrations and movements of game animals both inside and outside of Death Valley National Park.

For the Timbisha people, as well as perhaps others elsewhere in the Great Basin, it is important management should "show," thereby creating, at least in certain circumstances, habitats that appear to be tended as opposed to what they feel is unkempt. Elders explain that

plants need to "feel" the presence of people—they are used to it—
and that is how plant-human interrelationships are at least in part
maintained. The other side is that they need to "hear" from people:
hear the prayers of thanksgiving and the talk required before
collecting medicinal plants or foods. Plants are not destroyed when
people harvest or care for them in proper ways; they are actually
enhanced. To use some of the more modern phraseology of people-
plant relationships (see Ucko 1989:xii–xiii), the Timbisha Shoshone
"domesticate" their environments. They have not necessarily
created anthropogenic environments of the types seen in parts of
California or the Southwest (see examples cited in Blackburn and
Anderson 1993; Nabhan et al. 1982), but they have altered conditions to fit their standards of a managed landscape. Whether there
are any negative or additional positive benefits beyond those suggested remains to be determined.

THE PRESENT STATE OF INDIGENOUS
KNOWLEDGE OF BIODIVERSITY

Although there have not been any studies explicitly conducted to
assess the present state of knowledge of biodiversity among the
Indian peoples of the Great Basin, some data have been gathered.
Several factors can be identified as contributing to the erosion of
information about plants and animals among the people. The first
major factor, and one that has been ongoing in the region since
settlement, is reservation confinement. A second is general cultural
change in the areas of diet and medicinal use. And a third, which
greatly affects both knowledge retention and the ability to pass
information to a new generation, is language loss. None of these
factors is unique to the Great Basin, or particularly new to the story
of Native America generally, but each has played out in this region
in some interesting ways.

Already in the 1960s, when I began ethnobotanical fieldwork in the region, the effects of reservation confinement and dietary and medicinal change were apparent, as I noted they had been even for the ethnographers working thirty years earlier. Language loss was not yet in a critical state, although signs of erosion were quite apparent. In the early 1970s, after finding the "foods" and "medicines" samples collected by Powers, Lowie, and Barrett along with their plant lexicons, I attempted to identify their materials in the field with people then considered knowledgeable in these matters. Using the Native terms as guides, I questioned Northern Paiute people at Pyramid Lake, Fallon, and Walker River about the plants collected in 1875, 1914, 1916, and even later by additional fieldworkers. Although retentions were slightly different for each period and set collected, overall roughly 60% of the plant names were still recognized. However, less than 40% of those could still be field collected or be discussed by people in terms of their harvesting and preparation. Overall, losses to knowledge were near 50% in this sample of 140 items. The toll was highest in seed plants and medicines, with a number dropping out of active use or, in the case of medicines, showing a reduction or shift in use from what was previously reported.

Stephen Powers, who made his field collection in 1875, roughly twenty-five years after the Pyramid Lake and Walker River reservations had been established, noted that people attributed some of the changes that had already taken place in medicinal use to an increase in diseases brought about by reduced personal cleanliness in turn brought about by reservation confinement and the encumbrance of clothing (Fowler and Fowler 1970). Powers also noted that "[o]pthalmia [*sic*] overtops all other [diseases] together, if not in fatality, at least in prevalence" on both reserves and that the people stated that this was not the case in former times, when "phthises and rheumatism" were the common complaints (Fowler and Fowler 1970:131). The people attributed this increase to the necessity of using big sagebrush as fuel wood, which burns with an acrid smoke, as opposed to their former use of greasewood (*Sacrobatus vermiculatus*), which was much more clean burning. They also noted increases in dust due to the wagon and horse traffic in the district, also an eye irritant. By Barrett's time (1916), the common disease being treated with natural remedies was tuberculosis, although other complaints, such as syphilis and gonorrhea, were still extant.

Barrett's food sample collection is of interest for yet another reason: the obvious admixture of cultivated plants such as wheat and barley in his seed specimens. Six of Barrett's twenty-two Northern Paiute seed food specimens contain wheat and/or barley in quantities up to 50%. Both wheat and barley were being grown on the reservations by this time, and people suggested that they were popular because they were so similar to native seeds in appearance and in processing. By roughly the 1940s, these grains had all but replaced wild seeds in the diet.

Reservation confinement was perhaps also affecting local floras in important ways. In the 1930s, people at Pyramid Lake began complaining that local stocks of favored bitterroots (*Lewisia rediviva*), yampa (*Perderidia bolanderi*), onions (*Allium* spp.), and biscuit roots (*Lomatium* spp.) were failing, as were the seed favorites Indian ricegrass (*Oryzopsis hymenoides*) and white-stemmed blazing star. Although the data are far from clear on this point, we might at least suggest that Native gathering pressure over eighty years was partially responsible. For although there were new cultivated crops in the years around the turn of the century (including wheat, barley, oats, and potatoes), more people were resident within this restricted area than probably had ever been the case in precontact times. Even if they continued to gather a little, it could have been significant. The other culprit was likely the introduction of cattle to the reservation. The situation for ricegrass got so bad at Pyramid Lake that in 1938 the women on the Walker River Reservation gathered over 500 lbs of ricegrass seed and sold it to the Bureau of Indian Affairs to aid in reseeding the Pyramid Lake Reservation (Murphy n.d.). Overgrazing continued to take its toll on plant communities on both reservations until little subsistence collecting was possible. Food plants and medicines came to be regarded more as occasional than as necessary, although collecting a few such as pine nuts (Fowler 1992), acorns (Rucks 1995), some roots (Couture, Ricks, and Housley 1986), and a few medicines (for example, *Lomatium dissectum*) remains an important marker of ethnicity to the present.

Language loss has become critical in nearly the whole of the Great Basin in the last ten to fifteen years. Among the Northern Paiute, it is severe, with most communities having fewer than 10% of their populations as active speakers (Abel and Fowler 1994). Without language, in the form of lexicon and text, it is difficult to pass down information from one generation to the next. Plant vocabulary is particularly vulnerable here, as people can still discuss animals using their common English names. But there are so many plants that do not carry English common names, or that are known by more than one common name, or that Indian people do not know by a common name that it makes the retention of Native names for them particularly crucial. In addition, people need to be out in the country, interacting with the plants in front of members of younger generations, for a major sense of plant use and interrelationships to remain. Children need to hear the prayers and see the whole plant processing procedure, not just the final result. That has occurred with pine nuts to a greater degree than with any other plant, and thus a number of people today still know a good deal about pine nuts (see fig. 4.2). They look forward to going to the hills and camping with their families each fall, attending the pine nut harvest festival at the Walker River Reservation every September (even if no one can offer an old-time version of the pine nut blessing any longer [Fowler and Abel 1997]), and tasting the result of a fruitful harvest.

Fig. 4.2. Mrs. Wuzzie George winnowing pine nuts (*Pinus monophylla*) in the Sweetwater Range, Nevada, 1969. Margaret Wheat Collection. Special Collections, University of Nevada–Reno.

CONTINUING CONTRIBUTIONS OF NATIVE KNOWLEDGE

Lest the foregoing sound too pessimistic, it is useful to consider the continued contributions that Native peoples and their indigenous knowledge can still make to issues affecting biodiversity. One major contribution is to ideas about the management of resources, both plant and animal. A second includes the continuing need to catalogue the knowledge that remains for the purposes of reviving that knowledge among Native children as well as instructing non-Indians, when that is allowed. And a third is educating various publics about the important role that Native peoples have played

Fig. 4.3. Mrs. Wuzzie George collecting tule (*Scirpus acutus*) rhizomes, Stillwater Marsh, Nevada, 1970. Margaret Wheat Collection. Special Collections, University of Nevada–Reno.

in discovering the nature and uses of biota in the region and can still play through their ethic in their continued success.

The issue of resource management, or what should better be co-management of resources on former and present-day Native lands, continues to be a major one, especially in certain parts of the Great Basin. In Death Valley, the Timbisha Shoshone Tribe has called for true co-management of its former territory and resources (such as pinyon, mesquite, deer, bighorn, etc.) on National Park Service lands as well as those adjacent lands controlled by the Bureau of Land Management, the U.S. Forest Service, and the U.S. Fish and Wildlife Service (Boland et al. 1995). The Tribe feels that it has never lost its custodial obligation to its homeland and that it would be seriously remiss if it did not push for a say in its future. Members would like to trim and manage the mesquite, whip the pinyon trees, burn the marshes now choked with cattail, and conduct limited small and large game hunts. They feel that a philosophy of benign neglect has not contributed to the health of the land and resources and that something must be done. They have other information, such as the history and movement of big game herds in the region, that they feel should be of considerable interest to game managers in the agencies. Elderly members of the tribe have still retained important knowledge of former practices and times, even if they have not been allowed to exercise this knowledge since the 1940s.

The Western Shoshone National Council, an overarching political organization made up of some twenty-three member Shoshone tribes in Nevada and California, has had similar but less focused discussions with various agencies in Nevada and through them won the right (for a few years at least) to regulate their own fishing and hunting on public lands (Fowler 1995a). They and other Native peoples in the state are continually upset that commercial pine nut pickers are allowed into the region and damage the trees, while they have to get permits to pick in certain areas and cannot follow old harvesting and preparation practices. Given that 87% of the state of Nevada is public land, they reason that they retain certain aboriginal rights and entitlements with reference to it. Some Western Shoshone communities, such as Gosiute, Yomba, and Owyhee, are still relatively rural, and people there are likely to retain practical knowledge and the essential spiritual attachment to their lands.

Neither the Timbisha Shoshone nor the Western Shoshone National Council have gotten very far in their discussions with agencies. Agency personnel still feel that they know best what is good for the country and resources, and they are frightened to try any alternatives. They continually cite their "public trust responsibilities" as an excuse for not trying something new—or in this case something old, such as Native management techniques. Both sides distrust each other, and little happens as a result. Undoubtedly there are still new indigenous management ideas to be learned from the elders, if only someone will listen.

The need to continue to catalogue Native information about the biodiversity in the Great Basin should be clear from previous statements as to the state of our knowledge. Despite reservation confinement, culture change, and language loss, Native people still hold important knowledge about the natural world. For what individuals may lack in quantity at present, they could easily make up in quality if someone would really listen. They may only know a few plants or the habits of a few animals, but they probably know them well. One important thing that they often know is the former distribution of a plant or an animal, because their attachment to the land has been long-term. Many native species are being extirpated from former habitats, even if they are not officially threatened or endangered.

But Native knowledge needs to be preserved for use in the Native communities as well as, perhaps, by outsiders. With language loss and cultural change, young people have a need to know. They need language- and culture-based curricula for schools, summer programs, and after-school training. Then they can take the place of their elders as the intermediaries between the world of plants and animals and that of humans. They can tell stories about the activities and antics of the animals in times passed and pass on the "right way" to collect willows for basketry, roots and seeds for foods, and medicines. Then the plants and animals will "feel" their presence and give of themselves again. Non-Indians cannot expect to share in all of that knowledge; some of it is private, family based, or meant to be known between a master and an apprentice.

But several publics need to know something about the richness of indigenous Great Basin knowledge of the natural world. Agency people need to learn about what was known in the past as well as how to listen to Native people in the present. They need to know how to bend a few rules for the betterment of the environment. If they do not want to adopt co-management plans wholeheartedly, they should at least share the power of decisionmaking in a few cases to make a start. Resource managers and biologists need to learn specifically from Native knowledge and not dismiss it out of hand as uninformed. They should look to the spiritual side, to "ecologies of the heart" (Anderson 1996). Environmentalists, too, should listen to opinions about wise and informed use of resources and not assume that if left to its own devices the natural world will achieve some pristine state that probably never really existed. But, in general, all interested parties should listen to each other, show respect for what the others know, how and why they know it, and what difference it makes. Perhaps then we will all truly "live by them," and some real progress will be made in both assessing and protecting biodiversity and cultural diversity in the Great Basin.

NOTES

1. See Berlin (1992) for a discussion of the utilitarian vs. the intellectualist approaches to ethnobiology, usually defined from the point of view of the investigator, but meant here also as a Native perspective.

2. The history of exploration and settlement is treated in several chapters in the *Handbook of North American Indians*, vol. 11 (*Great Basin*). See d'Azevedo (1986a).

3. Other measures of knowledge of biodiversity could be developed, including an examination of the plant/animal nomenclature for evidences of knowledge of ecological interrelationships (see Nabhan, this volume), research into ideas of succession such as, perhaps, those associated with burning, and more concepts of ethnoecology in general.

4. King (1996), based on a review of selected published sources, lists at most twelve more species utilized for manufactures that are not otherwise utilized.

5. Wallace (1980) offers a preliminary discussion of Timbisha Shoshone agriculture, but see also Fowler et al. (1994). Based on present evidence, it seems doubtful that it predates by much the 1840s.

REFERENCES CITED

Abel, Harold, and Catherine S. Fowler. 1994. The Status of Northern Paiute. Unpublished paper. Symposium on Threatened and Endangered Languages of the Americas and Their Future, International Congress of Americanists, Stockholm, July.

Anderson, E. N. 1996. *Ecologies of the Heart*. New York: Oxford University Press.

Berlin, Brent. 1992. *Ethnobiological Classification: The Principles of Categorization of Plants and Animals in Traditional Societies*. Princeton: Princeton University Press.

Blackburn, T. C., and K. Anderson (comps. and eds.). 1993. *Before the Wilderness: Environmental Management by Native Californians*. Menlo Park: Ballena Press.

Boland, Richard, and the Land Restoration Committee. 1995. Outline of a Proposed Study to Be Conducted by the United States Department of Interior in Consultation with the Timbisha Shoshone Land Restoration Committee of Lands Suitable to Be Reserved for the Timbisha Shoshone Tribe as Provided for in the California Desert Protection Act 01 1994 [Public Law 103-433]. Timbisha Shoshone Tribe, Death Valley California, May.

Bolton, Herbert E. 1950. Pageant in the Wilderness: The Story of the Escalante Expedition to the Interior Basin, 1776, including the Diary and Itinerary of Father Escalante. *Utah Historical Quarterly* (Salt Lake City) 18(1–4):1–265.

Bye, Robert A., Jr. 1972. Ethnobotany of the Southern Paiute Indians in the 1870s: With a Note on the Early Ethnobotanical Contributions of Dr. Edward Palmer. In *Great Basin Cultural Ecology: A Symposium*, edited by Don D. Fowler, pp. 87–104. Publications in the Social Sciences 8. Reno: Desert Research Institute.

Chamberlin, Ralph V. 1909. Some Plant Names of the Ute Indians. *American Anthropologist* 11(1):27–40.

———. 1911. Ethno-botany of the Gosiute Indians. *Memoirs of the American Anthropological Association* 2(5):329–405. (Also 1905, University of Utah Biological Series.)

Couture, Marilyn. 1978. Recent and Contemporary Foraging Practices of the Harney Valley Paiute. Master's thesis. Portland State University, Portland, Ore.

Couture, Marilyn D., Mary F. Ricks, and Loucile Housley. 1986. Foraging
  Behavior of a Contemporary Northern Great Basin Population. *Journal
  of California and Great Basin Anthropology* 8(2):150–60.
Coville, F. V. 1891. Death Valley Expedition Itinerary. Unpublished MS,
  United States Fish and Wildlife Service, 1860–1861. Smithsonian Institution Archives, Washington, D.C.
————. 1892. The Panamint Indians of California. *American Anthropologist*,
  o.s. 5:351–35.
d'Azevedo, Warren L. 1986a. Introduction. In *Handbook of North American
  Indians*, edited by W. C. Sturtevant, vol. 11 (Great Basin), edited by W.
  L. d'Azevedo, pp. 1–14. Washington, D.C.: Smithsonian Institution.
————. 1986b. Washoe. In *Handbook of North American Indians*, edited by W.
  C. Sturtevant, vol. 11 (*Great Basin*), edited by W. L. d'Azevedo, pp.
  466–98. Washington, D.C.: Smithsonian Institution.
Downs, James F. 1961. The Effect of Animal Husbandry on Two American
  Indian Tribes: Washo and Navaho. Ph.D. dissertation. University of
  California, Berkeley.
————. 1966. The Significance of Environmental Manipulation in Great
  Basin Cultural Development. In *The Current Status of Anthropological
  Research in the Great Basin: 1964*, edited by Warren L. d'Azevedo et al.,
  pp. 39–56. Social Sciences and Humanities Publication No. 1. Reno:
  Desert Research Institute.
Driver, H. E. 1937. Culture Element Distributions: VI, Southern Sierra
  Nevada. *University of California Anthropological Records* (Berkeley)
  1:53–154.
Drucker, Philip. 1937. Culture Element Distributions, V: Southern Cali-
  fornia. *University of California Anthropological Records* (Berkeley) 1:1–52.
Dutcher, B. H. 1893. Piñon Gathering among the Panamint Indians.
  American Anthropologist, o.s. 6:377–80.
Euler, Robert C. 1966. Southern Paiute Ethnohistory. *University of Utah
  Anthropological Papers* (Salt Lake City) 78:v–139 and 2 appendices.
Fisher, C. E. 1977. Mesquite and Modern Man in Southwestern North
  America. In *Mesquite: Its Biology in Two Desert Ecosystems*, edited by B. B.
  Simpson, pp. 177–88. Stroudsburg, Pa.: Dowden, Hutchinson and Ross.
Fowler, Catherine S. n.d. Unpublished Fieldnotes, Southern Paiute,
  Northern Paiute and Western Shoshone, 1964–95. Notebooks in author's
  possession, University of Nevada, Reno.
————. 1972. Comparative Numic Ethnobiology. Ph.D. dissertation.
  University of Pittsburgh.

————. 1986. Subsistence. In *Handbook of North American Indians*, edited by W. C. Sturtevant, vol. 11 (*Great Basin*), edited by W. L. d'Azevedo, pp. 64–97. Washington, D.C.: Smithsonian Institution.

————. 1990a. *Tule Technology: Northern Paiute Uses of Marsh Resources in Western Nevada*. Smithsonian Folklife Studies No. 6. Washington, D.C.: Smithsonian Institution Press.

————. 1990b. *Willard Z. Park's Ethnographic Notes on the Northern Paiute of Western Nevada, 1933–1940*. Anthropological Papers 114. Salt Lake City: University of Utah Press.

————. 1992a. *In the Shadow of Fox Peak: An Ethnography of the Cattail-Eater Northern Paiute People of Stillwater Marsh*. Cultural Resources Series No. 5. Portland: U.S. Fish and Wildlife Service.

————. 1992b. Kai Pasapana ("Don't Dry Out"): Northern Paiute Pine Nut Ceremonies. Paper presented at the Great Basin Anthropological Conference, Boise, Idaho, October.

————. 1995a. *Native Americans and Yucca Mountain*. Y MRDB #21. Carson City: Nevada Nuclear Waste Projects Office.

————. 1995b. Some Notes on Ethnographic Subsistence Systems in Mojavean Environments in the Great Basin. *Journal of Ethnobiology* 15(1):99–117.

————. 1996. Historical Perspectives on Timbisha Shoshone Land Management Practices, Death Valley, California. In *Case Studies in Environmental Archaeology*, edited by Elizabeth J. Reitz, Lee A. Newsom, and Sylvia J. Scudder, pp. 87–101. New York: Plenum Press.

Fowler, Catherine S., and Harold Abel. 1997. Northern Paiute Prayer: Some Features of the Genre. In *Western American Indian Language Studies: Essays in Honor of Wick R. Miller*, edited by Tom Willett and Eugene Casad. Salt Lake City: University of Utah Press, in press.

Fowler, Catherine S., Molly Dufort, Mary Rusco, and the Historic Preservation Committee, Timbisha Shoshone Tribe. 1994. Residence without Reservation: Traditional Land Use Study of the Timbisha Shoshone of Death Valley National Monument, CA.: Phase I. Submitted to the Applied Ethnology Program, National Park Service, Washington, D.C.

————. 1995. Timbisha Shoshone Homelands: A Study of Twelve Subareas. Report for the Timbisha Shoshone Tribe, Death Valley, California.

Fowler, Catherine S., and Joy H. Leland. 1967. Some Northern Paiute Native Categories. *Ethnology* 6(4):381–404.

Fowler, Don D., and Catherine S. Fowler (eds.). 1970. Stephen Powers' "The Life and Culture of the Washoe and Paiutes." *Ethnohistory* 17(3–4):117–49.

————. 1971. *Anthropology of the Numa: John Wesley Powell's Manuscripts on the Numic Peoples of Western North America, 1868–1880*. Smithsonian Contributions to Anthropology 14. Washington, D.C.: Smithsonian Institution.

Frémont, John C. 1845. *Report of the Exploring Expedition to the Rocky Mountains in the Year 1842 and to Oregon and Northern California in the Years 1843–1844*. Washington, D.C.: Gales and Seaton.

Grayson, Donald K. 1993. *The Desert's Past: A Natural Prehistory of the Great Basin*. Washington, D.C.: Smithsonian Institution Press.

Heizer, Robert F. (ed.). 1979. *Indian Names for Plants and Animals among Californian and Other Western North American Tribes, by C. Hart Merriam*. Publications in Archaeology, Ethnology and History 14. Socorro: Ballena Press.

Irwin, C. (ed.). 1980. *The Shoshone Indians of Inyo County, California: The Kerr Manuscript*. Publications in Archaeology, Ethnology and History 15. Socorro: Ballena Press.

Jacobsen, William H., Jr. 1955. Washoe Terms for Plants and Animals. Unpublished manuscript in author's possession, University of Nevada, Reno.

————. 1986. Washoe Language. In *Handbook of North American Indians*, edited by W. C. Sturtevant, vol. 11 (*Great Basin*), edited by W. L. d'Azevedo, pp. 107–12. Washington, D.C.: Smithsonian Institution.

Jaeger, Edmond C. 1957. *The North American Deserts*. Stanford: Stanford University Press.

Kartesz, John T. 1987. A Flora of Nevada. Ph.D. dissertation. University of Nevada, Reno.

Kelly, Isabel T. 1932. Ethnography of the Surprise Valley Paiute. *University of California Publications in American Archaeology and Ethnology* (Berkeley) 31(3):67–210.

————. 1964. *Southern Paiute Ethnography*. Anthropological Papers 69. Salt Lake City: University of Utah Press.

King, Glenda L. 1996. Great Basin Ethnobotany: A Computerized Database. Master of Liberal Arts thesis. University of Oklahoma, Norman.

Lawton, Harry W., Phillip J. Wilke, Mary DeDecker, and William M. Mason. 1976. Agriculture among the Paiute of Owens Valley. *Journal of California and Great Basin Anthropology* 3(1):13–50.

Lowie, Robert H. 1909. The Northern Shoshone. *Anthropological Papers of the American Museum of Natural History* (New York) 2(2):165–306.

―――. 1924. Notes on Shoshonean Ethnography. *Anthropological Papers of the American Museum of Natural History* (New York) 20(3):185–314.

―――. 1939. Ethnographic Notes on the Washo. *University of California Publications in American Archaeology and Ethnology* (Berkeley) 36(5): 301–52.

Miller, Wick R. 1986. Numic Languages. In *Handbook of North American Indians*, edited by W. C. Sturtevant, vol. 11 (*Great Basin*), edited by W. L. d'Azevedo, pp. 98–106. Washington, D.C.: Smithsonian Institution.

Mooney, H. A., B. B. Simpson, and O. T. Solbrig. 1977. Phenology, Morphology, Physiology. In *Mesquite: Its Biology in Two Desert Ecosystems*, edited by B. B. Simpson, pp. 26–43. Stroudsburg, Pa.: Dowden, Hutchinson and Ross.

Moorman, Daniel. 1991. The Medical Flora of Native North America: An Analysis. *Journal of Ethnopharmacology* 31:1–42.

Murphy, Edith V. n.d. Notes on Pyramid Lake Ethnobotany. Unpublished notebook in C. S. Fowler's possession, University of Nevada, Reno (dates 1938–40).

Nabhan, G. P., A. M. Rea, K. L. Reichhardt, E. Mellink, and C. F. Hutchinson. 1982. Papago Influences on Habitat and Biotic Diversity: Quitovac Oasis Ethnoecology. *Journal of Ethnobiology* 2:124–43.

Powers, Stephen. 1873–75. Aboriginal Botany. *California Academy of Science Proceedings* (San Francisco) 5:373–79.

Rucks, Penelope. 1995. Washoe Uses of Ground Stone. Master of Arts thesis. University of Nevada, Reno.

Shimkin, Demitri. 1947. Wind River Shoshone Ethnogeography. *University of California Anthropological Records* (Berkeley) 5(4):245–88.

Simpson, J. H. 1876. *Report of Explorations across the Great Basin of the Territory of Utah for a Direct Wagon-Route from Camp Floyd to Genoa, in Carson Valley, in 1859*. Washington, D.C.: U.S. Government Printing Office.

Smith, Janet H. 1972. Native Pharmacopoeia of the Eastern Great Basin: A Report of Work in Progress. In *Great Basin Cultural Ecology: A Symposium*, edited by D. D. Fowler, pp. 73–86. Desert Research Institute Social Sciences and Humanities Publications 8. Reno: Desert Research Institute.

Steward, Julian H. 1930. Irrigation without Agriculture. *Papers of the Michigan Academy of Science, Arts, and Letters* (Ann Arbor) 12:149–56.

————. 1933. Ethnography of the Owens Valley Paiute. *University of California Publications in American Archaeology and Ethnology* 33(3): 233–350.

————. 1938. *Basin-Plateau Aboriginal Sociopolitical Groups*. Bulletin 120. Washington, D.C.: Bureau of American Ethnology.

————. 1941. Cultural Element Distributions, XIII: Nevada Shoshone. *University of California Anthropological Records* (Berkeley) 4:209–360.

————. 1943. Culture Element Distributions, XXIII: Northern and Gosiute Shoshone. *University of California Anthropological Records* (Berkeley) 8(3):263–392.

Stewart, Omer C. 1941. Culture Element Distributions, XIV: Northern Paiute. *University of California Anthropological Records* (Berkeley) 4(3):361–446.

————. 1942. Culture Element Distributions, XVIII: Ute–Southern Paiute. *University of California Anthropological Records* (Berkeley) 6(4):231–356.

————. 1944. Washo–Northern Paiute Peyotism: A Study in Acculturation. *University of California Publications in American Archaeology and Ethnology* (Berkeley) 40(3):63–142.

————. 1955. Forest and Grass Burning in the Mountain West. *Southwestern Lore* 21(1):5–9.

Train, Percy, James A. Henrichs, and W. Andrew Archer. 1941. *Medicinal Uses of Plants by Indian Tribes of Nevada*. Contributions toward a Flora of Nevada 33. Beltsville: Bureau of Plant Industry.

Ucko, Peter. 1989. Foreword. In *Foraging and Farming: The Evolution of Plant Exploitation*, edited by D. Harris and G. C. Hillman, pp. ix–xviii. London: Unwin Hyman.

Wallace, W. J. 1980. Death Valley Indian Farming. *Journal of California and Great Basin Anthropology* 2:269–72.

Zigmond, Maurice. 1981. *Kawaiisu Ethnobotany*. Salt Lake City: University of Utah Press.

CHAPTER FIVE

"Just Like a Garden"

Traditional Resource Management and Biodiversity Conservation on the Interior Plateau of British Columbia

SANDRA L. PEACOCK AND NANCY J. TURNER

They [Stl'atl'imx, or Lillooet] burned them [the hills] so that they would get good crops there. They told others who went there, "Do the same at your place, do the same at your place." Their own hills were just like a garden.

THE LATE BAPTISTE RITCHIE,

LIL'WAT [STL'ATL'IMX] ELDER, 1971

INTRODUCTION

It has always been puzzling to us that the most productive, prolific areas to find particular edible or useful plants, especially wild root vegetables, are invariably in those localities where they have been traditionally harvested in immense quantities. One might logically assume that such populations, having been intensively exploited, might show decline compared to places where they were not harvested, but this does not seem to be the case. This observation is supported by many elders, who insist that the best places to collect particular plant resources today are where they have always been harvested.

Elders also observe that, since the harvesting of many culturally important plants has decreased, or ceased altogether, plants are not as plentiful and habitats not as productive. This depletion of traditional resources is attributed to several causes, one of the major ones being that people no longer look after the plants as they did in the past. Practices such as landscape burning, pruning, tilling, and even picking are said to improve the resources, making them more bountiful and enhancing their quality.

These observations, combined with a growing body of ethnobotanical evidence from British Columbia (Gottesfeld 1994a, 1994b; Turner 1997a, 1998, 1999; Turner et al. 1980, 1990), suggest indigenous peoples actively managed the resources of their environment to ensure a reliable, predictable supply of culturally significant plants—whether for food, materials, or medicines. Management decisions were not solely economic ones, but were embedded in social contexts and encoded in religious philosophies and oral traditions. These strategies, whether intentionally or incidentally, promoted and conserved biological diversity across the landscape.

In this chapter, we present evidence that aboriginal peoples of British Columbia's Interior Plateau have traditionally been active managers of their plant resources and that within the present century there has been a deterioration of certain habitats and resources due, in part, to the cessation of management practices as well as the impacts of industrial society. First, we provide a brief description of the Interior Plateau region, its environment, and its indigenous peoples. Next, we outline the culturally important plant resources of the Plateau and examine the practices used to manage these resources at the population, community, and landscape levels. We discuss the relationships of these management strategies to the creation and maintenance of biodiversity and identify the issues relating to them, including recent environmental deterioration and

biodiversity. Finally, recommendations for reinstatement of some
traditional management practices and philosophies in eco-restoration
are provided.

THE PEOPLES OF THE INTERIOR PLATEAU

The Interior Plateau of British Columbia is defined by its physiography as well as by the cultural traditions shared by its indigenous
peoples. It covers a vast, diverse area of south-central British
Columbia, situated between the Coast and Cascade Mountains to
the west and the Rocky Mountains to the east. The landscape is
characterized by gently rolling uplands, punctuated by highlands
and mountains and dissected by the deeply incised river valleys
and lakes of the Fraser, Thompson, and Columbia river drainages.
In all, the Interior Plateau encompasses three degrees of latitude
and nine degrees of longitude (Parish et al. 1996).

This juxtaposition of low-, mid-, and high-elevation environments and variable topography results in a diversity of flora and
fauna throughout the region. Dry valleys, grasslands and shrub-
steppe, extensive plateau lands, upland forests, and high mountain
ranges are all found within the boundaries of the Interior Plateau.
In all, the territory encompasses nine major biogeoclimatic zones:
Bunchgrass; Ponderosa Pine; Interior Douglas-fir; Montane Spruce;
Engelmann Spruce–Subalpine Fir; Interior Cedar-Hemlock; Sub-
Boreal Pine–Spruce; Sub-Boreal Spruce; and Alpine Tundra (British
Columbia Ministry of Forests 1988; Meidinger and Pojar 1991). Each
of these zones is represented by characteristic plant and animal
species, and each provided particular resources to the traditional
Plateau economy.

Culturally, the Interior Plateau is considered part of the Plateau
Culture Area as originally defined by A. L. Kroeber (1939). The
southern portion, the focus of this discussion, is the traditional
territory of Interior Salish–speaking peoples, including the

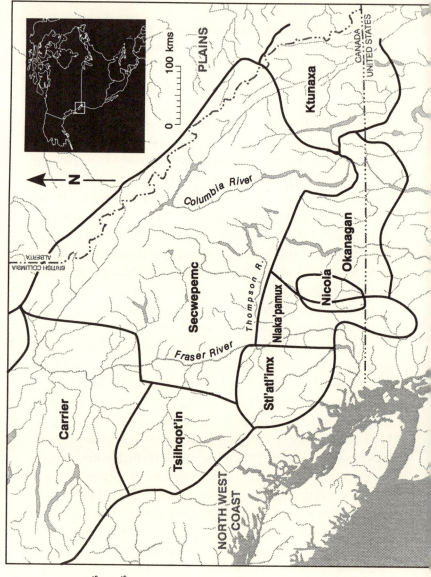

Map 5.1. The traditional territories of the Interior Salish peoples and neighboring groups as recorded by Teit (1900:450).

Secwepemc (Shuswap) and their neighbors the Stl'atl'imx (Lillooet), the Nlaka'pamux (Thompson), and the Okanagan. These peoples shared many cultural traditions, including a diversified gathering-fishing-hunting economy, with intensive use of wild plant foods.

At the time of European contact, the Interior Salish peoples were seasonally transhumant, living in semipermanent villages along the major river systems of the Plateau, as their ancestors had for generations. These villages, consisting of groups of extended family pithouse dwellings, were occupied during the winter months. Families dispersed from these locales over the harvesting season to hunt, fish, and gather plants. The diverse environment—and, as we shall see, peoples' management strategies—created "patches" of resources that were both spatially and temporally distributed; thus, task groups moved to riverine, lacustrine, up-land, and montane ecosystems at various times throughout the year to take advantage of different plant and animal resources through the growing seasons. Specific resource harvesting locales were visited year after year, in a patterned and predictable seasonal round. As G. Palmer (1975a:213) notes, "the zoned pattern of resources in the [Canadian] Plateau allowed a typical riverine community to exploit almost any type of habitat occurring in the Plateau within the distance of a few miles. This situation favoured economic diversification. . . ."

PLANT RESOURCES AND MANAGEMENT STRATEGIES

Plants were essential to all aspects of life on the Plateau, with over 300 different species whose roots, shoots, leaves, berries, and/or wood were utilized as foods, materials, and medicines. As indicated in table 5.1, various management strategies were utilized to main-tain and enhance these plant resources, ranging from maintenance of particular habitats using fire to practices affecting only the

Fig. 5.1. Nlaka'pamux woman digging roots at Botanie Valley, an important root gathering ground managed by Interior Salish peoples. Reproduced from Teit 1900.

Fig. 5.2. Balsamroot or spring sunflower (*Balsamorhiza sagittata*), a former root staple traditionally pitcooked in earth ovens.

resource species themselves. These management activities may be grouped into three categories on the basis of spatial scale:

1. Population management: activities designed to enhance the reliability and productivity of any culturally significant species at the population level.
2. Community management: strategies that create and maintain diversity in selected habitats or locales, often successional, where populations of culturally significant plant resources occur.
3. Landscape management: The totality of peoples' management effects, including systems of decisionmaking and social sanctions that control the management and harvesting of plant resources in various habitats throughout a large geographic area, such as a traditional territory.

TABLE 5.1.

Summary of Culturally Important Plants of the British Columbia Interior Plateau with Associated Management Practices

Category	Use and Approx. No. of Species	Examples Species (Common Name)	Management Notes
Food	Berries (Total ~50)	*Amelanchier alnifolia* (saskatoon, serviceberry) *Fragaria* spp. (wild strawberry) *Prunus virginiana* (choke cherry) *Ribes inerme, R. irriguum* (wild gooseberry) *Rubus idaeus* (wild raspberry) *Rubus leucodermis* (blackcap) *Shepherdia canadensis* (soapberry) *Vaccinium membranaceum* (black huckleberry) *Vaccinium oxycoccus* (bog cranberry)	all except wild strawberry are woody perennials; fruit picking generally did not impact plants; diversification and use of alternative species in poor crop years was practiced; seasonal rounds; most said to be enhanced by periodic landscape burning; some (e.g., soapberry, huckleberries) were pruned periodically
Food	Seeds and nuts (total ~6–8)	*Balsamorhiza sagittata* (balsamroot) *Corylus cornuta* (hazelnut) *Pinus albicaulis* (whitebark pine)	hazelnut bushes were burned individually; hazelnuts and pine seeds gathered (sparingly) from rodent caches
Food	Root vegetables (Total ~35)	*Allium cernuum* (nodding onion) *Balsamorhiza sagittata* (balsamroot) *Calochortus macrocarpus* (mariposa lily) *Cirsium undulatum* (wild thistle) *Claytonia lanceolata* (spring beauty) *Erythronium grandiflorum* (avalanche lily) *Fritillaria lanceolata* (chocolate lily) *Lewisia rediviva* (bitterroot) *Lilium columbianum* (tiger lily) *Lomatium macrocarpum* (desert parsley) *Potentilla anserina* (silverweed)	all are herbaceous perennials with bulbs, corms, rhizomes, tubers, or taproots; all selectively harvested by season, age, size, life-cycle stage; part of seasonal round harvesting cycles; most said to be enhanced by periodic landscape burning; propagules often incidentally or intentionally replanted; some weeded during harvest; specific sites harvested in several-year cycles

		Sagittaria latifolia (wapato) *Sium suave* (water-parsnip)	
Food	Green vegetables (Total ~18)	*Balsamorhiza sagittata* (balsamroot) *Epilobium angustifolium* (fireweed) *Heracleum lanatum* (cow-parsnip) *Lomatium nudicaule* ("Indian-celery") *Opuntia* spp. (prickly-pear cactus) *Rubus* spp. (raspberry, blackcap, thimbleberry) *Typha latifolia* (cattail)	all are herbaceous perennials or woody perennials (*Rubus* spp.); all selectively harvested as shoots or leaves by season, age, size, life-cycle stage; part of seasonal round harvesting cycles; some said to be enhanced by picking; cactus propagules incidentally replanted
Food	Tree inner bark (Total ~7)	*Pinus contorta* (lodgepole pine) *Pinus ponderosa* (ponderosa pine) *Populus balsamifera* (cottonwood)	all tree species; harvested by partial bark and cambium removal, but not girdling; selectively harvested by season; part of seasonal round harvesting cycles
Food	Lichen (1)	*Bryoria fremontii* (black tree lichen)	selectively harvested by abundance, taste, season, tree species, location; pulled from coniferous tree branches, allowing regeneration from remaining thallus
Food	Mushrooms (Total ~8)	*Pleurotus ostreatus* (oyster mushroom) *Tricholoma magnivelare* (pine mushroom) *Tricholoma populinum* (cottonwood mushroom)	seasonally available; selectively harvested by size, age; cut and ground litter recovered for multiple harvests (for ground mushrooms)
Food	Casual foods, flavorings and sweeteners, emergency foods, beverage plants (Total ~50)	*Arctostaphylos uva-ursi* (kinnikinnick: leaves thirst quencher) *Ledum glandulosum* (trapper's tea: beverage) *Larix occidentalis* (western larch: chewing gum) *Pseudotsuga menziesii* (Douglas-fir: sugar)	variously herbaceous or woody perennials; leaves, gum, shoots, or other parts selectively harvested by season or at times of need; seldom harvested intensively in any locality

TABLE 5.1. (continued)

CATEGORY	USE AND APPROX. NO. OF SPECIES	EXAMPLES SPECIES (COMMON NAME)	MANAGEMENT NOTES
Smoking	Tobaccos and tobacco flavorings (Total ~10)	*Arctostaphylos uva-ursi* (kinnikinnick: leaves smoked) *Cornus sericea* (red-osier dogwood: inner bark smoked) *Nicotiana attenuata* (tobacco; leaves smoked) *Ligusticum canbyi* (Canby's lovage: roots smoked) *Lomatium nudicaule* (seeds as tobacco flavoring)	*Nicotiana* formerly cultivated, annual; others are perennials, materials harvested selectively from living plants; *Ligusticum* roots highly valued; tops stuck back in ground by some people after harvesting root; dug after flowering
Materials	Pit-cooking matting (Total ~12)	*Agropyron spicatum* (bluebunch wheatgrass) *Cornus sericea* (red-osier dogwood: branches) *Penstemon fruticosus* (shrubby penstemon: leafy shoots) *Pseudotsuga menziesii* (Douglas-fir: boughs) *Pinus ponderosa* (ponderosa pine: needles) *Rosa* spp. (wild rose: branches)	all herbaceous woody perennials; materials harvested selectively from living plants as plucking or "pruning" or (for ponderosa pine) as fallen needles
Materials	Woods for construction and manufacture (Total ~25)	*Acer glabrum* (Rocky Mountain maple) *Amelanchier alnifolia* (saskatoon or serviceberry) *Cornus sericea* (red-osier dogwood) *Crataegus douglasii* (black hawthorn) *Juniperus scopulorum* (Rocky Mountain juniper) *Pinus ponderosa* (ponderosa pine) *Populus balsamifera* (cottonwood) *Pseudotsuga menziesii* (Douglas-fir) *Taxus brevifolia* (Pacific yew)	all trees or shrubs; many harvested or coppiced as branches or stems from living plants; some dead trunks selected (as opposed to cutting live trees); trees selectively cut (e.g., cottonwood for dugout canoes)
Materials	Woods and others for fuel, tinder (Total ~25)	*Artemisia tridentata* (big sagebrush) *Betula papyrifera* (paper birch) *Juniperus scopulorum* (Rocky Mountain juniper) *Pinus* spp. (pines)	most are trees or woody perennials; materials often harvested from downed/dead trees or selectively as branches from living trees

		Populus balsamifera (cottonwood) *Pseudotsuga menziesii* (Douglas-fir) *Salix lasiandra* (Pacific willow)	
Materials	Bark sheets for manufacture or lining caches (Total ~10)	*Abies lasiocarpa* (subalpine fir) *Betula papyrifera* (paper birch) *Pinus monticola* (white pine) *Populus balsamifera* (cottonwood) *Prunus emarginata* (bitter cherry)	all trees; birch and cherry outer bark only removed, without killing tree; others removed in large sheets, which would kill trees if living; possibly dying or dead trees selected for cottonwood bark; barks harvested selectively by size, season, tree characteristics
Materials	Stem, leaf, root fibers / fibrous tissues (Total ~25)	*Acer glabrum* (Rocky Mountain maple: inner bark) *Apocynum cannabinum* (Indian-hemp: stem fiber) *Elaeagnus commutata* (silverberry: inner bark) *Picea engelmannii* (Engelmann spruce: roots) *Salix exigua* (sandbar willow: stems) *Scirpus lacustris* (tule: stems) *Thuja plicata* (western red-cedar: roots) *Typha latifolia* (cattail: leaves)	all are woody or herbaceous perennials; materials cut (stems, leaves) or pulled in strips (barks) from living plants by pruning; herbaceous materials harvested selectively by size, season, plant growth form, habitat
Materials	Dyes, stains (Total ~25)	*Alnus* spp. (alders: bark) *Echinodontium tinctorium* (Indian paint fungus) *Letharia vulpina* (wolf lichen) *Mahonia aquifolium* (Oregon-grape: inner bark)	various types of materials; harvested selectively and sporadically as required
Materials	Adhesives, caulking, waterproofing agents (Total ~10)	*Abies lasiocarpa* (subalpine fir: liquid pitch) *Pinus contorta* (lodgepole pine: pitch) *Populus balsamifera* (cottonwood bud resin) *Pseudotsuga menziesii* (Douglas-fir: pitch)	harvested selectively from living trees

TABLE 5.1. (continued)

Category	Use and Approx. No. of Species	Examples Species (Common Name)	Management Notes
Materials	Scents, cleansing agents, Miscellaneous (Total ~125)	*Abies lasiocarpa* (subalpine fir: boughs as scent) *Anaphalis margaritacea* (pearly everlasting: flowering tops, leaves as menstrual padding) *Artemisia tridentata* (big sagebrush: leaves as scent) *Equisetum hiemale* (scouring rush: abrasive) *Juniperus scopulorum* (Rocky Mountain juniper: boughs as scent) *Lomatium dissectum* (chocolate-tips: roots as fish poison) *Mentha arvensis* (Canada mint: tops as scent) *Typha latifolia* (cattail: seed fluff as diapering) *Urtica dioica* (stinging nettle: tops as cleansing agent) (see Turner et al. 1990:38–40 for more examples)	various herbaceous or woody perennials; most materials selectively harvested from living plants; usually harvested by season, life-cycle stage
Medicines	Whole plants or leafy branches (Total: ~250–300 plant preparations)[a]	*Artemisia dracunculus* (wild tarragon: wash for sores) *Ceanothus velutinus* (snowbrush: tonic, general illness) *Clematis ligusticifolia* (white clematis: wash for sores, scalp) *Gaillardia aristata* (brown-eyed Susan: influenza, tonic)	various herbaceous or woody perennials; most materials selectively harvested from living plants; usually harvested by season, life-cycle stage
Medicines	Bark tissues (Total ~50–60)	*Abies lasiocarpa* (subalpine fir: coughs, tuberculosis, many ailments) *Cornus sericea* (red-osier dogwood: poultice; coughs) *Oplopanax horridus* (devil's-club: diabetes, stomach problems) *Populus balsamifera* (cottonwood: tonic) *Rhamnus purshiana* (cascara: laxative)	barks usually removed from whole twigs or as portions from trunk; trees not girdled; harvested selectively from a number of individual plants

Medicines	Pitch, resin, latex (Total ~35)	*Abies lasiocarpa* (subalpine fir: sores) *Pinus contorta* (lodgepole pine: salve, colds) *Pseudotsuga menziesii* (Douglas-fir: salve, colds)	pitch removed from injured or insect-damaged trees or from bark blisters
Medicines	"Roots" (Total ~100–125)	*Balsamorhiza sagittata* (balsamroot: sores) *Heuchera cylindrica* (alumroot: sores) *Ligusticum canbyi* (Canby's lovage: colds, sores) *Valeriana sitchensis* (mountain valerian: colds) *Veratrum viride* (false hellebore: arthritis: TOXIC)	virtually all are herbaceous perennials; roots selectively harvested by size, life-cycle stage; fragments left behind often capable of regeneration; *Ligusticum* said to be enhanced by burning, and tops replanted
Medicines	Leaves and/or shoots (Total ~75)	*Chimaphila umbellata* (pipsissewa: childbirth); *Equisetum hiemale* (scouring rush: childbirth; eye medicine) *Urtica dioica* (stinging nettle: leafy shoots for arthritis)	herbaceous or woody perennials; leaves/shoots harvested selectively from living plants, which can then regenerate
Medicines	Flowers, fruits (Total ~35–40)	*Achillea millefolium* (yarrow flowers: kidney, toothache; leaves, roots also used) *Shepherdia canadensis* (soapberries: indigestion, ulcers) *Symphoricarpos albus* (waxberry: eye medicine)	herbaceous or woody perennials; flowers/fruits harvested from living plants, by season, life-cycle stage
Medicines	Miscellaneous, or unspecified incl. fungi (Total ~30–35)	*Lycoperdon perlatum* (puffball: spores as poultice for burns, sores)	gathered sporadically or incidentally

SOURCE: Based on Turner 1979a, 1998; Turner et al. 1980, 1985, 1990; Turner and Ignace, unpublished notes, 1996.

[a] Note that these numbers are only approximations, based on the summaries calculated for Nlaka'pamux (Thompson) herbal medicines. They are based not on species *per se*, but on the numbers of particular medicinal preparations used in treating a specific illness or condition (see Turner et al. 1990:43–54). Although each cultural group has its own traditional medicines, the Nlaka'pamux medicines seem generally representative of the species, plant parts, and applications used in other areas of the British Columbia Plateau. The examples provided are generally of species and medicines widely used by Plateau peoples.

We recognize that these management activities are not mutually exclusive, but interact with one another in promoting biological diversity, whether intentionally or incidentally. Management activities at the population level will have an impact on the composition of the community, which will, in turn, be reflected on the landscape. Similarly, decisions concerning the overall timing of management and harvesting of resources in a traditional territory will have repercussions at the community and population levels.

POPULATION MANAGEMENT

The fundamental unit of management was the species. Populations of plants with cultural utility were encouraged through a number of strategies associated with aboriginal harvesting practices. These strategies were based on both biological and cultural considerations and were employed to ensure the continued productivity of key resources. They include the selective harvesting of plants based on well-defined criteria; a number of extractive techniques that increased, rather than decreased, overall population levels; and a system of scheduling that regulated the timing and frequency of the harvest.

Harvest Criteria

The harvesting of plant resources was, and is, selective, being neither random nor all-encompassing. The criteria used to select plants for harvest varied considerably between species and depending upon the type of plant resource and its intended use. Cultural preferences, the physiology of the plant, and environmental factors all influenced the selection process (e.g., Turner 1992a). However, in general, the most important criteria were the yearly growth cycle, reproductive status (e.g., flowering versus nonflowering), and maturity and size. Habitat preference also played a role.

The yearly growth cycles of culturally important species were well known and carefully monitored, as the desired qualities of a particular resource varied throughout its development, either seasonally (spring versus summer) or yearly as the plant matured. On a seasonal basis, variations in growth cycles meant certain species could only be harvested during a short period at any given location even though the plant might be present throughout the year. The green shoots of cow-parsnip (*Heracleum lanatum*), for example, were harvested in early spring, before the plant flowered. After this, the stalks became unpalatable and undesirable. On a yearly basis, variations in growth often meant that a particular plant was left to mature for several years prior to harvesting.

The reproductive status of an individual plant, which is linked to growth cycles, was also an important criterion for selection. For example, a number of important root vegetables were harvested only after the plant had gone to seed. In addition, many medicinal roots were collected after flowering, at which point the roots were considered more potent. Similarly, the leaves of nonfruiting cattail (*Typha latifolia*) plants were selected for harvest over the fruiting ones. There were also cultural prohibitions against harvesting certain plants at certain reproductive stages. For example, women were to avoid collecting the "male" (flowering or fruiting) individuals of desert parsley (*Lomatium macrocarpum*) in favor of the "female" vegetative ones.

Plants were also selectively harvested based on size preferences. According to Secwepemc elder Mary Thomas, multiflowered (and therefore large-bulbed) individuals of avalanche lily (*Erythronium grandiflorum*) were preferred. Similarly, only the "carrot-sized" roots of balsamroot (*Balsamorhiza sagittata*) were dug, leaving the larger "mothers" to flower and go to seed. Elders consistently report that in root collecting the medium-sized individuals were picked, leaving the smaller roots to regenerate and the largest plants to go to seed. Mary Thomas, for example, recalls digging chocolate lily (*Fritillaria lanceolata*), spring beauty (*Claytonia lanceolata*), and avalanche lily with her grandmother, who taught her to leave the smallest bulbs and corms. In fact, her grandmother would sort through the children's baskets at the end of the day, removing the smallest "roots" and replanting them.

Habitat preference was another criterion used in selective harvesting. Plants growing in a specific location were often preferred to their counterparts in other regions. Medicinal plants were considered purer and more potent when collected from higher elevations in the mountains. Berries from certain locales were said to taste sweeter than others. Indian-hemp (*Apocynum cannabinum*), an important fiber plant, was said to be tallest and thickest in damp areas, while those found on sidehills were bushier and not as desirable. Further, if a habitat was particularly productive for one root, it was generally productive for other species as well, a fact that tended to concentrate harvesting activities on the landscape.

Extractive Technologies

The specific tools and techniques used to harvest plant resources varied according to the species and the intended use of the plant. However, the net result of harvesting was to create a disturbance regime within any given plant population. This was accomplished through digging, tilling, weeding, pruning, coppicing, and, in some instances, the selective burning or pest management of individual plants.

Digging was the most common harvesting technique and was used to collect a wide variety of edible roots and medicinal plants. A digging stick, "a pointed stick about four feet in length, with a crutch-shaped handle" (Dawson 1892:19), commonly manufactured from the fire-hardened wood of shrubs such as saskatoon (*Amelanchier alnifolia*) or black hawthorn (*Crataegus douglasii*), with a handle of birch (*Betula* sp.) or sometimes antler or goat horn, was the basic tool (see fig. 5.1). It was used to pry roots out of the ground, an extremely effective technique for extracting large tap-

Fig. 5.3. Secwepemc elder Mary Thomas holding a "carrot-sized" balsamroot taproot.

rooted species such as balsamroot or those with deep roots such as desert parsley.

An alternative method of root digging involved cutting a small patch of turf around a number of roots, flipping it over, and removing the appropriate-sized roots from the underside. This was commonly practiced with spring beauty and chocolate lily, whose "roots" grow just below the ground surface. With avalanche lily, a large clump of turf was removed, then the bulbs were dug out from the subsurface soil. Dirt and small "roots" were replanted, but the turf was left off, as a form of weeding. Elders also mention that they frequently weeded during root digging to remove unwanted, nonutilitarian species, especially grasses.

Pruning or coppicing was another form of harvesting practiced on the shoots and stems of herbaceous and woody perennials used as food and materials. Cow parsnip was picked in its shoot stage in the spring, then left to mature and flower, die back, and shoot up again the following year. This management approach is very similar to that for a well-known domesticated perennial vegetable, asparagus (*Asparagus officinalis*).

Stems of shrubs such as red-osier dogwood (*Cornus stolonifera*), used for sweatlodge frames, saskatoon (*Amelanchier alnifolia*), used for arrows and other implements, and sandbar willow (*Salix exigua*), used for rope, were also cut from living plants. Mary Thomas recalls her mother observing large, bushy overgrown saskatoon bushes and saying, "It's time to cut them back." She then cut the older stems to the ground, and the next year the shoots that grew up were just right for basket rim hoops. A few years later, berry production on these bushes was excellent in terms of both quantity and quality of the fruit. Tule (*Scirpus lacustris*), cattail (*Typha latifolia*), and Indian-hemp (*Apocynum cannabinum*), other culturally important herbaceous perennials, were sought for their stems, leaves, and stem fiber, respectively, and were cut in enormous quantities at their full maturity in late summer and fall. Since their rhizomes were not impacted, however, they would grow up anew each spring.

Certain species of berries, such as soapberry (*Shepherdia canadensis*) and huckleberries (*Vaccinium* spp.), were harvested by breaking off the berry-laden branches. This, too, was a form of pruning. Hazelnut (*Corylus cornuta*) and perhaps other fruiting bushes were burned individually as well to encourage vigorous new growth in the following years (Turner 1999).

The bark and wood of a wide range of trees were also important to Plateau peoples. Bark sheets of birch (*Betula papyrifera*) and bitter cherry (*Prunus emarginata*) were harvested for use in basketry and other purposes, but only the outer bark was taken; the inner bark was left to protect the tree and to allow it to continue to grow (Turner 1997b, 1998).

Bark removed totally, either to access inner bark and cambium for food (e.g., lodgepole pine, *Pinus contorta*) or for use as medicine (e.g., cascara, *Rhamnus purshiana*), was generally taken in small patches, so that the tree was not girdled and would be able to heal after a while. Living trees with characteristic scars of bark removal are seen throughout the Plateau (e.g., Cole and Lockner 1989).

Of course, trees needed for the wood of their trunks, or those whose bark could not be removed in part, were cut or girdled, but this was evidently done selectively. By at least one account, people sometimes purposefully used windfalls and dead or dying trees to avoid killing living ones.

Scheduling

The scheduling of plant harvesting was regulated by a number of constraints. On one hand, the timing and frequency of collecting were imposed by the life cycles of the plants themselves, which varied between species and according to the micro-environment (e.g., aspect, precipitation, elevation) of a harvesting locale. These, in turn, had to be balanced with cultural preferences for species at certain growth stages, as well as with conflicts that might arise when several species were available simultaneously for harvesting in different locales.

Fig. 5.4. Soapberry (*Shepherdia canadensis*), an important source of food, beverage, and medicines, was managed through pruning and burning.

Decisions concerning where, when, and what to harvest were dictated by cultural preferences and necessity, but limited by the spatial and temporal availability of the plant resources. This required indigenous peoples to move extensively from resource patch to resource patch throughout their traditional territory on a seasonal basis. Elder Mary Thomas recalled, for example, that in her area Secwepemc women first dug desert parsley roots in the valley bottoms, then the lower-elevation spring beauty corms and avalanche lily bulbs, then balsamroot, all at lower elevations. By this time the saskatoons, soapberries, and some of the other berries were ready to be picked. In midsummer, people would move up to the mountains and dig more spring beauty and avalanche lily "roots." After this, the huckleberries were ready to be picked, as well as some of the other later-ripening fruits such as high-bush cranberries (*Viburnum opulus*) and hazelnuts. Similar rounds of progressive resource access are noted for other British Columbia Plateau peoples (Turner et al. 1980, 1990; Turner 1992b), as well as for peoples to the south on the Columbia Plateau (Hunn et al. 1990; Marshall 1977).

Decisions concerning how much and how often to harvest were closely linked with fluctuations in the annual productivity of resources. The people of the Plateau were well aware of the cyclical nature of the yield of many key plant resources. Fruits are well known for having multiyear cycles of heavy and light bearing years; people's use of saskatoons, huckleberries, and other alternative species reflected these cycles. The cycles of productivity were also known for species and populations that had been burned. Furthermore, specific root digging beds, once harvested, were left to develop for a few "fallow" years before people returned to the exact spot. Thus, seasonal movements, in conjunction with the rotation of resource patches, ensured the continued productivity of a specific population (this is discussed in greater detail in the section on Landscape Management).

COMMUNITY MANAGEMENT

On a somewhat larger scale, the management of plant communities encompassed the practices described above, but in this instance people were managing to create a particular habitat type or successional stage, rather than to increase the production of individual species *per se.*

Controlled burning was the most common form of community-level management practiced by Interior Plateau peoples. The extensive use of controlled burns to create and maintain ecologically heterogeneous mosaics is discussed in detail elsewhere (Turner 1999), and readers are referred to this reference for a more detailed treatment of the subject. Baptiste Ritchie's (1971) "Burning Mountainsides for Better Crops" gives eloquent evidence for community-level management practiced by Stl'atl'imx people, and other elders confirm similar uses of fire in various parts of the Plateau. It was widely recognized that fire, through clearing brush and providing a quick source of nutrients, can stimulate the growth of certain complexes of plants, as can pruning and thinning. Ritchie, on one occasion, recalled:

> When they used to burn that grass above timberline they used to say the Indian Potatoes [*Claytonia lanceolata*] were as big as your fist. Now they are only that big [i.e., small], because they are not cultivated. They would burn every five or six years. The ground can only support so much. Now it's only timber grows. It takes away from the other. (Baptiste Ritchie, transcription from taped interview with Dorothy Kennedy, May 1977)

Secwepemc elder Mary Thomas recalled that fire not only stimulated the growth of huckleberries and blueberries (*Vaccinium* spp.), root vegetables, and mushrooms, but also, her mother told her, killed harmful plant-eating insects that accumulated in a given area.

In fact, her father used to travel all around their lands by horseback each spring, setting fire to the tent caterpillar webs on the choke cherry trees. Competing annual species, too, might be suppressed by burning. In all, at least nineteen species of plants, including eleven fruiting shrubs, one herbaceous fruit (strawberry, *Fragaria* spp.), and seven herbaceous "edible root" species, have been identified by various sources as having their production enhanced by periodic burning (Turner 1999).

The success of this management technique rested in the selection of habitat, as well as in the timing and intensity of the burn. Ethnographic evidence indicates that people typically burned to increase productivity of certain berries and root foods (see table 5.1), species that commonly occur in montane, subalpine, and alpine areas throughout the Plateau in upland meadows, open forests, and along the edge of mature forests. Thus, burning was designed to create and maintain productive parkland and ecotones.

The timing of fires was carefully controlled by specialists within the community. Fires were usually set in early spring or late fall when there was sufficient moisture to prevent the spread of the fire and to minimize its intensity, avoiding damage to the soils below. The late Annie York, Nlaka'pamux elder of Spuzzum in the Fraser Canyon, recalled the practice of landscape burning from her early childhood, between seventy and eighty years ago:

> They wait until close to fall. They know just when to burn. And then two or three years after, lots of huckleberries, lots of blueberries. . . . And the *skamec* [*Erythronium grandiflorum*], that's when it grows, when you burn. I've seen it, when the old people used to do it. I was just a little girl. I'd go up the mountain with granny. After we'd pick berries, my uncle would say, "It's going to rain pretty soon; time to burn" [so the fire will not spread too much]. He stays up [after we have finished]. Then, we go back the next year, it's all burned. Now, it turns into bush. That's why we don't get many

berries any more. We're not allowed to burn. [We get] some, but not the same as it used to be. They [berries] do [grow] after logging, but its not the right kind. . . .

The intensity of these aboriginal fires was also linked to the frequency with which people burned. Generally, berry patches were burned every eight to ten years and allowed to regenerate for two to three years before harvesting. As mentioned earlier, this period of "fallow" was accompanied by the rotation of harvesting locales in the seasonal round.

LANDSCAPE MANAGEMENT

As previously discussed, both population and community management activities influenced the overall composition of the landscape. However, indigenous peoples of the Plateau also employed a number of resource management strategies on a broad scale, such as within a traditional territory, which, in turn, influenced species and community productivity and diversity. These included a planned and patterned seasonal round, the rotation of harvesting locales, controlling access to resource patches, and religious ceremonies and moral sanctions (e.g., Turner 1997).

The seasonal movements of people across the landscape were linked to the temporal and spatial availability of culturally important plant resources, as outlined earlier. Forests and woodlands of different types, grasslands, upland meadows, and wetlands were all recognized by indigenous peoples as being valuable habitats for plant resources. Ecological variation and succession and the interrelationships among plants, other lifeforms, and the physical environment were central to peoples' knowledge and lifestyles. It was widely recognized that certain plants grow in association with each other and that often life cycles of various plants and animals coincide. Nlaka'pamux elder Annie York, for example, noted that "all plants have relatives, all of them," in reference to companion plants always found growing together, such as bitterroot (*Lewisia rediviva*), an important root vegetable, and miner's lettuce (*Claytonia perfoliata*) (Turner et al. 1990). Growth and productivity are dependent on local weather conditions as well as aspect, moisture, climate, and genetic variation. The cyclical nature of plant resources and runs of salmon and population profiles of game were also recognized.

All of these factors came into play in broad-scale sustainable resource use. The seasonal round, and the limited periods it entailed for people to focus on particular resources in a particular area, was important in restricting the quantities of a resource harvested at one time in one place. Further, peoples' movements from one area to another through the seasons, and the alternation or rotation of specific harvesting locations over multiyear cycles, were in fact forms of broad-scale resource management and were comparable to the swidden agriculture practices of many tropical forest peoples (see Posey 1990).

Limiting or controlling access to productive resource locales was another mechanism that ensured resources were sustainably utilized. Although root digging grounds and berry picking areas were considered common tribal property, access to those areas was carefully monitored. For example, G. M. Dawson (1892:21) notes that among the Secwepemc "the picking of each kind of berry is regulated by custom. For each recognized berrying ground some experienced old woman takes charge and watches the ripening of the fruit. Finally, when it is full time, word is sent to the other neighbouring Indians and the harvest begins." A similar system existed amongst the Nlaka'pamux; James Teit (1900) notes that women of one village could pick in the berry patches of another as long as they did so at the proper season.

In addition, large and valuable berrying-spots were looked after by the chief of the band in whose district they were situated. The chief watched for the ripening of the berries and sent young men to watch and report on the various locations throughout the territory.

From time to time, they would bring in branches to show the chief. When the berries were just about ripe, the chief sent word that on a certain day the berrying would commence at a particular berry patch. Women would come from all over to begin picking and preserving. Then the women would move to the next patch, as directed by the chief, until the berrying had finished (Hill-Tout 1978).

Root digging grounds, where important root foods were abundant, were well known and regularly visited and managed. Further, it appears each group using the area had a designated harvesting locale. For example, Teit (1900:294) writes:

> Botani Valley, situated in the mountains. . . . Has been from time immemorial a gathering place for the upper divisions of the tribe [Nlaka'pamux or Thompson], chiefly for root-digging during the months of May and June. Sometimes over a thousand Indians, representing all divisions of the tribe, would gather there. . . . Each division had, besides, its separate and recognized camping ground.

Controlled access to root and berry resources was, in fact, a form of stewardship, managed by the chief of the band or a designated representative. This form of management parallels the _hahuulhi_ system of the Nuu-Chah-Nulth peoples of Vancouver Island, whereby a hereditary chief "owned" resources and resource-rich areas, but also had responsibilities to maintain them and share them with his people (Scientific Panel for Sustainable Forest Practices in Clayoquot Sound 1995; Turner and Peacock in press). Further, as villages and bands were composed of two or more related families, it can be suggested, following Lilian Ackermann (1994), that access to key plant resources was controlled and regulated through kinship systems.

Finally, resource management was ensured through the religious principles and moral precepts of the Plateau people. On the Plateau, as with many indigenous cultures, the manner in which people interacted with the landscape was inextricably linked to spiritual beliefs, which were embodied in public ceremonies and oral traditions. These guided people in their day-to-day interactions with the natural environment, a point made very eloquently in Gene Anderson's (1996) *Ecologies of the Heart* and well documented in cultures around the world (e.g., Gadgil et al. 1993).

Among the Interior Salish peoples, First Foods Ceremonies were one of the more prominent mechanisms used to control harvesting. Charles Hill-Tout (1978) summarizes these as follows:

> As far as I could learn, the hunting, fishing and berry grounds of the Thompson [Nlaka'pamux] were common property. But no one under penalty of a severe punishment could take a fish, pick a berry, or dig a root until after the Feasts of First Fruits had been held.
>
> These feasts were conducted as follows: When the salmon, for instance, begin to run, the word is brought to the divisional chiefs that the fish are coming up river. Messengers are then sent to the neighbouring villages, calling a meeting of the people on a certain day, at which all must attend at the appointed place. When the day has arrived and the people have assembled, the head chief, attended by the other lesser ones and the elders, opens the ceremony at daybreak by a long prayer. When the prayer is being said everybody must stand with eyes reverently closed. . . .
>
> Exactly to whom these prayers were addressed my informant could not tell me. All I could gather was that the "old Indians" believed in some great and beneficent power who dwelt behind the clouds, and who gave them the salmon, fruits, roots, etc., who, if they showed themselves ungrateful or unthankful, could, and might, withdraw his gifts from them.

In addition to these public ceremonies, people were taught, through oral traditions, to understand and appreciate their connections with the "natural" world and to respect and honor those ties. This philosophy is captured in the story of the Old-One and his role in creating the earth, the sky, and the people.

> Now Old-One appeared, and transformed Sun, Moon, and Stars into those we see in the sky at the present day, and placed them all so that they should look on the Earth-woman, and she could look at them. He said, "Henceforth you shall not desert people, nor hide yourselves, but shall remain where you can always been seen at night or by day. Henceforth you will look down on the Earth."
>
> Then he transformed the woman into the present earth. Her hair became the trees and grass; her flesh, the clay; her bones, the rocks; and her blood, the springs of water. Old-One said, "Henceforth you will be the earth, and people will live on you, and trample on your belly. You will be as their mother, for from you, bodies will spring, and to you they will go back. People will live as in your bosom, and sleep on your lap. They will derive nourishment from you, for you are fat; and they will utilize all parts of your body. . . ."
>
> After this, the earth gave birth to people, who were very similar in form to ourselves; but they knew nothing, and required neither food nor drink. They had no appetites, desires, knowledge, or thoughts. Then Old-One travelled over the world and among the people, giving them appetites and desires, and causing all kinds of birds and fish to appear, to which he gave names, and ascribed them all certain positions and functions. He said to the people, "Where you see fish jump, there you will find water to drink. It will quench your thirst and keep you alive." He taught the women how to make birch baskets, mats, and lodges and how to dig roots, gather berries and cure them. He taught the men how to make fire, catch fish, shoot, snare, trap and spear game. . . .

When he had finished teaching them, he bade them good-by, saying, "I leave you now, but if you forget any of the arts I have taught you, or if you are in distress and require my aid, I will come again to you. The sun is your father, and the earth is your mother. When you die, you will return to your mother's body. You will be covered with her flesh as a blanket, under which your bones will rest in peace." (Teit 1912:321)

This view of the earth as a transformed person is further exemplified in Teit's unpublished notation on Nlaka'pamux sanctions against wanton destruction of plants: ". . . flowers, plants and grass especially the latter are the covering or blanket of the earth. If too much plucked or ruthlessly destroyed earth sorry and weeps[.] It rains or is angry & makes rain, fog & bad weather" (James Teit, ethnographer, unpublished notes on Nlaka'pamux, or Thompson, plant knowledge, ca. 1900, cited from Turner et al. 1990:54). Nellie Taylor, Mary Thomas, and Annie York were routinely taught from their childhood days to respect the plants and animals and never to waste them or use them foolishly (Turner et al. 1995).

SUMMARY OF PLANT MANAGEMENT STRATEGIES

In summary, the traditional plant management activities practiced by the aboriginal peoples of the Interior Plateau ensured a reliable, predictable, and productive supply of culturally important plant species.

At the population level, plant management was practiced through harvesting strategies dictated by both cultural and biological factors. Harvesting created disturbance regimes that had both intentional and incidental but generally positive effects on the productivity of targeted species. By selecting individuals at certain life cycles, or according to age and size, indigenous peoples thinned the populations, decreasing intraspecies competition. Weeding also decreased competition between desired and undesired species, giving the culturally important plants a competitive advantage. Pruning and coppicing of herbaceous plants and shrubs encouraged the growth of new shoots, leaving the root systems intact, as did the burning of selected individuals such as hazelnut bushes. The intentional replanting of "roots" and their propagules was also an important factor in maintaining population productivity.

Incidental impacts of harvesting practices included localized soil disturbances from digging and tilling. In addition, the accidental detachment of portions of taproots, tubers, corms, and bulbs would enable vegetative reproduction of the species. In our experience, it is difficult to extract the entire root: often a small portion is left behind to regenerate vegetatively. Further, harvesting of some species was done at a time when seeds were in production, and the activities associated with harvesting—digging, tilling, turning over the turf—would help to distribute seeds and propagules.

Not only did people actually seem to enhance the growth and abundance of particular species through time, but they may have, in some instances, extended the range of particular species through purposeful or accidental transport and replanting. Today some people like Mary Thomas have transplanted spring beauty, wild onions, bitterroot, and avalanche lily into their gardens. In the past, such root vegetables were commonly stored by burying them fresh in underground caches (Dawson 1892; Teit 1900, 1906, 1909; Turner et al. 1980, 1990). Caches that were not emptied in one season might well produce growing plants in the succeeding years.

The use of controlled fires to manage plant communities is well documented for indigenous peoples throughout the world (e.g., Anderson 1993a; Boyd 1986; Day 1953; Gottesfeld 1994a, 1994b; Lewis 1973, 1977, 1982; Lewis and Ferguson 1988; Timbrook et al. 1982). It is not surprising, then, that this was one of the most important management tools of the Plateau peoples, who burned upland habitats at specified times of the year and at regular inter-vals to enhance the productivity of roots and berries. The continued productivity of these habitats was ensured through alternating harvest locales.

Finally, while these plant management techniques had economic motives, they were embedded in a larger decisionmaking system structured by religious and moral ideologies. These principles guided people's interactions with the natural environment and ensured careful, considered, and considerate use of plant resources.

INFLUENCES OF PLANT MANAGEMENT STRATEGIES ON BIODIVERSITY

Based on the preceding discussion, it is clear the indigenous peoples of the interior of British Columbia were active managers of plant resources at the population, community, and landscape levels. But what was the influence of these management strategies on biodiversity?

Biodiversity may be measured in a number of ways, including:

- Genetic diversity: the genetic variation within a population, or the variety of species, genera, and families within a community;
- Species diversity: the number of species in a community and their relative abundance;
- Structural diversity: variations in how plant communities are structured, both horizontally and vertically.

Disturbance is one of the principal factors influencing biodiversity. As mentioned previously, indigenous plant management techniques are forms of human disturbance that can influence which species occur in a particular habitat as well as the relative abundance of those species. Disturbances such as those created by traditional management practices tend to be occasional and spatially focused. This has the effect of creating mosaics, increasing habitat diversity within a landscape, and, as a consequence, increasing species diversity.

At the population level, selective harvesting practices are the main form of disturbance. Digging, tilling, weeding, and pruning alter the composition and structure of the population and, ultimately, of the larger community. Of particular interest is the fact that, without exception, the species managed are perennials. Unlike many annuals, most perennials have a range of regenerative and reproductive strategies and, consequently, can respond to harvesting in several ways. Virtually all of them have a capacity for regeneration through various means, from regrowth of shoots and leaves from underground or aerial parts, to healing over of tree trunks when bark patches are removed, to the more obvious abilities for propagation from seed or spore. Many are very long-lived. As a result, traditional harvesting technologies did not necessarily remove the individual or its genetic material from the population, as seeds, root fragments, and rhizomes were left behind (we liken this to the botanical equivalent of dairy farming!). Traditional disturbance regimes, therefore, can actually stimulate growth, enhancing the population and maintaining genetic diversity.

At the community level, frequent, low-intensity fires disrupted successional sequences in the habitat and reduced the overall dominance of a particular community type, such as coniferous forest, on the landscape. These actions, along with repeated harvesting in preferred locales, created patches of "cultivated" habitats, which are diverse in terms of their species and structure. Further, a mosaic of "cultivated" or managed and "natural" or unmanaged habitats would result in a greater genetic diversity.

The key to the use of disturbance regimes in promoting biodiversity is regulating the intensity (size) and frequency of the disturbance events in the community. When there is very little disturbance, species with a competitive advantage will eventually take over. If there is a high level of disturbance, species that can recover from disturbance quickly will take over. Thus, the size and frequency of disturbance change the distribution of species in a given area.

This is where landscape management becomes important. Traditional landscape management strategies monitored the frequency and intensity of harvesting and burning practices on a regional scale to ensure appropriate levels were maintained. Rotating use of harvesting grounds and burning locales on multiyear cycles, and controlled access to resource areas, resulted in intermediate levels of disturbance. These management principles were ultimately embedded in religious ideologies and enforced through social mechanisms.

In summary, indigenous peoples of British Columbia's Interior Plateau were much more active managers of their environment than traditional views of hunter-gatherers of the region would allow (see, for example, Hayden's [1992:535] treatment of the impacts of root harvesting on plant species). In these models, hunter-gatherers are seen as adapting to their environment, not modifying it. However, as Richard Ford (1985) and others (Harris 1989; Rindos 1984) have pointed out, the plant management activities of hunter-gatherers are guided by the same dynamics as those of horticultural and agricultural peoples, but at differing degrees of intensity. Based on Ford's model, we suggest the indigenous peoples of the Plateau were essentially cultivators who managed and maintained plant resources to ensure a predictable, productive, and continued supply of culturally significant plant species. Further, through the use of these sophisticated strategies and disturbance regimes, aboriginal peoples of British Columbia domesticated their environment to a certain extent and, in doing so, helped to conserve genetic, specific, and structural biodiversity.

BIODIVERSITY CONSERVATION: PAST, PRESENT, AND FUTURE

The evidence presented thus far indicates that the biodiversity observed by the first Europeans in the interior of British Columbia was the result of generations of careful use and management of the plant resources by the indigenous peoples of the region. However, it is difficult to estimate the antiquity of these practices with any certainty. The historic pattern of winter villages and subsistence based on the use of plant, ungulate, and salmon resources may be traced back at least 3,000 to 4,000 years in the archaeological record (Pokotylo and Mitchell 1998; Stryd and Rousseau 1996).

At present, the best evidence for plant resource management is inferred from the archaeological remains of earth ovens, which appear approximately 3,000 years ago and are thought to represent ethnographically documented processes of wild root food production (Peacock 1996, 1998; Pokotylo and Froese 1983). Since these features were used until historic times to process large quantities of root foods (including balsamroot, avalanche lily, spring beauty, and tiger lily, *Lilium columbianum*), we suggest that these root resources have been harvested sustainably for at least 3,000 years and that in order to do this plant resource management strategies must have been practiced. Several digging stick handles have been recovered from archaeological contexts dating to this same period (Pokotylo and Mitchell 1998; Richards and Rousseau 1987), suggesting a continuity in harvesting technologies from this time.

Therefore, although we cannot demonstrate conclusively that indigenous peoples were actively managing the plant resources of the Interior Plateau in the distant past, we do know that people have been exploiting certain root resources for at least 3,000 years and have certainly utilized plants as foods, materials, and medicines since the initial peopling of the region some 10,000 years ago.

Unfortunately, many circumstances have changed since traditional plant resource management methods were developed and practiced widely. Indigenous peoples throughout British Columbia have lost access to their homelands and struggle to maintain the traditions of their ancestors against the pressures of the social and economic changes accompanying the rapid industrialization of the Plateau landscape. The net result is a loss of productivity and bio-

diversity in traditional harvesting locales as management techniques at population, community, and landscape levels are no
longer practiced.

Burning, for example, is prohibited, and many elders have
expressed deep regret that they are no longer allowed to follow
their traditional burning practices. They are convinced that loss of
control of their traditional lands and prohibitions against landscape
burning have caused severe deterioration of traditional plant foods.
For example, Baptiste Ritchie (1971) stated:

> But now, because the white man really watches us, we don't
> burn anything. We realize already, it seems the things that
> were eaten by our forefathers have disappeared from the
> places where they burned. It seems that already almost
> everything has disappeared. Maybe it is because it's weedy.
> All kinds of things grow and they don't burn. If you go to
> burn then you get into trouble because the white men want
> to grow trees.

Similarly, Annie York noted that Frozen Lake near Yale used to
be a prime huckleberry picking spot, but it is not as good as it used
to be. "Before, it was plentiful, [when] they used to burn. Now,
nobody burns." Botanie Mountain, near Lytton, was another area
where burning was practiced, but now, according to Annie, the
skamec (avalanche lily) is not as good, nor as plentiful (Turner et al.
1990:123).

Similar observations have been made concerning the deterioration of berry picking locales:

> Where we used to pick berries, oh, they were really plentiful!
> Right here where our house is situated now [in Mount
> Currie], that is where we used to come to pick berries, like
> gooseberries [*sxniz'—Ribes divaricatum*]. Now there are no
> gooseberries near us. Now the other berries are the same.

They have all disappeared. We named other grounds of ours around here; called them "The Picking Places" because that is where we went to pick berries. Now you will not find one single berry there. (Ritchie 1971)

The cessation of management practices and the effects of live-stock grazing and introduced weeds such as knapweed (*Centaurea* spp.), mustards (*Sisymbrium* spp., *Brassica* spp.), couchgrass (*Agropyron repens*), and European thistles (*Cirsium* spp.) have also had a detrimental impact on traditional root resources. Elders have noted a significant deterioration in the quality and quantity of root foods (specifically spring beauty; avalanche lily; water parsnip, *Sium suave*; and wapato, *Sagittaria latifolia*) and medicines (such as valerian, *Valeriana sitchensis*) in traditional harvesting areas due to trampling by horses and cattle and the invasion of weedy species (cf. Turner et al. 1990). Mary Thomas discusses the difficulties associated with collecting traditional root foods such as spring beauty and avalanche lily today:

Everything is deteriorating—the surface of the soil where we used to gather our food, there's about 4–6 inches of thick, thick sod and all introduced. And on top of that the cattle walk on it, and it's packing it to the point where there's very little air goes into the ground, very little rain, and it's choking out all the natural foods, and it's going deeper and deeper, and the deeper they go the smaller they're getting.

British Columbia's active forest industry has also had a profound impact on traditional plant use as more and more of the old-growth forests are cleared, essentially eliminating them as resource harvesting locales. Mary Thomas discusses the loss of the forests and the impact on her people:

The old growth had a lot to offer, but now that we haven't got that old growth, all those things that used to be had—

maybe took it for granted it was going to be there all the time. We don't realize what we did to Mother Nature after cutting down all that old growth; for survival—a lot of them offered something that helped keep our health balanced. There's a lot of things we can't find anymore, because of the [loss of] old growth. It has its purpose, not only by being a big tree; there were things that came out of that tree that helped the other plants around it. So without the old growth I guess we're losing a lot. I haven't got anything against logging but we also have to remember what its purpose was for.

The use of herbicides and pesticides in forestry and agricultural activities is also taking its toll on traditional plant foods. Elders note that many types of berries, notably Oregon-grape (*Mahonia aquifolium*), black huckleberries, and saskatoons, are quite wormy and of lower quality these days. They attribute this to the insecticides being used on forests, which are killing the birds that controlled the insects.

The solutions to these problems are not simple or straightforward. While it is tempting to suggest that traditional plant management strategies simply be reintroduced in eco-restoration projects, such methods may not always be advantageous today when lands and resources are controlled by outsiders, when seasonal rounds and land occupancy are disrupted, and when traditional economies have often been partially or wholly replaced by mainstream industrial economies. Widespread cutting of forests, use of herbicides and pesticides, encroachment of mines and urban development, intensive grazing by cattle, sheep, and horses, clearing and tilling the land for commercial agricultural use, and the concomitant introduction of a complex of aggressive weeds all pose major management problems for traditional plant resources and habitats. Resources that used to be abundant—old-growth cedars for their roots, birches for their bark, large plants of avalanche lily and spring beauty, wapato and large water parsnip from the wetlands, large patches of Indian-hemp, special medicines like Canby's lovage (*Ligusticum canbyi*)—are now difficult to access at all, let alone manage by traditional methods.

As in the case of a garden that falls into disuse, restoring the productivity and biodiversity of the landscape will take time and effort. The first step in such restoration efforts, we suggest, is to return the "gardens" to their original managers. Indigenous peoples must be given greater control in decisionmaking processes impacting their traditional territories (e.g., Hyndman 1994; Stevens 1995; Turner and Thomas 1996; Turner et al. in press). This requires that First Nations peoples be equal partners in these processes and that their traditional ecological knowledge and management techniques be recognized as valid and valuable, equivalent in many respects to modern scientific knowledge (e.g., Scientific Panel for Sustainable Forest Practices in Clayoquot Sound 1995).

Second, the mismanagement of the "gardens" must stop. Activities that prevent the use of habitats by indigenous peoples, such as clear-cutting forests, extensive and intensive livestock grazing, and the use of chemical agents, must be replaced with plant management strategies such as controlled burning, selective harvesting, and rotating harvest locales. We must begin to manage the landscape, and to do so we must manage at the population and community levels, guided by a conservation ethic.

Thus, we need to encourage the elders in aboriginal communities to continue practicing traditional harvesting methods and plant management techniques and to teach these to their children and grandchildren. We need to promote traditional diets and medicines and the health benefits associated with these (e.g., Kuhnlein and Turner 1991; Nuxalk Food and Nutrition Program 1984).

Finally, we suggest that current notions of parks and protected areas be reconsidered. It is clear from this discussion, and from the work of numerous others (e.g., Anderson 1993a, 1993b, 1993c; Blackburn and Anderson 1993; Young et al. 1991; Young and Ross 1994), that much of what early explorers and conservationists perceived as "wilderness" was in fact a landscape that had been actively managed by indigenous peoples for thousands of years. In British Columbia, evidence points to the active use and manage-ment of plant resources for probably dozens of generations and suggests that the biodiversity of the region was a result of this interaction between people and plants.

Unfortunately, the idea that "use ensures abundance" remains antithetical to the ideals of most conservation efforts. The practice of traditional harvesting or other plant management strategies is commonly prohibited in protected areas, such as provincial and federal parks, in British Columbia. However, it is increasingly recognized that these protected areas are becoming less productive as succession reaches a climax stage, reducing the genetic, specific, and structural diversity of the landscape. In fact, several mountain parks (e.g., Banff and Waterton Lakes, Alberta) have reintroduced landscape burning in efforts to maintain parkland habitat, although these strategies were not based explicitly on aboriginal techniques.

We recommend, therefore, that current management practices in protected areas be revised to permit access to indigenous peoples for harvesting and the reinstatement of traditional plant resource management strategies.

CONCLUSIONS

The aboriginal peoples of the British Columbia's Interior Plateau have been active managers of their plant resources for thousands of years. This challenges traditional notions that hunter-gatherers simply "adapted to" the environment and suggests that Plateau peoples were essentially cultivating significant plant resources. Plant management strategies ensured a reliable, predictable, and continued supply of key resources for food, materials, and medi-cine. Population and community-level management practices such as selective harvesting, digging, weeding and pruning, controlled

burning, and rotating harvesting locales created ecologically heterogenous mosaics and enhanced the productivity and diversity of
plant resources within these areas. Management decisions were not
based solely on economic motives, but were embedded in social
contexts and encoded in religious philosophies that ensured the
sustainable use of these resources.

As indigenous peoples lost access to their homelands and the
ability to practice traditional plant management strategies, however,
the biodiversity of the region, based on their own observations,
began to decline, a trend that continues today. Removal of lands
through industry or conversion to protected areas, the invasion of
introduced weeds and livestock, and a prohibition on controlled
burning all contribute to a decrease in productivity and biodiversity
observed by elders throughout traditional territories.

The lesson, therefore, is that, just like a garden, the landscape
must be carefully used and maintained to be productive and diverse.
Conservation efforts at the landscape level must begin locally.
Indigenous peoples must be given greater control over traditional
territories and be actively involved in reintroducing traditional plant
management systems, such as harvesting and burning, in order to
enhance the productivity and biodiversity of the area.

The diversity of plant communities on the Plateau is closely
linked to the cultural systems of its indigenous inhabitants. Without
a land base on which to practice traditional lifestyles, however,
indigenous peoples are in danger of losing their cultural diversity
and the environment, its biological diversity.

ACKNOWLEDGMENTS

We are indebted to many people who contributed to this work,
especially the aboriginal elders whose knowledge and experiences
are cited and incorporated. These include Baptiste Ritchie, Sam
Mitchell, Charlie Mack Seymour, Alex Peters, Margaret Lester,

Edith O'Donaghey, Bill Edwards, Dez Peters, Sr. (Stl'atl'imx); Aimee August, Nellie Taylor, Mary Thomas (Secwepemc); Annie York, Hilda Austin, Mabel Joe, Louie Philips, Julia Kilroy, Bernadette Antoine (Nlaka'pamux); and Martin Louie and Selina Timoyakin (Okanagan).

We are grateful to Marianne B. Ignace and Chief Ron Ignace and to Richard Ford, Kat Anderson, Eugene Anderson, Kay Fowler, and Gary Nabhan, whose work and thoughts inspired us and guided the direction of our own research. We also thank Chief Manny Jules and the Band Council of the Kamloops Indian Band, as well as John Jules, Cultural Resource Management coordinator, for supporting our research on the ethnobotany and archaeology of the Kamloops peoples' traditional root processing grounds. The work of Dorothy Kennedy and Randy Bouchard, particularly their interviews with Baptiste Ritchie and other elders regarding burning, is also gratefully acknowledged. Paul Minnis and Wayne Elisens of the University of Oklahoma are acknowledged for organizing the symposium on "Biodiversity and Native North America." The research for this paper was funded in part by research grants from the Social Sciences and Humanities Research Council of Canada and by a University of Victoria Faculty Research grant to Nancy Turner. Sandra Peacock was funded, in part, by a Doctoral Fellowship and a Postdoctoral Fellowship from the Social Sciences and Humanities Research Council of Canada.

REFERENCES CITED

Ackermann, Lilian. 1994. Nonunilinear Descent Groups in the Plateau Culture Area. *American Ethnologist* 221(2):286–309.

Anderson, Eugene N. 1996. *Ecologies of the Heart: Emotion, Belief and the Environment*. New York: Oxford University Press.

Anderson, M. K. 1993a. California Indian Horticulture: Management and Use of Redbud by the Southern Sierra Miwok. *Journal of Ethnobiology* 11(1):145–57.

————. 1993b. The Experimental Approach to Assessment of the Potential Ecological Effects of Horticultural Practices by Indigenous Peoples on California Wildlands. Ph.D. dissertation. Wildland Resource Science, University of California, Berkeley.

————. 1993c. Native Californians as Ancient and Contemporary Cultivators. In *Before the Wilderness: Environmental Management by Native Californians*, edited by T. C. Blackburn and M. K. Anderson, pp. 151–74. Menlo Park, Calif.: Ballena Press.

Blackburn, Thomas C., and Kat Anderson (eds.). 1993. *Before the Wilderness: Environmental Management by Native Californians*. Menlo Park, Calif.: Ballena Press.

Boyd, Robert. 1986. Strategies of Indian Burning in the Willamette Valley. *Canadian Journal of Anthropology/Revue Canadienne d'Anthropologie* 5(1):65–77.

British Columbia Ministry of Forests. 1988. *Biogeoclimatic Zones of British Columbia 1988* (annotated map). Victoria, B.C.: Research Branch, Ministry of Forests.

Cole, Douglas, and Bradley Lockner (eds.). 1989. *The Journals of George M. Dawson, British Columbia, 1875–1878*. Vol. 2. Vancouver: UBC Press.

Dawson, G. M. 1892. Notes on the Shuswap People of British Columbia. *Transactions of the Royal Society of Canada*, section 2:3–46.

Day, Gordon M. 1953. The Indian as an Ecological Factor in the Northeastern Forest. *Ecology* 34(2):329–46.

Ford, Richard I. 1985. The Processes of Plant Food Production in Prehistoric North America. In *Prehistoric Food Production in North America*, edited by R. I. Ford, pp. 1–18. Anthropological Papers No. 75. Ann Arbor: University of Michigan Museum of Anthropology.

Fowler, Catherine, and Nancy J. Turner. In press. Indigenous Knowledge Systems: Other Ways of Knowing. In *Cambridge Encyclopedia of Hunters and Gatherers*, edited by Richard B. Lee and Richard H. Daly. Cambridge: Cambridge University Press.

Gadgil, Madhav, Fikret Berkes, and Carl Folke. 1993. Indigenous Knowledge for Biodiversity Conservation. *Ambio* 22(2–3):151–56.

Gottesfeld, L. M. Johnson. 1994a. Aboriginal Burning for Vegetation Management in Northwest British Columbia. *Human Ecology* 22(2): 171–88.

————. 1994b. Conservation, Territory, and Traditional Beliefs: An Analysis of Gitksan and Wet'suwet'en Subsistence, Northwest British Columbia, Canada. *Human Ecology* 22(4):443–65.

Harris, David. 1989. An Evolutionary Continuum of People-Plant Interactions. In *Foraging and Farming: The Evolution of Plant Exploitation*, edited
by D. R. Harris and G. C. Hillman, pp. 11–26. London: Unwin, Hyman.

Hayden, B. (ed.). 1992. *Complex Cultures of the British Columbia Plateau:
Traditional Stl'atl'imx Resource Use*. Vancouver: University of British
Columbia Press.

Hill-Tout, Charles. 1978. *The Salish People*. Vol. 1. *The Thompson and
Okanagan*. Edited by Ralph Maud. Vancouver, B.C.: Talonbooks.

Hunn, Eugene S., with James Selam and Family. 1990. *Nch'i-Wana, "The
Big River": Mid-Columbia Indians and Their Land*. Seattle: University of
Washington Press.

Hyndman, David. 1994. Commentary: Conservation through Self-
Determination: Promoting the Interdependence of Cultural and Biological Diversity. *Human Organization* 53(3):296–302.

Kroeber, A. L. 1939. *Cultural and Natural Areas in Native North America*.
University of California Publications in American Archaeology and
Ethnology 38. N.p.

Kuhnlein, Harriet V., and Nancy J. Turner. 1991. *Traditional Plant Foods of
Canadian Indigenous Peoples: Nutrition, Botany and Use*. Vol. 8. Food and
Nutrition in History and Anthropology, edited by Solomon Katz.
Philadelphia: Gordon and Breach Science Publishers.

Lewis, Henry T. 1973. Patterns of Indian Burning in California. *Ecology and
Ethnohistory*. Anthropological Papers No. 1. Socorro, Calif.: Ballena
Press.

———. 1977. Maskuta: The Ecology of Indian Fires in Northern Alberta.
Western Canadian Journal of Anthropology 7(1):15–52.

———. 1982. *A Time for Burning*. Occasional Publication No. 17. Boreal
Institute for Northern Studies. Edmonton: University of Alberta.

Lewis, Henry T., and Theresa A. Ferguson. 1988. Yards, Corridors, and
Mosaics: How to Burn a Boreal Forest. *Human Ecology* 16(1):57–77.

Marshall, A. G. 1977. Nez Perce Social Groups: An Ecological Interpretation. Ph.D. dissertation. Department of Anthropology, Washington
State University, Pullman.

Meidinger, Del, and Jim Pojar (eds.). 1991. *Ecosystems of British Columbia*.
Victoria: British Columbia Ministry of Forests.

Nuxalk Food and Nutrition Program. 1984. *Nuxalk Food and Nutrition
Handbook*. Bella Coola, B.C.: The Nuxalk Nation.

Palmer, Gary. 1975a. Cultural Ecology in the Canadian Plateau: Pre-contact
to the Early Contact Period in the Territory of the Southern Shuswap

Indians of British Columbia. *Northwest Anthropological Research Notes* 9(2):199–245.

———. 1975b. Shuswap Indian Ethnobotany. *Syesis* 8:29–81.

Parish, Roberta, Ray Coupe, and Dennis Lloyd (eds.). 1996. *Plants of Southern Interior British Columbia.* Vancouver: B.C. Ministry of Forests and Lone Pine Publishing.

Peacock, Sandra. 1996. It's the Pits: Innovations in Plateau Plant Processing. Paper presented at the 29th Annual Chacmool Conference, University of Calgary Archaeological Association in Calgary, Alberta, November.

———. 1998. Putting Down Roots: The Emergence of Wild Plant Food Production on the Canadian Plateau. Ph.D. dissertation. Interdisciplinary, Faculty of Graduate Studies, University of Victoria, Victoria, B.C.

———. In press. Perusing the Pits: The Evidence for Prehistoric Geophyte Processing on the Canadian Plateau. In *The Archaeobotany of Temperate-Zone Hunter-Gatherers,* edited by Jon Hather and Sarah Mason. London: Institute of Archaeology.

Pokotylo, David L., and Patricia D. Froese. 1983. Archaeological Evidence for Prehistoric Root Gathering on the Southern Interior Plateau of British Columbia: A Case Study from Upper Hat Creek Valley. *Canadian Journal of Archaeology* 7(2):127–57.

Pokotylo, D., and D. Mitchell. 1998. Prehistory of the Northern Plateau. In *Handbook of North American Indians* (gen. ed. W. C. Sturtevant), vol. 12: *Plateau,* edited by D. E. Walker, pp. 81–102. Washington D.C.: Smithsonian Institution.

Posey, Darrell Addison. 1990. The Science of the Mebêngôkre. *Orion Nature Quarterly* 9(3):16–23.

Ray, Verne. 1939. *Cultural Relations in the Plateau of Northwestern America.* Publications of the Frederick Hodge Anniversary Publication Fund 3. Los Angeles: Southwest Museum.

Richards, Thomas, and Michael Rousseau. 1987. *Late Prehistoric Cultural Horizons on the Canadian Plateau.* Department of Archaeology Publication No. 16. Burnaby, B.C.: Simon Fraser University.

Rindos, David. 1984. *The Origins of Agriculture: An Evolutionary Perspective.* New York: Academic Press.

Ritchie, Baptiste. 1971. Burning Mountainsides for Better Crops. In Leo John Swoboda, Lillooet Phonology, Texts and Dictionary, pp. 182–91. Master of Arts thesis. Department of Linguistics, University of British Columbia, Vancouver.

Scientific Panel for Sustainable Forest Practices in Clayoquot Sound. 1995. *First Nations' Perspectives on Forest Practices in Clayoquot Sound*. Report 3. Victoria, B.C.: Scientific Panel for Sustainable Forest Practices in Clayoquot Sound.

Stevens, Michelle. 1995. A Step toward Integration of Indigenous Knowledge Systems into Restoration Efforts. Conference Report, Indigenous People's Program. Society of Ecological Restoration. Seattle, Washington.

Stryd, Arnoud H., and Michael Rousseau. 1996. The Early Prehistory of the Mid Fraser–Thompson River Area of British Columbia. In *Early Human Occupation in British Columbia*, edited by Roy L. Carlson and Luke Dalla Bona, pp. 177–204. Vancouver: University of British Columbia Press.

Teit, James A. 1900. *The Thompson Indians of British Columbia*. Memoir of the American Museum of Natural History, vol. 1, part 4. New York: G. E. Stechert and Co.

———. 1906. *The Lillooet Indians*. Memoir of the American Museum of Natural History, vol. 2, part 6. New York: G. E. Stechert and Co.

———. 1909. *The Shuswap*. Memoir of the American Museum of Natural History, vol. 2, part 7. New York: G. E. Stechert and Co.

———. 1912. *Mythology of the Thompson Indians*, vol. 7, part 2. The Jesup North Pacific Expedition. Edited by Franz Boas. Memoir of the American Museum of Natural History. New York: G. E. Stechert and Co.

Timbrook, Jan, John R. Johnson, and David D. Earle. 1982. Vegetation Burning by the Chumash. *Journal of California and Great Basin Anthropology* 4(2):163–86.

Turner, Nancy J. 1992a. "Just When the Wild Roses Bloom": The Legacy of a Lillooet Basket Weaver. *TEK TALK: A Newsletter of Traditional Ecological Knowledge* (UNESCO, World Congress for Education & Communication on Environment & Development) 1(2):5–7.

———. 1992b. Plant Resources of the Stl'atl'imx (Fraser River Lillooet) People: A Window into the Past. In *Complex Cultures of the British Columbia Plateau: Traditional Stl'atl'imx Resource Use*, edited by B. Hayden, pp. 405–69. Vancouver: University of British Columbia Press.

———. 1996. "Dans une Hotte": L'importance de la vannerie dans l'économie des peuples chasseurs-pêcheurs-cueilleurs du Nord-Ouest de l'Amérique du Nord ("Into a Basket Carried on the Back": Importance of Basketry in Foraging/Hunting/Fishing Economies in Northwestern North America). *Anthropologie et Sociétés* (Special Issue on

Contemporary Ecological Anthropology: Theories, Methods and Research Fields, Montréal, Québec) 20(3):55–84 (in French).

———. 1997a. *Food Plants of Interior First Peoples*. Rev. ed. Vancouver: University of British Columbia Press; Victoria: Royal British Columbia Museum. (Orig. published in 1978 by B.C. Provincial Museum.)

———. 1997b. Traditional Ecological Knowledge. In *The Rain Forests of Home: Profile of a North American Bioregion*, edited by Peter K. Schoonmaker, Bettina Von Hagen, and Edward C. Wolf, Ecotrust, pp. 275–98. Covelo, Calif., and Washington, D.C.: Island Press.

———. 1998. *Plant Technology of British Columbia First Peoples*. Rev. ed. Vancouver: University of British Columbia Press; Victoria: Royal British Columbia Museum. (Orig. published in 1979 by B.C. Provincial Museum.)

———. 1999. "Time to Burn": Traditional Use of Fire to Enhance Resource Production by Aboriginal Peoples in British Columbia. In *Indians, Fire and the Land in the Pacific Northwest*, edited by Robert Boyd, pp. 185–218. Corvallis: Oregon State University Press. (Revised and expanded version of "Burning Mountainsides for Better Crops." *Archaeology in Montana* [1991].)

Turner, Nancy J., Randy Bouchard, and Dorothy I. D. Kennedy. 1980. *Ethnobotany of the Okanagan-Colville Indians of British Columbia and Washington*. Occasional Paper No. 21. Victoria: British Columbia Provincial Museum (now Royal British Columbia Museum).

Turner, Nancy J., Marianne Boelscher Ignace, and Ron Ignace. 1995. "To Preserve and Maintain for the Generations to Come": Strategies for Sustainable Resource Use among Aboriginal Peoples of British Columbia. Paper presented at Society of Ethnobiology, 18th Annual Conference, Tucson, Arizona, March.

Turner, Nancy J., Marianne B. Ignace, and Ronald Ignace. In press. Traditional Ecological Knowledge and Wisdom of Aboriginal Peoples in British Columbia. For Special Issue of *Ecological Applications*, edited by Jesse Ford.

Turner, Nancy J., Harriet V. Kuhnlein, and Keith N. Egger. 1985. The Cottonwood Mushroom (*Tricholoma populinum* Lange): A Food Resource of the Interior Salish Indian Peoples of British Columbia. *Canadian Journal of Botany* 65:921–27.

Turner, Nancy J., and Sandra L. Peacock. In press. The Perennial Paradox: Traditional Plant Management on the Northwest Coast. In *"Keeping It Living": Indigenous Plant Management on the Northwest*

Coast, edited by Douglas Deur and Nancy J. Turner. Seattle: University of Washington Press.

Turner, Nancy J., and Mary Thomas. 1996. Incorporating Traditional Knowledge into Modern Conservation Programs: Examples from Northwestern North America. Botanical Society of America Annual Conference, Economic Botany Symposium, University of Washington, Seattle, August.

Turner, Nancy J., Laurence C. Thompson, M. Terry Thompson, and Annie Z. York. 1990. *Thompson Ethnobotany: Knowledge and Usage of Plants by the Thompson Indians of British Columbia*. Memoir No. 3. Victoria: Royal British Columbia Museum.

Young, Elspeth, and Helen Ross. 1994. Using the Aboriginal Rangelands: "Insider" Realities and "Outsider" Perceptions. *Rangeland Journal* 16(2):184–97.

Young, Elspeth, Helen Ross, J. Johnston, and J. Kesteven. 1991. Caring for Country: Aborigines and Land Management. AGPS, Canberra, Australian Capital Territory.

CHAPTER SIX

IWÍGARA

A Rarámuri Cognitive Model of Biodiversity and Its Effects on Land Management

ENRIQUE SALMÓN

INTRODUCTION

Western cultural models of nature separate humans from nature, while indigenous models include humans as one aspect of the complexity of nature. The cognitive model of nature among the Rarámuri of Chihuahua, Mexico, is founded on the concept of *iwígara*. As in other indigenous models, humans are on an equal standing with the rest of the natural world. The word *iwígara* can closely resemble the Western notion of biodiversity and stands equal to biodiversity as a unique model of the natural world. In addition, *iwígara* influences Rarámuri approaches to caring for the land or land management.

A Rarámuri cognitive model of *iwígara* is presented first. The model reveals how differently an indigenous culture perceives and is influenced by the local environment. The obvious difference is that the Rarámuri view themselves as an integral part of the life and place where they live. Next, the model is applied to Rarámuri land management practices, which, again, differ from Western constructs of management that imply a separate mode of thinking and, there-fore, of approaching the land. Land management is not a practice to the Rarámuri: it is a culturally encoded ethic of spiritual and practical knowledge and thinking that shapes how they approach their land.

The land of the Rarámuri, the northern Sierra Madre Occidental, rests within the Mexican states of Chihuahua, southeastern Sonora, and northeastern Sinaloa (Salmón 1977) (see map 6.1). The Rarámuri people live in small, scattered agricultural settlements called rancherías (Salmón 1977). The rancherías are generally dispersed along the western Sierra Madre, which extends south from Arizona into Mexico. These mountains are characterized by their deep and narrow barrancas (canyons) that were cut and gouged by the many rivers that drain the area into the Sea of Cortez. These rivers include the Río Fuerte, Río Yaqui, Río Mayo, Río Urique, and Río Verde (Bennett and Zingg 1935).

The mountains are Tertiary volcanic tufa that developed into the formidable barrancas, which make life and travel difficult for the Rarámuri. Some barrancas descend as deep as 3,000 feet, often providing two distinct ecological regions for the Rarámuri to inhabit: the highlands and the gorges. In the woods of the cool highlands stand several varieties of hard and softwood trees, the most numerous being pines and oaks. The most common species of pine is *Pinus ayacahuite*, which reaches a height of 60 feet and is valued for its straight grain, and the Douglas-fir (*Pseudotsuga mucronata*). Other smaller conifers exist here, including the stunted cedar (*Juniperus mexicana*). The two most common oaks are *Quercus fulva* and *Quercus incarnata* (black oak), which add color to the highlands during the autumnal change. The highlands are under-storied by many species of plants, shrubs, and cacti. Ball cacti (*Echinocereus* sp.) are abundant, as is the nopal (*Opuntia* sp.), which is prized for its fruit, the tuna, which is carefully freed of its spines then cooked and eaten by the Rarámuri. On the hillsides are yucca (*Yucca decipens*) and sotol (*Dasylirion simplex*), both used for their

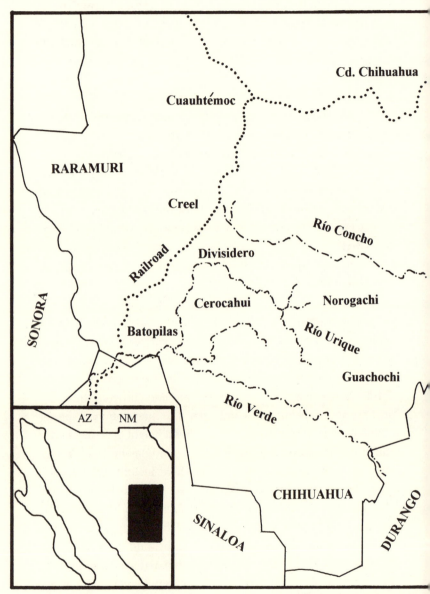

Map 6.1. The Sierra Tarahumara.

fibrous leaves; two types of agave (*Agave schottii* and *Agave patonii*); and manzanilla (*Arctostaphylos pungens*). Along the high streams and rivers stand pussy willow (*Salix lasiolepis*) and choke cherry (*Prunus virens*) (Bennett and Zingg 1935).

In the winter, many Rarámuri migrate to their caves located in the walls of the deep barrancas to escape the cold highlands. A distinct change from alpine to tropical flora is seen as one encounters the dramatic altitudinal shift in the descent. The giant agave, sotol, and cacti still exist on the canyon walls, but deeper in the canyon are found different species of trees and shrubs: the fragrant laurel tree (*Litsea glaucescens*) and also the brazilwood tree (*Haematoxylum brasiletto*), valued for its hardness. The several shrubs common to the gorges include physic nut (*Jatropha curcus*), used as a Mexican folk remedy, cotton plant (*Gossypium mexicanum*), wild tobacco (*Nicotiana glauca*), and indigo (*Indigofera suffruticosa*) (Bennett and Zingg 1935).

The northern Sierra Madre Occidental represents a biologically rich zone of contiguous montane woodland that reaches north from southern Mexico nearly to the U.S. border (Felger and Dahl 1994). The complex geography, topography, and elevational changes result in the astounding amount of biodiversity in the region. "No less than eight physiognomic vegetation types can be found" there, including montane evergreen forest, oak-coniferous woodland, tropical deciduous forest, oak savanna, chaparral, short-grass prairie, subtropical thornscrub, and subtropical desert fringe (Felger and Dahl 1994). The Madrean region of northwest Mexico houses two of the richest floras of Mexico, which "ranks as one of three top megadiversity centers in the world" (Ramamoorthy, Bye, et al. 1993; see also Felger and Dahl 1994). It is estimated that 4,000 vascular plant species are found in the region, 150 of which are endemic (Felger and Dahl 1994). In the Rarámuri region of the central Sierra Tarahumara alone, as many as 1,900 plant species can be found (Felger and Dahl 1994). Many varieties of insects have been identified, along with 65 species of reptiles and amphibians, 17 of which are endemic. Between 260 to 295 species of breeding birds inhabit the region, while many more migrate to or visit the area. Ninety-two different mammals roam the area, including several that are rare or threatened.

The region is also rich in useful plants. Eighteen land races of prehispanic crops grow in the Sierra Madres (Felger and Dahl 1994), including the genera *Agave*, *Lepidium*, *Hyptis*, and *Panicum*. Other plants used for medicine and food include species from the Cactaceae, Asteraceae, Fabaceae, Lamiaceae, and Solanaceae. Wild relatives of domesticated plants occur in the area, which include cucurbits and species of *Agave*, *Phaseolus*, *Prunus*, and *Solanum*.

Not to be omitted are the indigenous people who inhabit the region. It is being recognized that biologically diverse regions of the world are usually inhabited by distinctive cultural groups who have managed to hold onto their traditions, including their languages, which carry the centuries of culturally encoded knowledge of their bioregions (Martinez 1994; Nabhan 1995). Nabhan notes that it "has been documented that 16 of the top twenty-five countries ranked for endemic languages also rank in the top 25 countries for flowering plant diversity" (Nabhan 1995:4). In the Sierra Madre Occidental, four culturally distinctive groups who have held onto their languages survive. If the region is stretched west to the Sea of Cortez, three more cultures can be added. The link between biodiversity and cultural diversity in the Sierra Madres can be established without difficulty.

The Rarámuri number between 40,000 to 60,000 people (Kennedy 1978; Rascón 1979). They subsist on an agricultural economy growing mainly maize, wheat, sugarcane, squash, melons, beans, potatoes, and chiles (Pennington 1963). They also gather wild plants for food, seasonings, medicine, and ceremonies (Bye 1976, 1985; Salmón 1995). Their society and culture are basically the same as they were in the sixteenth century. W. L. Merrill (1988) states that "the Raramuri of the sixteenth century would have little difficulty recognizing their descendants of the twentieth." Unfortunately, mining operations and lumber roads have encroached into the Rarámuri region, bringing mestizo language, values, and technological innovation. Domesticated animals have been introduced to some Rarámuri living closer to the mestizo settlements, as well as more Christian theology (Merrill 1988). These introductions have not altered Rarámuri culture very much, however. Technological innovations in the form of metal axes and plows have only allowed the Rarámuri to clear more land for growing and to produce a higher yield of crops. The domesticated animals have made some Rarámuri more seasonally mobile, following their animals into the lower barrancas to escape the bite of winter (Merrill 1988).

BUILDING A MODEL

Cultural models are cognitive patterned diagrams culturally embodied in the members of a social group. Models are generally endowed with small groups of related concepts, usually three to seven. But each concept may itself be a complex schema. For example, a Western model of nature is made up of several concepts, which include material benefits, recreation, ecology-science, aesthetics, symbolism, dominion, humanization, morals, and fear. Each concept is complex but, at the same time, is related to other members of the model. In addition, the model of nature can play a role in other cultural models.

Cultural models suggest and determine how a culture, and individuals from that culture, will interact with, in this case, the natural world. Models influence culturally shared thought, reactions, actions, and understandings. Models are culturally constructed pillars of conventional common thought. They presume and assume probability and cause; they give weight to rules and metaphor. Presented with a common situation, two individuals from distinctive cultures will approach the situation differently according to the way in which their cultural models influence their assessment of the situation.

IWÍGARA

The Rarámuri speak a Uto-Aztecan language, which implies that they arrived in their region of Mexico with a wave of others of the same language stock, including the Papago, Yoeme, Mayo, and Huichol, at an early date (Jenkinson 1972; Kennedy 1978). In a study of the Uto-Aztecan speech community, linguist Jane Hill noted strong associations with flowers in song and oratory. She found many references to flowers and "beautiful landscapes," natural phenomena, animals, crystals, fire, gender identity, and prototypical landscapes (Hill 1992). Flowers are also associated with the spirit world. Although Hill never suggested it, this implies that references

Fig. 6.1. Rarámuri *yúmari* ceremony.

Fig. 6.2. Dancing at *yúmari*. This is the only Rarámuri ceremony at which women are allowed to dance.

to flowers can be metaphors of a deeply ingrained relationship to the biodiversity of the regions where the Uto-Aztecan speakers live.

In my own study of Rarámuri language, references to flowers in song and oratory are numerous (Salmón 1991, 1995). In one specific *yúmari* song, reference is made to sumati okilivea, the beautiful lily. Women do not dance except for *yúmari*. They dance in a continual *iwí* (circle) while two male singers and chanters dance within the moving circle. The songs ask that the land be nourished and that the land nourish the people. As the songs are performed, the *iwí* continues to turn. The *iwí* represents the fertility of the land. *Iwí* can convey other meanings, however. It translates roughly into the idea of binding with a lasso. But it also means to unite, to join, to connect. Another meaning of *iwí* is to breathe, inhale/exhale, or respire.

Iwí also makes reference to the Rarámuri concept of soul, which can be an elusive concept. It means different things depending on the individual. Generally, however, it is understood that the soul, or *iwí*, sustains the body with the breath of life. Everything that breathes has a soul. Plants, animals, humans, stones, and the land all share the same breath. When humans and animals die, their souls become butterflies that visit the living. The butterflies will also travel to the Milky Way, where past souls of the ancestors reside.

Iwí is also the word used to identify a caterpillar that weaves its cocoons on the madrone tree. The metamorphosis of the caterpillar implies that there is a whole morphological process of change, death, birth, and rebirth associated with the concept of *iwí*. *Iwí* is the soul or essence of life everywhere. *Iwígara* then channels the idea that all life, spiritual and physical, is interconnected in a continual cycle. *Iwí* is the prefix to *iwígara* (see fig. 6.3).

Iwígara expresses the Rarámuri belief that all living things share the same life-sustaining breath and play a role in the complexity of life. To the Western-minded, *iwígara* might most closely resemble the concept of "biodiversity." To the leading thinkers on biodiversity, it seems to mean the variety of life in its multiformed ecological roles and genetic patterns. In addition, most are correctly concerned about the increasing loss of biodiversity, but they usually speak of it in terms of the intrinsic value of animal, plant, or insect species lost (Kellert and Wilson 1993; Wilson 1988). Rarely are humans a part of their calculations, except to mention how species loss will negatively affect humanity, implying that humans are separate from nature.

The Western model of biodiversity is a direct result of the influence of Christianity, which assumes that humanity is not equal to the natural world. Like the Christian God who has dominion over his creation, humans have dominion over the creatures of the world. The model is a multileveled one that places humans near the top of the hierarchy, one level below God. The other concepts of

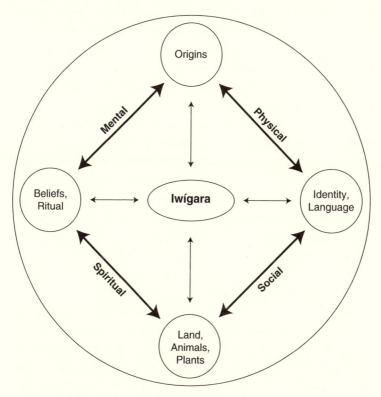

Fig. 6.3. The Rarámuri cultural model of *iwígara*.

this model are all related to this general separation from nature. In contrast, indigenous models are generally not multileveled but, rather, multisegmented, much like a Venn diagram, which overlaps several aspects of a domain on an equal plane. Neither aspect is larger or more important than the other. Each has its role to play, which will affect the others.

To the Rarámuri, the cultural model of *iwígara* encompasses many ideas and ways of thinking unique to the place where they live. Rituals and ceremonies, the language, and, therefore, Rarámuri thought are influenced by the centuries of a psychically encoded relationship with the Sierra Madres. *Iwígara* reflects the Rarámuri sense of realities in terms of their belief in the total interconnectedness and integration of all life in the Sierra Madres, physical and spiritual. *Iwígara* calls on each Rarámuri to realize automatically the human place in and influences on the environment. The word simultaneously activates several Rarámuri mental spaces, drawing from cultural models, including Rarámuri and earthly origins, relationships to animals and plants, the place of nurturing, and the entities to which the Rarámuri look for guidance.

To add another corollary, to the Rarámuri, *numatí*, things of the natural world, are relatives in a realistic sense. Rarámuri self-identity stems from the realization that plants and animals were and are their relatives. In a previous world, people were part plant. When the Rarámuri emerged into this world, many of those plants followed. They live today as humans of a different form. Peyote (*Lophophora williamsii*), datura (*Datura* sp.), maize (*Zea mays*), morning glory (*Ipomoea purpurea*), and brazilwood (*Haematoxylon brasiletto*) are all humans. Rarámuri feel related to these plants as if they were cousins and siblings (Levi 1993).

The natural world, therefore, is not one of wonder, but of familiarity. The human niche is only one of a myriad of united niches that work together to continue the process of *iwígara*. If one aspect of the lasso is removed, the integrity of the circle is threatened and all other aspects are weakened. The notion of biodiversity *per se* does not exist in the Rarámuri cultural model of nature. This is because it is not flexible enough to accommodate the complexities of realizing that everything living is a relative that shares our breath. But biodiversity can be encompassed by *iwígara*—all is bound, connected, and affected by a sharing breath.

Studies of environmental effects on language (Ellen 1986; Hunn 1982; Morris 1984; Posey 1984) and thought have suggested either that taxonomies and lexicons are a result of the human recognition of the "discontinuities" of nature in "gross morphological form or that they result from human adaptation to and recognition of environmental utility" (Posey 1984:123). Although contradictory, both approaches imply that lexicons are a result of a human need to categorize biodiversity; that humans act upon an inactive bioregion to categorize it.

Benjamin Whorf was the first to suggest that language and thought are intertwined (Whorf 1950, 1956). Later F. J. Varela et al. suggested that language and thought are embodied in experiences with the environment: experiences actually are embodied in the human being, becoming thoughts, models, language, then actions (Varela et al. 1993). Included in this discussion should be the notion that humans not only impose order on their local environments but also are afforded information about their surroundings by the surroundings themselves.

The concept of an environment that affords information to humans is somewhat independent. But there are others who allow this idea credence. While researching the ecology of visual perception, Dr. J. Gibson of Cornell University discovered not only that the human eye is connected to a brain that passively sorts and classifies the information fed into it, but also that human visual perception is the result of a complex system that uses the eye as only the "central organ" of a visual system relying equally on the remaining sensory systems of the human body (Gibson 1979). Vision and, therefore, thought about what one is seeing are the result of an active and dynamic relationship between the person and the bioregional influences present. In *The Ecological Approach to Visual Perception*, Gibson suggests that "the affordances of the environment are what it offers the animal, what it provides or furnishes" (Gibson 1979:56).

Local environments can influence human thought through the production of raw material humans use to create and shape expressions of self and their relationship to the land (Kellert 1997). What humans perceive around them is what they use to build metaphors that expedite communication. The resulting lexicon can only identify what is there or what is believed to be there, although humans never entirely categorize all that is there. Gregory Cajete states that "our physical makeup and the nature of our psyche are formed in direct ways by the distinct climate, soil, geography and living things of a place" (Cajete 1994:44).

Although Cajete speaks from the perspective of an indigenous educator and scholar, his opinions are mirrored by non-native scholars. Environmental writer and Yale University professor Stephen Kellert notes that symbols derived from nature play a role in the development of human language: children rely on the diversity of nature to help them in the developmental "tasks of ordering, sorting, and naming, all fundamental in the development of language." He states that "the human emotional and intellectual need for varied distinctions . . . appears to be matched only by the rich diversity and complexity encountered in the natural world" (Kellert and Wilson 1993). As a result of his linguistic work with Anglo, O'odham, Hispanic, and Yaqui (Yaqui/Mayo) children, Gary Nabhan reflects on the importance of nature in child language development: "The playful exploration of habitat by cohorts of children, as well as the gradual accumulation of an oral tradition about the land, have been essential to child development for over a million years, as the emergence of language allowed the telling of stories and an expression of kinships with the earth" (Nabhan and Trimble 1994). Finally, Keith Basso suggests that the Western Apache maintain a reciprocal relationship with their land: they are "inhabitants of their landscape" and "are thus inhabited by it as well." Basso adds that this reciprocal relationship is one "in which individuals invest themselves in the landscape while incorporating its meaning into their own most fundamental experience" (Basso 1996:102).

It can be asserted that language influences thought and that language comes partly from experience with one's environment. In northwest Mexico, Uto-Aztecan cultural models of the land and the flower world reflect their centuries of experience with their place. Rarámuri experiences developed into the model of *iwígara*, their notion of biodiversity.

IWÍGARA AND MANAGING THE LAND

For the Rarámuri, food and medicine are intertwining necessities of life. Food is often a component of healing and an important aspect of healing ceremonies. Food and healing are symbols of the Rarámuri's relationship to their natural environment and their mode of living with their place. The uses of natural foods and medicine influence how the Rarámuri perceive their place in the Sierra Madres. Their knowledge of the foods and medicinal plants embodies their relationship and, therefore, their model of self-identification with their place and their manner of using what nature has offered. The foundation for their model of land management stems directly from the notion of *iwígara*.

The Rarámuri use around 350 different plant species for food and medicine (Salmón 1995). I will not delve into the myriad of plant uses, but one plant, maize, may serve as an example of the Rarámuri model of plants and land management. Maize is a staple food of the Rarámuri. It is eaten raw, made into tortillas, used in soups and in tamales. As a medicine, the meal itself is sprinkled onto patients as a blessing. The tassels are used in a recipe with other plants to cure dysentery and for kidney problems. No ceremony would be complete without an offering of tortillas and *suwi-ki* to the Creator. *Suwi-ki*, consumed at all healing and nonhealing ceremonies, is a beerlike beverage made from maize. *Suwi-ki* is at the center of Rarámuri rituals and ceremonies; without it, the Rarámuri would not be able to assure the health of the Creator, who provides rain, sun, and other necessities of life. *Suwi-ki* is also at the center of community activities, including planting, harvesting, and all ceremonies and dances. Community activities strengthen the Rarámuri's sense of identity and relationship to each other, to their land, and to their spiritual universe (Kennedy 1978).

It was the Creator who supplied food, medicine, and life to the people; it is understood that he must be cared for. Each day the Creator faces a fight with his evil brother over who controls the

Fig. 6.4. Olla (clay jar) full of fermenting corn beer.

earth. If the Creator were to lose his daily battle, the rains would stop and the land would dry up. Fortunately, the Creator of the Rarámuri manages to prevail each day. This is only because he has help from the Rarámuri in the form of dances, song, offerings of food, and the consumption of *suwi-ki*.

Suwi-ki in this sense becomes a sacrament. Through its consumption, the Rarámuri return, symbolically, to their origins as the children of maize. They rekindle, with each drink, the belief that they are part maize. Through the sacrament, dances, and songs associated with the *suwi-ki*, the Creator is strengthened and is able to overcome his evil brother, ensuring rain and, therefore, the life of the land and the plants, animals, and people. An important cycle of existence is assured with the consumption of *suwi-ki*. More importantly, the Rarámuri thereby maintain their relationship with their world while they continue to fit harmoniously into it without disturbing it.

The foundation for this model of mutually assured existence emanates directly from the notion of *iwígara*. The Creator's daily battle—which leads to rain, which leads to the growth of maize, which leads to the consumption of *suwi-ki*, which leads to the strength of the Creator—is a continuous interconnected cycle of breath and life. Rarámuri land management, then, is only one latent effect of a need to continue the cycle of breath.

The physical application of *iwígara* is at the heart of Rarámuri land management philosophy. It is *iwígara* that guides agriculture, medicine, and foraging. The use of plants for healing and for food offers a foundational relationship from which the Rarámuri view themselves as participants in the natural community. The Rarámuri perceive the land as a relative who must be cared for and nurtured. Rarámuri cultural history tells how the people emerged into this world from ears of corn. Another version tells how the people were put upon the land by the Creator with corn in their ears. The Rarámuri understand that they were placed here as caretakers of their land but also to aid in the health of the Creator, who works hard each day to provide for the land and its inhabitants.

Fig. 6.5. Blessing the fields at *yúmari*.

In return for Rarámuri care, the land provides a cornucopia. *Sepé* (wild greens) are collected by nearly all Rarámuri to augment the daily diet. *Sunú* (maize) is a staple eaten at nearly every meal. The Rarámuri grow beans, potatoes, squashes, wheat, and a variety of other products both Old and New World in origin. The land also permits the raising of goats, sheep, chickens, and pigs. Some Rarámuri raise cows and horses.

This rich area offers wild products, most of which are exploited by the Rarámuri. One of the most important plants is the relative *hikuli*, peyote (*Lophophora williamsii*). The use of peyote remains a focus in some communities in the Sierra. But its use is declining as outside pressures increase. Peyote yields are on the decline across northwest Mexico as more recreational users and Native American

Church members to the north demand it. One of the most important medicinals is *chuchupate* (*Ligusticum porteri*), also called *wásia* by the Rarámuri and *osha* by Hispanics. It is used for nearly every ailment and carried by all healers to repel sorcerers and snakes. Many plant specialists conceal their favorite arroyos or corners of the pine-oak forests where they collect *chuchupate*. This is out of respect for the plant but also to lessen the impact of non-native harvesters, who are causing a decline of *chuchupate* as well. Other natural materials include *bisíkori* (piñon) for building and fuel, sagebrush, and weaving materials: sotol, pine needles, and yucca. The Rarámuri weave items for household use, but many baskets and other crafts are sold to the exploding tourist industry to supplement their meager incomes.

Iwígara may be difficult to understand for the Western-minded. Notes from my discussions with two Rarámuri colleagues may clarify this concept.

Each day Jesusita travels the spine of the world (her reference to the Sierra Madres). She is *ybero*, an herbalist. In her shadow quickly strides her little *u'usu* (granddaughter). Together they collect edible greens, which will be dried and stored then eaten later. They recognize and harvest many plants, which they use for colds, arthritis, baskets, stomachaches, corn beer, bruises, the blood, and headaches. Their collecting trips are not specially appointed times, nor are they specifically planned. They collect plants as they are walking to the Conusupo (trading post), as they come over to visit, or in-between times, when they enjoy stopping by the creek to toss rocks into the water. I once came upon Jesusita and her shadow at the creek. They were laughing, enjoying the splashes their efforts were producing. Jesusita showed no sign of her sixty-six years. I asked, "What are you doing?"

Jesusita said, "Just throwing."

Her reply was from someone whose dimension of time was in synchrony with the cycles of the land. Her knowledge of the use of plants in her bioregion is not just a stored collection of facts, recipes,

and illness. It is the result of a lifelong relationship she has cultivated with her home. Her granddaughter's relationship with the
land has long since sprouted and is growing strongly; she often
corrects Jesusita's mistaken identifications of plants and their uses.
Jesusita's shadow is her only apprentice.

When Jesusita speaks of the land, the religious and romantic
overtones so prevalent in Western environmental conversation are
absent. For her, the land exists in the same manner as do her family,
her chickens, the river, and the sky. No hierarchy of privilege places
one above or below another. To Jesusita, *iwígara* binds and manages
the interconnectedness of all life. Within this web, there are particular ways that living things relate with one another. All individual
life plays a role in the cycle: people should collect plants in the same
manner that fish should breathe water and birds collect seeds and
eat bugs. These are things we are meant to do and are supposed to
do. As caretakers of the land, then, we should collect plants in a
proper manner so as to fulfill our role.

When discussing plant collecting, Jesusita becomes cautious and
reminds me that the collecting is done only at certain times and in
certain places to avoid disturbing or offending the plants or the
places where the plants grow. Jesusita prefers to collect her pine
needles (*Pinus leiophylla*), for example, which she uses for basket
weaving, at only a handful of places, all a half-day's walk from her
community. In this way she prevents overharvesting of the needles
and maintains a relationship with all the directions from her home.

Rarámuri women use several other natural materials for
weaving. Sotol (*Dasylirion simplex*), yucca (*Yucca decipens*), and
beargrass (*Nolina matapensis*) are the three most widely used basket
materials, along with pine needles. There has been a large tourist
demand for Rarámuri baskets since the Chihuahua-Pacífico Rail-
road opened the region to tourism in the 1960s. They are sold on a
daily basis along the railway, in the numerous gift shops in the
region, and to the traders who ship them by the railcar-load to the
United States. It would seem that overharvesting of weaving

materials might be a hazard. Yet the materials, found in the pine forests and along the walls of the barrancas, are carefully managed. This is due largely to the collection philosophy expressed by Jesusita.

Overharvesting is an enduring concern in the Sierra Tarahumara, where arable land is cherished and where the pressures of logging and narcotrafficking are making sustainable horticulture tenuous. Yet, for centuries up to the modern period, the Rarámuri have managed and harvested the Sierra and barrancas in a manner that is sustainable. Pockets of small fields grew and continue to grow in the bottomlands and arroyos of the Sierra while milpas (terraces), some at 45-degree angles, pose a bright green contrast to the oak forests along the upper reaches of the barrancas. Making optimum use of arable land is a skill that grew out of centuries of a relationship to the Sierra and a philosophy of *iwígara* born from the place.

A neighbor of Jesusita's, Lencho, also prefers to collect some of his medicinal plants from a particular *rincón*, or corner, of a large arroyo. He collects from other favorite locations as well, all of which he says are places in which the best plants grow.

Walking to his *rincón* one day, we passed by several plants of the same species we were intending to harvest. When questioned as to why we did not collect those plants, Lencho asserted that "those plants are not right for harvest because they are in the wrong place." Later examination revealed that the populations of plants that we passed were low when compared to those that were eventually harvested.

There is an intuitive understanding that harvesting threatened populations is not ecologically sound. Yet Lencho would not explain the situation is this manner. He suggested that the *iwígara* in these low population areas was "weak" and must, therefore, be allowed to strengthen before the plants there would be of any use.

Wild edible plants are treated with the same respect as the medicinals. When collecting wild onions (*Allium lingifolium*), the Rarámuri often select the larger bulbs, leaving the smaller ones in the ground to promote a second harvest. In addition, the Rarámuri use digging sticks to harvest the bulbs. The ground in which the onions grow is continuously disturbed, encouraging further growth of the plants. A symbiotic relationship exists between the Rarámuri and the onions. Disturbance of the sod and selective harvesting encourage the populations and assure a harvest of onions (Bye 1976).

Jesusita, Lencho, and other Rarámuri represent a tradition of conservation that relies on a reciprocal relationship with nature, where the idea of *iwígara* becomes an affirmation of caretaking responsibilities and an assurance of sustainable subsistence and harvesting. It is a realization that the Sierra Madres are a place of nurturing, full of relatives with whom all breath is shared.

CONCLUSION

The Rarámuri of northwest Mexico maintain daily direct contact with their natural world. Through centuries of experience with the resources in their region, they have maintained culturally encoded and detailed ecological knowledge. The northern Sierra Madre Occidental is rich in useful plants but also in indigenous communities. It is now being recognized by the ethnobotanical community that there is a strong link between biodiversity and cultural diversity.

The Rarámuri speak a Uto-Aztecan language, with the implication that lexical references to flowers are metaphors for a deeply ingrained relationship to the biodiversity of the regions where they live. References to flowers in Rarámuri song and oratory are numerous. The songs refer to the notion of binding the lasso and cycles, based on the idea of *iwígara*. The term *iwígara* expresses the belief that all life shares the same breath: all living things are related and play a role in the complexity of life. *Iwígara* might most closely resemble the concept of biodiversity. The two concepts are constructs of culture, however, and do not imply the same meaning or influences on actions. The concept of *iwígara* spawns many ideas and ways of thinking unique to the place where the Rarámuri live. Rituals and ceremonies, the language, and, therefore, Rarámuri thought are influenced by the lands, animals, and winds with which they live. *Iwígara* conveys the idea that all life, spiritual and physical, is interconnected in a continual cycle, and the Rarámuri act according to the cultural models derived from this philosophy.

The Rarámuri use food and medicinal plants in a number of ways. The food and medicine, both of which come from the land, embody the Rarámuri relationship to the Sierra Madres and their self-identity. The foundation for their model of use or land management stems directly from the notion of *iwígara*. The relationship with their perfect flower world occurs while they continue to fit into their harmonious world without disturbing it. The Creator's daily battle is a continuous interconnected cycle of breath and life. *Iwígara* guides agriculture, medicine, and foraging.

The relationship of the Rarámuri with their place is one of reciprocity with total engagement on each side, a relationship full of wonder and stewardship. I hope that Western land managers will begin to learn and understand indigenous philosophies concerning the land and apply some new approaches. Our place of nurturing can nurture only as long as we take care of it. The Rarámuri will continue to dance, to nurture the land, and to live.

REFERENCES CITED

Basso, K. 1996. *Wisdom Sits in Places: Landscape and Language among the Western Apache*. Albuquerque: University of New Mexico Press.

Bennett, W., and R. Zingg. 1935. *The Tarahumara: An Indian Tribe of Northern Mexico*. Chicago: University of Chicago Press.

Bye, R. 1976. Ethnoecology of the Tarahumara of Chihuahua, Mexico. Cambridge, Mass.: Harvard University Press.

———. 1985. *Medicinal Plants of the Tarahumara Indians of Chihuahua, Mexico. Two Mummies from Chihuahua, Mexico*. Papers, No. 19. San Diego: San Diego Museum of Man.

Cajete, G. 1994. *Look to the Mountain: An Ecology of Indigenous Education*. Durango: Kivaki Press.

Ellen, R. F. 1986. Ethnobiology, Cognition, and the Structure of Prehension: Some General Theoretical Notes. *Journal of Ethnobiology* 6(1):83.

Felger, R., and E. K. Dahl 1994. Northern Sierra Madre Occidental and Its Apachean Outliers: A Neglected Center of Biodiversity. Unpublished report distributed by Native Seeds/SEARCH, Tucson, Ariz.

Gibson, J. 1979. *The Ecological Approach to Visual Perception*. Boston: Houghton-Mifflin.

Hill, J. H. 1992. The Flower World of Old Uto-Aztecan. *Journal of Anthropological Research* 48(2):117.

Hunn, E. 1982. The Utilitarian Factor in Folk Biological Classification. *American Anthropologist* 84(4):830.

Jenkinson, M. 1972. The Glory of the Long Distance Runner. *Natural History* 81(1):55.

Kellert, S. R. 1997. *Kinship to Mastery: Biophilia in Human Evolution and Development*. Washington, D.C., and Covelo, Calif.: Island Press and Shearwater Books.

Kellert, S. R., and E. O. Wilson (eds.). 1993. *The Biophilia Hypothesis*. Washington, D.C., and Covelo, Calif.: Island Press and Shearwater Books.

Kennedy, J. G. 1978. *Tarahumara of the Sierra Madre: Beer, Ecology, and Social Organization*. Arlington Heights: AHM Publishing Corporation.

Levi, J. M. 1993. *Pillars of the Sky: The Genealogy of Ethnic Identity among the Raramuri-Simaroni (Tarahumara/Gentiles) of Northwest Mexico*. Cambridge, Mass.: Harvard University Press.

Martinez, D. 1994. *Karuk Tribal Module for the Main Stem River Watershed Analysis: Karuk Ancestral Lands and People as Reference Ecosystem for Eco-cultural Restoration in Collaborative Ecosystem Management*. Prepared by the Karuk Tribe of Northern California under the Auspices of Cultural Solutions for the U.S. Klamath Nation Forest.

Merrill, W. L. 1988. *Raramuri Souls: Knowledge and Social Process in Northern Mexico*. Washington, D.C.: Smithsonian Institution Press.

Momaday, N. S. 1992. *In the Presence of the Sun*. New York: St. Martin's Press.

Morris, B. 1984. The Pragmatics of Folk Classification. *Journal of Ethnobiology* 4(1):45.

Nabhan, G. P. 1995. Rare Plants and Vanishing Traditional Ecological Knowledge. Unpublished manuscript for symposium in Norman, Okla.

Nabhan, G. P., and S. Trimble 1994. *The Geography of Childhood: Why Children Need Wild Places.* Boston: Beacon Press.

Pennington, C. W. 1963. *The Tarahumara of Mexico: Their Environment and Material Culture.* Salt Lake City: University of Utah Press.

Posey, D. A. 1984. Hierarchy and Utility in a Folk Biological Taxonomic System: Patterns in Classification of Arthropods by the Kayapo Indians of Brazil. *Journal of Ethnobiology* 4(2):123.

Ramamoorthy, T. P., R. Bye, et al. 1993. *Biological Diversity of Mexico: Origins and Distribution:* Oxford: Oxford University Press.

Randall, R., and E. Hunn 1984. Do Life-Forms Evolve or Do Uses for Life? Some Doubts about Brown's Universals Hypothesis. *American Ethnologist* 11:329.

Rascón, F. I. 1979. *Cerocahui: Una comunidad en la Tarahumara.* Chihuahua: Centro Librero La Prensa.

Restak, R. 1984. *The Brain.* Toronto: Bantam Books.

Salmón, E. 1991. Tarahumara Healing Practices. *Shaman's Drum* (Summer) 24:34.

————. 1995. Cures of the Copper Canyon: Medicinal Plants of the Tarahumara with Potential Toxicity. *Herbalgram* 34:44–55.

Salmón, R. 1977. Tarahumara Resistance to Mission Congregation in Northern New Spain. *Ethnohistory* 24(4):379.

Varela, F., E. Thompson, et al. 1993. *The Embodied Mind: Cognitive Science and Human Experience.* Cambridge, Mass.: MIT Press.

Whorf, B. 1950. *Time, Space, and Language: Culture in Crisis.* New York: Harper and Brothers.

————. 1956. *Language, Thought, and Reality.* Cambridge, Mass.: MIT Press.

Wilson, E. O. (ed.). 1988. *Biodiversity.* Washington, D.C.: National Academy Press.

Prehistory and Biodiversity

HUMAN DISTURBANCE AND BIODIVERSITY

A Case Study from Northern New Mexico

RICHARD I. FORD

Many naturalists assume that they can reconstruct the biota and biological landscape of precontact America. Rarely do their scenarios consider the ancestors of Native Americans as having had an active role in the construction of the environment. Instead, they are viewed as super conservationists or as passive recipients of what nature dealt. They were pawns in the games nature played: if there was a drought, they accepted it; if it became cold, they accepted it; if species disappeared, they accepted it. Fatalism was their lot, if not their religion. Thus, some believe biodiversity and the management of natural resources today can ignore the actions of the prehistoric denizens of North America.

But the story changes if we start with the hypothesis that Native people were active players in nature who transformed the landscape by a variety of techniques for purposes of survival. Through their behavior, targeted biological resources were exploited, new species were introduced, and others had their distributions altered. Some may even have become locally extinct. The image changes to one of managers or custodians rather than passive recipients who had no role in the creation of biodiversity in America.

Both positions are amenable to testing by using anthropological theory and the techniques of paleobiology that are part of the arsenal of archaeological research methods that can reveal prehistoric behavior toward the natural world and its impact on the landscape. The results can be compared to the statements of Native Americans themselves (e.g., Deloria 1995) and the research of ethnoscientists who are examining similar contradictions today (e.g., Nabhan 1989).

PREHISTORIC CULTURAL TOPOGRAPHY

Landscape archaeology is commonly practiced by prehistorians, especially in Europe. One important observation that we have learned from ethnological studies of living people is that they do not use natural resources randomly. The world is a cultural creation, a way of intellectualizing the environment. Because Pre-Columbian Americans lacked the instrumentation Western scientists possess, not all physical forces were recognized (e.g., gravity), and their classifications of plants and animals may have categories not recognized in the taxonomies constructed by Western-trained biologists. But the world was knowable through human physiological senses and comprehended through local systems of knowledge, commonly called culture. Prehistoric cultural perceptions and explanations about the environment probably were not extensive, if ethnography is a guide, but they did require short-term predictions about natural events (e.g., rainfall or cold weather), the availability of useful resources, and the perpetuation of life for all creatures as they defined them. To achieve these cultural realities, or even predictions, required a careful monitoring of the natural world, such as noting the arrival of certain birds, the appearance of specific stars or constellations, or the religious control of physical elements perceived as needed by agricultural crops or as detrimental to their successful harvest. As part of the cultural transformation of place, sacred areas were designated or created on the landscape where rituals, often directed toward the control and propitiation of life-giving forces of nature, were performed.

The assumption cannot be sustained that the present landscape is the same as it was even several hundred years ago. Geological forces have altered it, albeit the rates of change differ according to physiography and climate. Prehistoric humans also have a place in the equation for changing the physical world. Their involvement is rarely accidental and is usually purposeful, based upon their culture. When people have a major role in altering the physiography of an environment in the precontact past, we refer to this as pre- historic cultural topography. This is a valuable working concept because it allows us to examine human-induced physical environ- mental change, whether for agriculture, habitation, or ritual, and the consequences it has for biodiversity.

Archaeology has the techniques for investigating the biological genera composition of any geographic locality. Paleobiology is the investigation of the plants and animals that occupied an area under investigation in the past. The tools include the recovery of macro- remains through small-aperture sieving and one of several methods of flotation or water separation. Both plant and animal evidence in the form of seeds, charcoal and plant food debris and bones, fish scales, and exoskeletons can be recovered. Microremains, such as pollen, phytoliths, and diatoms, while requiring a separate sampling strategy, allow further discovery of the living world and its bio- logical diversity (Pearsall 1989). Together these forms of evidence, when well dated, can allow a reconstruction of the biodiversity of a locality in the past.

An explanation for this reconstruction depends upon recog- nizing the landform and climatic parameters at the time when sites in the situation of a regional analysis were occupied. Pre- historic cultural topography provides a method of description that considers past human behavior and its physical environmental consequences and a theory of interpretation to account for the biota and its transformation as a consequence of culturally defined actions.

A CASE STUDY OF PREHISTORIC CULTURAL TOPOGRAPHY AND BIODIVERSITY

As a case study we will examine the prehistoric cultural landscape and the resulting biodiversity of northern New Mexico and in particular the Rio del Oso River drainage. Archaeological aerial and pedestrian surveys of northern New Mexico have revealed extensive landscape alteration from the late twelfth century to contact (Wills et al. 1990). Particularly noteworthy are the water control devices found from the Taos district down to Jemez and Zia. These cover La Bajada mesa, Abiquiu mesa, and most terraces along tributary streams to the Rio Grande that cut through the Santa Fe geological formation, including the Rio del Oso valley. The altered physiography constitutes part of what we are calling prehistoric cultural topography. An extensive survey conducted by Kurt Anschuetz (1998) as part of a major University of Michigan project has revealed extensive landscape alterations.

The Rio del Oso is an eastward-flowing tributary of the Rio Chama and is located between Española and Abiquiu, New Mexico. Most of the valley is managed by the Española District of the Santa Fe National Forest, United States Department of Agriculture. Where it joins the Chama, the elevation is 1,800 m (5,500 ft) above mean sea level, but it quickly rises into the Jemez Mountains, where it originates from springs on Tsikomo Mountain at 3,660 m (11,000 ft). Over its 30 km course, it passes through spruce (*Pseudotsuga menziesii*), fir (*Abies concolor*), and aspen (*Populus tremuloides*) forests and western yellow pine (*Pinus ponderosa*) and pinyon-juniper ecozones. The majority of the drainage below 2,100 m consists of pinyon-juniper. Various shrubs comprise the understory in each forest type. Forbs and grasses are not numerous today because of extensive cattle grazing. A riparian gallery forest of Fremont cotton-wood (*Populus fremontii*) and willow (*Salix exigua*) outlines the river's course to the Rio Chama. The mountains are home to bears and mountain lions. The lower reaches have foxes and coyotes. The ungulates are deer and elk. Both are found throughout the valley according to season, with a presence of both in the higher elevations in summer and the lower elevations, including prehistoric inhabi-tation areas, in wintertime. Other smaller animals present include jackrabbits, cottontails, badgers, and ground squirrels. Birds, reptiles, amphibians, and even fish (an isolated population of New Mexico cutthroat trout) are also present. Despite cattle grazing, occasional horses, hunters, trucks, and all-terrain vehicles (ATVs), the area has more biodiversity than most other areas at this eleva-tion in New Mexico. It has few outside visitors, as the extensive, undisturbed archaeological surface sites testify.

However, the depopulated human presence in the valley and its apparent serenity now should not deceive us. From the eighteenth century until the middle of this century, there were several moderate-sized Spanish villages in the valley. The Spanish herded sheep until World War II and raised crops by gravity-flow canal irrigation and rainfall farming at elevations up to 2,300 meters. Archaeological photographs from A.D. 1910 show that much of the valley was deforested for pasturage and firewood until fairly recently. In addition to the Spanish settlers, Native people have also used the valley in the historic period. During the Pueblo Rebellion, at least one large site was reoccupied, but the temporal extent of the occupation and its environmental impact are still to be determined (Jeancon 1912). People from San Juan Pueblo have continuously hunted and collected wild plants for medicines, tools, and food in the valley from prehistoric times until the present, according to their stories. Recent archaeological surveys have also revealed the tipi villages of at least one band of (Jicarilla) Apache, which occupied the valley in the late 1800s. Since A.D. 1700 this valley has witnessed extensive use of its biological resources until today, when there is less pressure on the land than at any time in the previous 300 years.

Archaeological reconnaissance has demonstrated that the late prehistoric period witnessed even more alterations to the land than occurred in historic times. In the fifteenth century, three major Pueblos occupied in the valley, and the total population exceeded any count in historic times. By A.D. 1250, it appears that defor-estation of the lower 10 kilometers of the valley had begun for purposes of creating agricultural fields. Boulders with "slicks" on their sides, presumably for sharpening stone axes, appear in asso-ciation with the initial construction of water control devices.

The prehistoric cultural topography of the Rio del Oso drainage was extensive. The cultural basis for transforming the landscape appears to be to control the availability of precipitation and water for crops. Numerous shrines and petroglyphs with water symbols, at least as interpreted by contemporary Pueblo ethnography, are found associated with prehistoric field areas in the valley and some of the Pueblo sites. Some of the shrines and rock art are located in or near seasonal holding areas for water. As part of the prehistoric need for water to nurture the crops, numerous devices for water control were constructed, and some are still in operation today. The development of a prehistoric cultural topographic landscape resulted in numerous areas of environmental disturbance that otherwise would not exist and produced important ecological habitats for plants and animals. The amount of construction is only now being recognized, although hints have been known since Adolph Ban-delier's pioneering survey of prehistoric Pueblos in New Mexico (Bandelier 1890–92) and the Tewa ethnogeography recorded by John Peabody Harrington (Harrington 1916). As examples of the prehistoric human effort involved, two features that relate to water control require gravel excavated from the Santa Fe formation ter-races and volcanic rock collected or quarried from basalt outcrops in the valley. Both were then transported to create new land surfaces where farming was conducted. Similarly, holding tanks for water

Fig. 7.1. A lithic mulch field in the Rio del Oso Valley, New Mexico. The field is lined by a cobble border. Large, flat stones placed across parts of the field's surface form deliberate cultural patterns, but their function has not been determined. They are a frequent occurrence on lithic mulch fields.

were excavated into hillsides to catch runoff water, and small ditches were constructed to lead it to the rock-lined fields.

The most extensive form of a new topography is lithic mulch gardens (see fig. 7.1). These are located throughout the lower 10 km of the Rio del Oso, with most of them built on the north side of the valley. They are squares ranging from a few meters to over 10 m on a side, with stone gravel piled some 10–20 cm above the original ground surface. Precipitation in the form of melting snow or rainfall percolated through the gravel and irrigated the sandy loam some 10–20 cm below. It is difficult for water to evaporate from the lithic surface, and the soil remains moist and accessible to plants far longer than on exposed soil surfaces (White et al. 1995). Furthermore, the stone holds the heat of the day and mitigates frost that might injure young plants or maturing crops (Anschuetz 1995).

These water control devices are not unique to the Rio del Oso valley. Square or subrectangular lithic mulch grids are found throughout northern New Mexico, although the prehistoric date of their construction varies and the variety of forms results in dissimilar patterns (compare Bugé 1984; Greiser and Moore 1995; Lightfoot and Eddy 1995; Maxwell 1995; Wills et al. 1990). In the Rio del Oso, the grids are usually outlined with cobbles and are subdivided into smaller internal squares of a meter or so. Along the nearby Rio Chama and Rio Ojo Caliente (Hibben 1937; Lang 1981), these gridded fields or gardens are more elaborate, with internal partitions and larger, flat stones within the grid construction. It appears that lithic mulch grids continued to expand or to be altered elsewhere after their construction, but their use ceased earlier in the Rio del Oso drainage.

Other landscape modification in the Rio del Oso includes cobble-outlined grids without interior gravel. These occasionally form a checkerboard by alternating with lithic mulch grids. Their care suggests that they were planted, but we know little about the crops or why this form was selected. We do know that today they serve as nurseries for conifer trees, while the lithic mulch fields support a luxuriant growth of grass (see fig. 7.2).

Barrow pits often occur along the edges of abandoned stream terraces and mesa sides. Prehistoric farmers appear to have excavated the gravel and cobble for mulch from these areas. The remnant pits served as microtopographic catchment basins and concentrated melt water from snow and runoff from rain in the bottom. These were planted, sometimes with small stone grids in the basement, as can be observed at Poshuouinge ruin, located along the Rio Chama (Jeancon 1923).

The sandy loam tops of the highest terraces on the north side of the Rio del Oso were cleared for rainfall fields, and stone spreaders are found there to distribute runoff water more evenly across the

Fig. 7.2. Cobble border grid. These planting areas are extensive in northern New Mexico. They continue to trap water hundreds of years after their construction and frequently serve as a nursery for conifer trees. Here a pinyon pine (*Pinus edulis*) is growing in the center of the grid.

land surface. Prehistoric farmers prepared the fields with special stone hoe-like, split-cobble tools that show sheen from working in the sand.

Another agricultural surface type was built above 2,000 m on 5th mesa in the form of terraces. These were constructed along the edges of the mesa with basalt cobbles and then filled with soil. Water from the mesa top ran into these culturally made areas and then percolated down through the soil from one level to the next. Our survey revealed that they were constructed to catch natural runoff of precipitation as it flowed over the mesa edges.

Reservoirs for temporary water storage were dug into the sides of terraces. From these rainfall-charged features, small irrigation channels were constructed to lead water down to the mulch grids on the next natural terrace below. These irrigation systems were very localized and did not connect the water from one field to the next. They appear to be the operation of a single farmer or family. The maintenance was minimal, and there was little sediment that would be transported. These reservoir/channel systems may have functioned for very brief periods during the agriculture calendar.

It was reported by Jean Jeancon (1911) that more traditional irrigation ditches lined the Rio del Oso within the valley and brought water to the fields. The prehistoric origin of these ditches cannot be confirmed, but they are present in the middle of the valley and were used by Spanish farmers as part of their agricultural system. In other prehistoric Pueblo areas, irrigation ditches formed distinct ecosystems and were ritually opened and closed and managed to assure the diversity of plants found along them. Disjunct species, such as the American plum (*Prunus americana*), continue to grow along ancient canals in Pueblo and Spanish villages far from their relatives east of the Rockies.

Dating water-control features in the Rio del Oso and elsewhere is difficult. Generally, cross-dated pottery sherds (e.g., Santa Fe B/W, Biscuit A, Biscuit B ceramic types) indicate that they were constructed between the thirteenth and fifteenth centuries. It appears that the lithic mulch grids were built first and the terraces last. However, all the above-mentioned components of a larger agricultural system of water management and landscape manipulation were used simultaneously and are in proximity to each of the major Pueblos in the valley (Anschuetz 1998).

These agricultural features supported anthropogenic plant communities at the time prehistoric people occupied the valley, and they are functioning today without human intervention to maintain diverse plant biotic resources. We have no excavation records of macroremains of the plants other than maize that were grown in these areas. Pollen samples have been taken from several of the lithic mulch grids, and the identifications reveal some surprises (Clary 1987; Dean 1994, 1997). Cotton (*Gossypium* sp.) is one of the cultivars that has been identified along with corn and cucurbita. This is a very high altitude for the successful growth of cotton, but the water-holding capacity of the lithic mulch fields and the heat transfer of the stone surface must have facilitated its maturation. Other pollen types include *Portulaca, Eriogonum*, chenopods, amaranths, and other ruderal plants that some readers might interpret as useless weeds. However, ethnobotany would suggest otherwise (Dunmire and Tierney 1995); these genera had dietary significance, and finding the pollen indicates that prehistoric farmers tolerated them growing in these grids until they flowered and perhaps even cultivated them as part of an anthropogenic ecosystem.

Although the people long ago abandoned these sites (in the late 1400s), the grids are still collecting and storing water in the sediment beneath the gravel. When viewed from above or from afar in the springtime, these terraces appear as green patches, more verdant that the nonmulched areas of soil (see fig. 7.3). The plant species are mostly dense patches of grama grass (*Bouteloua gracilis*). The prehistoric grids are also a unique habitat in the Rio del Oso for an endangered cactus, the grama grass cactus (*Pediocactus papyracantha*) (Benson 1969:186–88), which grows on these grids, where it escapes the hooves of cattle grazing the dense grass on the mulch grid. The continuing water-holding capacity of these prehistoric water control devices has assisted with reforestation. Some grids are rock outlines that hold runoff. Within them pinyon (*Pinus edulis*) and one-seed juniper (*Juniperus monosperma*) seedlings are well watered or have grown into mature trees, but they are absent from areas immediately outside the rock alignments.

The latent functions of prehistoric human water control structures are found throughout the northern New Mexico (Rio Chama: Hibben 1937; Ojo Caliente: Bugé 1984; Lang 1981; Maxwell 1995; Taos: Greiser and Moore 1995; Lightfoot and Eddy 1995). In all these areas, the features continue to control water and to support a flora that is otherwise sparse. They also serve as a refuge for rare species elsewhere. At Fort Burgwin in the Taos archaeological district,

Fig. 7.3. Lithic mulch grid next to plot without surface modification. The mulch field continues to irrigate the soil under the rocks and supports a dense growth of grama grass (*Bouteloua gracilis*). The unmodified soil surface has snakeweed (*Gutierrezia sarothrae*) and very sparse grasses growing on its surface.

similar grids are found. Here a disjunct species of a valuable medicinal plant, gayfeather (*Liatris punctata*), grows in a unique lithic mulch habitat far from any other populations. Its introduction and its history on these grids are unknown. A more detailed biological survey of these remnants of a prehistoric cultural topography would undoubtedly reveal that they are supporting populations of unique species not otherwise found growing in these areas.

Animal and bird populations may be affected by prehistoric landscape changes. Our observations in the Rio del Oso reveal that cottontails are the dominant rabbit in areas where the lithic mulch fields are prevalent, but jackrabbits prevail where the fields are absent and the forest has returned. Unless one acknowledges the cultural landscape transformations made more than 400 years ago, species distributions and population sizes can not be explained.

CONCLUSION

In a classic master's thesis, Richard Yarnell (1958) described a series of plants found growing on southwestern archaeological sites. It should have served decades ago as a guide for recognizing that prehistoric disturbance did not diminish biotic diversity; it enhanced it. Other papers from the Southwest document still other plants that were found in high frequency on archaeological sites, such as Parry's agave (*Agave parryi*: Minnis and Plog 1976) and cane cholla cactus (*Opuntia imbricata*: Housley 1974). Additionally, wolfberry (*Lycium pallidum*), squawbush (*Rhus trilobata*), wild potato (*Solanum jamesii*), wild tobacco (*Nicotiana attenuata*), and sagebrush (*Artemisia tridentata*) are noted for their association with prehistoric Pueblo sites and may have been introduced there, originally by accident, for economic purposes; but, once established, they have continued to flourish long after site abandonment. Now, some thirty years after Yarnell published his thesis, biodiversity is a major theme for resource managers and environmentalists. But as I have argued, it is a mistake to regard Native Americans as insignificant managers of biotic resources or as passive participants in the shaping of the landscape and the diversification of habitats. Human-induced disturbances are not necessarily bad for the environment, nor is their continuing signature on the landscape a sign of neglect. To the contrary, these inadvertent creative forces increase biodiversity and help to maintain it even as land use practices by different cultures change over time or disappear entirely. The late prehistoric human presence in the Rio del Oso disturbed the landscape, but it also enhanced biodiversity through niche creation as we view it at the end of the twentieth century.

REFERENCES CITED

Anschuetz, Kurt F. 1995. Saving a Rainy Day: The Integration of Diverse Agricultural Technologies to Harvest and Conserve Water in the Lower Rio Chama Valley, New Mexico. In *Soil, Water, Biology, and Belief in Prehistoric and Traditional Southwestern Agriculture*, edited by H. W. Toll, pp. 25–39. Special Publication 2. Albuquerque: New Mexico Archaeological Council.

————. 1998. Not Waiting for the Rain: Integrated Systems of Water Management by Pre-Columbian Pueblo Farmers in North Central New Mexico. 2 vols. Ph.D. dissertation. Department of Anthropology, University of Michigan, Ann Arbor.

Bandelier, Adolph F. 1890–92. *Final Report of Investigations among the Indians of the Southwestern United States, Carried on Mainly in the Years from 1880 to 1885*. 2 vols. American Series 3 and 4. Papers of the Archaeological Institute of America. Cambridge, Mass.: printed by J. Wilson.

Benson, Lyman. 1969. *The Cacti of Arizona*. Tucson: University of Arizona Press.

Bugé, David E. 1984. Prehistoric Subsistence Strategies in the Ojo Caliente Valley, New Mexico. In *Prehistoric Agricultural Strategies in the Southwest*, edited by S. K. Fish and P. R. Fish, pp. 37–43. Anthropological Research Papers 33. Tempe: Arizona State University.

Clary, Karen. 1987. Pollen Evidence for the Agricultural Utilization of Early Classic Period (A.D. 1350–1500) Anasazi Mulch Terrace Gardens, in the Vicinity of Medanales, New Mexico. MS on file, Castetter Laboratory for Ethnobotanical Studies, Department of Biology, University of New Mexico, Albuquerque.

Dean, Glenna. 1994. *Pollen Analysis of Nineteen Samples from Anasazi Agricultural Features at LA 71506, Rio del Oso Project, Rio Arriba County, New Mexico*. Technical Series Report 943. Santa Fe: Archeobotanical Services.

————. 1997. *Pollen Analysis of Ten Samples from Anasazi Agricultural Features at LA 101346 and LA 101348, Rio del Oso Project, Rio Arriba County, New Mexico*. Technical Series Report 971. Santa Fe: Archeobotanical Services.

Deloria, Vine, Jr. 1995. *Red Earth, White Lies*. New York: Scribner.

Dunmire, William W., and Gail D. Tierney. 1995. *Wild Plants of the Pueblo Province*. Santa Fe: Museum of New Mexico Press.

Greiser, Sally T., and James L. Moore. 1995. The Case for Prehistoric Irrigation in the Northern Southwest. In *Soil, Water, Biology, and Belief in Prehistoric and Traditional Southwestern Agriculture,* edited by H. W. Toll, pp. 189–95. Special Publication 2. Albuquerque: New Mexico Archaeological Council.

Harrington, John Peabody. 1916. *The Ethnogeography of the Tewa Indians.* Twenty-ninth Annual Report of the Bureau of American Ethnology for the Years 1907–8, pp. 29–636. Washington, D.C.: Bureau of American Ethnology.

Hibben, Frank C. 1937. *Excavation of the Riana Ruin and Chama Valley Survey.* Anthropological Series Bulletin 300. Albuquerque: University of New Mexico.

Housley, Louise K. 1974. *Opuntia imbricata* Distribution of Old Jemez Indian Habitation Sites. Master's thesis. Department of Biology, University of New Mexico, Albuquerque.

Jeancon, Jean A. 1911. Explorations in Chama Basin, New Mexico. *Records of the Past* 10:92–108.

———. 1912. Ruins of Pesedeuinge. *Records of the Past* 11:28–37.

———. 1923. *Excavations in the Chama Valley, New Mexico.* Bulletin 81. Washington, D.C.: Bureau of American Ethnology.

Lang, Richard W. 1981. *A Prehistoric Pueblo Garden Plot on the Rio Ojo Caliente, Rio Arriba County, New Mexico: Site 7, Features 1–2.* Contract Archeology Division Report 065. Santa Fe: School of American Research.

Lightfoot, D. R., and Frank W. Eddy. 1995. The Construction and Configuration of Anasazi Pebble-Mulch Gardens in the Northern Rio Grande. *American Antiquity* 60:459–70.

Maxwell, Timothy D. 1995. A Comparative Study of Prehistoric Farming Strategies. In *Soil, Water, Biology, and Belief in Prehistoric and Traditional Southwestern Agriculture,* edited by H. W. Toll, pp. 3–12. Special Publication 2. Albuquerque: New Mexico Archaeological Council.

Minnis, Paul E., and Stephen E. Plog. 1976. A Study of the Site Specific Distribution of *Agave parryi* in East Central Arizona. *Kiva* 41(3–4):299–308.

Nabhan, Gary Paul. 1989. *Enduring Seeds, Native American Agriculture and Wild Plant Conservation.* San Francisco: North Point Press.

Pearsall, Deborah M. 1989. *Paleoethnobotany: A Handbook of Procedures.* San Diego: Academic Press.

White, C. S., S. R. Lofton, and R. Aguilar. 1995. Ecology of Cobble Mulch Gardens: Structures for Modification of Soil Moisture Dynamics. MS on file, Department of Biology, University of New Mexico, Albuquerque.

Wills, W. H., T. A. Baker, and L. A. Baker. 1990. Aerial Perspectives on Prehistoric Agricultural Fields of the Middle Rio Grande Valley, New Mexico. In *Clues to the Past: Papers in Honor of William H. Sundt*, edited by M. S. Duran and D. T. Kirkpatrick, pp. 315–32. Papers 16. Albuquerque: Archaeological Society of New Mexico.

Yarnell, Richard A. 1958. Implications of Pueblo Indian Ruins as Plant Habitats. M.S. thesis. Department of Anthropology, University of New Mexico, Albuquerque.

CHAPTER EIGHT

LEVELS OF NATIVE BIODIVERSITY IN EASTERN NORTH AMERICA

GAYLE J. FRITZ

INTRODUCTION

Biological diversity can be assessed on several different levels. In the volume entitled *Environment*, coauthored by Peter Raven, Linda Berg, and George Johnson (1994), for example, biodiversity is discussed within species, among species, and among communities. The within-species level is called "genetic diversity." Determination of the total number of different species in an area is called "species diversity," a measurement known by ecologists as "species richness" or alpha-diversity (Whittaker 1972). Raven et al. (1994:344) use the term "ecosystem diversity" to encompass "the variety of ecosystems found on Earth: the forests, prairies, deserts, coral reefs, lakes, coastal estuaries, and other ecosystems of our planet."

All of these levels are important when thinking about the environments of American Indians in the Eastern Woodlands. The temperate and—in the extreme south—subtropical ecosystems of eastern North America are rich in natural resources, and their richness was augmented by the hundreds of thousands of people who lived there before European colonization. These societies spoke dozens of different languages and manifested impressive biological and cultural diversity of their own, making it an impossible task to do justice to this topic in one short chapter. I focus, therefore, on the most widespread type of human adaptation in the East at contact: the system of mixed farming and foraging that extended from the prairies in the west to the Atlantic seaboard and from the southern Great Lakes in the north down to the Gulf Coast.

Recent archaeological discoveries have made it necessary to reevaluate the timing and the nature of early plant domestication and indigenous gardening in this region, and we now see how agricultural intensification fit into the development of increasingly more sedentary, more populous, and politically more complex societies. It is important to spread this knowledge as widely as possible in order to dispel the myth still permeating the Euro-American psyche that Eastern American Indians were essentially nonagricultural and nomadic.

I rely on the concept of genetic diversity within species to present the evidence for local domestication of native plants beginning 5,000 to 7,000 years ago in the Midwest. I use the measurement of diversity among species to demonstrate the richness of early gardening strategies and their importance in the overall subsistence systems of which they were a part. I refer to this level as "community biodiversity" and focus on it also to monitor later developments such as the introduction of corn (*Zea mays* ssp. *mays*) and beans (*Phaseolus vulgaris*). At the level of eco-system biodiversity, I describe the mosaiclike landscape of agricultural fields, villages and ceremonial centers, managed woods, and larger expanses of forest that were used for hunting and that served as buffer zones between competing polities. I end by endeavoring to appreciate the impact American Indians in the East had on their land, cautioning against current tendencies to exaggerate and overextend the effects of these practices. Admittedly, the presence and practices of people had dramatic effects on sizable but localized patches during specific periods, but these localized conditions cannot be extended over half a continent for virtually the entire span of human occupation.

WITHIN-SPECIES GENETIC DIVERSITY:
THE DOMESTICATION OF NATIVE GOURDS
AND SEED PLANTS

The recognition of eastern North America as an independent center of plant domestication has been one of the most exciting archaeological revelations of the late twentieth century. When I started graduate school in 1980, we believed that a gourdy squash (*Cucurbita pepo*) was the earliest crop in what is now the United States, and we thought it had been introduced as an already domesticated plant from Mexico. Many people knew then that the sunflower (*Helianthus annuus* var. *macrocarpus*) and its relative sumpweed or marshelder (*Iva annua* var. *microcarpa*) had been domesticated thousands of years ago in the East, and a few researchers argued that a native chenopod now classified as *Chenopodium berlandieri* spp. *jonesianum* (Smith and Funk 1985) had been cultivated, possibly along with a few other weedy plants. The scale of gardening before the introduction of corn (*Zea mays* ssp. *mays*) and beans (*Phaseolus vulgaris*), however, was thought by most to be minimal.

Today we have a much stronger appreciation of the economic significance of plants domesticated in eastern North America. The gourdy squash still appears to be the earliest crop (see table 8.1), but its ancestor grew wild along the Gulf Coast in western Florida at the end of the Pleistocene era (Newsom et al. 1993). The natural range of wild pepo gourds 7,000 years ago is uncertain, but they probably grew along river and stream valleys well inland in Texas, Louisiana, and other coastal states, and they might have grown as far north as central Illinois, where thin rind fragments firmly identified as *Cucurbita pepo* have been directly dated by the Accelerator Mass Spectrometry (AMS) radiocarbon method to 5000 B.C. (Conard et al. 1984).

A hot debate is currently raging among archaeologists as to whether these mid-Holocene gourd fragments in the Midwest were cultivated or wild (Asch 1994; Asch and Asch Sidell 1992; Smith,

TABLE 8.1
Timing of Domestication and Adoption of
Crops in Eastern North America

Common Name	Scientific Name	Date by Which Crop Was Planted/Domesticated (uncal., B.P.)	Range of Wild Ancestor
Gourd/squash	*Cucurbita pepo* ssp. *ovifera*	5500 +/−1500[a]	Gulf Coast zone, Tamaulipas to Fla. (and inland?)
Bottle gourd	*Lagenaria siceraria*	4300 B.P.[b]	Africa, presumably
Sunflower	*Helianthus annuus* var. *macrocarpus*	4200 B.P.	Western North America
Sumpweed	*Iva annua* var. *macrocarpa*	4000 B.P.	Midwest, Southeast, S. Great Plains
Chenopod	*Chenopodium berlandieri* spp. *jonesianum*	3500 B.P.	Much of North America
Maygrass	*Phalaris caroliniana*	3000 B.P.	Southeast, Lower Mississippi River Valley, S. Plains

Knotweed	*Polygonum erectum*	2500 B.P.	Much of eastern North America
Little barley	*Hordeum pusillum*	2000 B.P.	Much of North America
Tobacco	*Nicotiana* sp.	2000 B.P. (at latest)	Several species native to W. North America; N. rustica native to South America
Maize	*Zea mays* ssp. *mays*	2000 B.P.	Mexico
Common beans	*Phaseolus vulgaris*	7000 B.P.	Mexico
Cushaw squash	*Cucurbita argyrosperma argyrosperma*	1000 B.P.	Mexico

---

[a] Asch (1994) believes the 7,000-year-old pepo squash rind in west-central Illinois came from cultivated gourds. Petersen and Asch Sidell (1996) belive the same for 5,700-year-old rind fragments from central Maine. Smith et al. (1992) believe all gourd remains in eastern North America predating 4300 B.P. were wild.

[b] Earlier bottle gourd at Windover, Florida, may have floated up on the beach; feral stands near the coast may have existed ephemerally.

Cowan, and Hoffman 1992). In a recent issue of *American Antiquity*, James Petersen and Nancy Asch Sidell (1996) report pepo gourd rind from the Sharrow site in central Maine (see map 8.1) directly dated to 5695 +/- 100 B.P. Because pepo gourds are not known to grow spontaneously in the Northeast, these authors support the scenario that "*Cucurbita* was cultivated at the Sharrow site." The squash seeds from the Phillips Spring site in Missouri, dating to 2300 B.C., are larger than wild seeds and therefore accepted as domesticated (Fritz 1997). So, if Archaic period foragers were distributing gourds from group to group for use as containers or rattles or net floats or bobbers or food, and these gourds were being cultivated in Maine by fisher-hunter-gatherers 5,700 years ago, the 7,000-year-old specimens in Illinois might have been cultivated as well.

Although early cultivation of gourds could have been a casual activity, resembling Edgar Anderson's (1952) Dump Heap Theory of Plant Domestication, it must have involved selection for fruits that had desirable sizes, shapes, colors, tastes, and so forth, and therefore resulted in increased genetic diversity. Biologists including Deena Decker-Walters (1990) and Hugh Wilson et al. (1992) have used isozymes and DNA analysis to determine which modern cultivars of squash and pumpkin are descendants of this eastern North American ancestor. An impressive number of varieties fall into this lineage, including yellow summer crooknecks, scallops and pattypans, acorn squashes, and most of the ornamental gourds. The earliest native North American cultigen, therefore, left a legacy of within-species biodiversity enjoyed by consumers around the world today.

An even more successful native eastern North American crop in today's global economy is the sunflower. Directly dated archaeological specimens from Tennessee show that sunflower seeds were well beyond the wild or weedy size by 2500 B.C. (Crites 1993). Sunflowers are immensely popular today, and the horticulture industry is busy seeking new ornamental varieties. Even in Pre-Columbian

Map 8.1. Eastern North America with locations of relevant sites and cultural areas.

times, American Indians avoided restricting the gene pool. Although archaeologists have found caches of relatively large achenes (seeds inside their fruit coats or "shells") in storage contexts, other samples, even some from late prehistoric sites, consist primarily of relatively small seeds, still too large to be anything but domesticated, yet unlikely to have come from large, monocephalic seed heads. In the Northeast, where Iroquoian people at contact used sunflower oil mostly as a dye and a cosmetic for enhancement of hair and skin (Heiser 1976), the seeds tend to be on the small side. Historic Hidatsa farmers in the Upper Missouri River drainage maintained populations with both large and small heads on the same plants, harvesting the seeds from the large heads first, but preferring the small seeds for their superior oil (Wilson 1987).

At least two and as many as five additional species of native seed plants were domesticated in eastern North America. Unfortunately, none of these survived as crops into modern times, and some appear to have declined during the centuries immediately preceding contact. Sumpweed is closely related to the sunflower, and its seeds may have had similar uses. Chenopod or goosefoot is in the same genus as the Andean grain quinoa (*Chenopodium quinoa*), and both are characterized by denser seed heads and seeds with dramatically thinner coats than their weedy ancestors. Erect knotweed (*Polygonum erectum*) has a buckwheatlike grain that seems to have undergone selection for size and for reduction of the numbers of thick-walled fruits produced on the same plants as fruits with thin pericarps (Lopinot et al. 1991).

Maygrass (*Phalaris caroliniana*) is an attractive early-season producer that is quite ubiquitous in archaeological sites well outside its modern range and sometimes in a clear storage context (Cowan 1978; Fritz 1986). It is the single most abundant seed by count in many sites in the American Bottom area of west-central Illinois, including the great site of Cahokia (Johannessen 1988; Lopinot 1991), co-occurring with other native crops and, after A.D. 800, with maize in a broad pattern, making it impossible for me to conceive of maygrass as anything but an important agricultural crop. Another early-season grass, little barley (*Hordeum pusillum*), also occurs commonly in agriculture-related contexts. Little barley has recently been proposed by Andrea Hunter (1992) to demonstrate morphological changes indicative of domestication, although these changes are subtle.

With so many opportunities for selection, exchange of seeds, range extension, and intraspecific crossing of varieties, the genetic diversity of all of these native species was enhanced. Although only the sunflowers and pepo squashes and gourds survive today as cultigens, botanists suspect that living populations of others, especially *Chenopodium berlandieri*, still exhibit traits such as synchronized fruiting that might well be genetic remnants of their agricultural ancestry (Wilson 1981).

COMMUNITY-LEVEL BIODIVERSITY (SPECIES RICHNESS): DIVERSIFIED FARMING AND FORAGING STRATEGIES

Production of native crops probably stayed on a fairly small scale until about 1200 B.C., but after that we see clear signs that gardening had become a significant component of the mixed subsistence systems of some human populations in the midlatitudinal zone of the Midwest and Midsouth (Fritz 1997; Gremillion 1997; Watson 1985; Yarnell 1974). The miners of gypsum and mirabilite who frequented the depths of Salts and Mammoth Caves in Kentucky in the middle of the first millennium B.C. regularly ate a mixture of chenopod, sunflower, sumpweed, squash, and maygrass seeds along with hickory nuts and wild or managed fleshy fruits (Watson and Yarnell 1986; Yarnell 1969, 1974). By approximately 100 B.C., native seed production had become important enough in many river valleys of interior eastern North America that some of us believe these crops were probably being grown in field-sized plots (see Smith 1992).

The increased quantities of storable surplus grain might have been critical in the rise of Hopewellian exchange and mortuary ceremonialism (Fritz and Smith 1988; Smith 1992). In Ohio, where the Hopewellian phenomenon was most dramatic and most complex, and in Illinois, where Havana Hopewell sites and settlement patterns exhibit fewer signs of internal ranking but strong integration, native crops were intensified to unprecedented levels (Asch and Asch 1985; Wymer 1992). Crop diversity remained high across the central riverine zone, with the gourds, the oil-rich sunflower and sumpweed seeds, and the carbohydrate- and protein-rich chenopod, maygrass, knotweed, and little barley seeds co-occurring at site after site where flotation is conducted. Maize was introduced into eastern North America at this time, approximately 2,000 years ago (Riley et al. 1994), possibly in conjunction with Hopewellian trade across the Plains, but all evidence leads to the conclusion that maize made no significant contribution to anybody's diet until hundreds of years later.

THE MIXED ECONOMY

Ten to twenty years ago, textbooks and articles minimized the economic importance of any kind of food production in eastern North America that did not include maize (Fiedel 1987; Ford 1977), and some archaeologists continue to be afflicted by the ethnocentric bias that I call "real men don't eat pigweed" (Fritz 1994a:40). In spite of a growing awareness that this region was a major center of indigenous agriculture before the arrival of maize, it seems likely that wild plants and, of course, animals were as important as the native seed crops in terms of caloric intake and time invested in their procurement. Subsistence systems of the early gardeners and farmers remained diversified in terms of the crops they planted as well as the wild resources they continued to harvest. Nuts were crucial sources of fats, proteins, and carbohydrates from early in the

Holocene into historic times, with hickory nuts (*Carya* spp.), walnuts (*Juglans nigra*), and acorns (*Quercus* spp.) showing up in most sites and hazelnuts (*Corylus americana*), chestnuts (*Castanea dentata*), and chinquapins (*Castanea pumila*) occurring in many sites within their more restricted ranges. Nuts—with proportions varying by genus across time and space—constituted a staple storable plant food wherever oak-hickory forests grew. This was true in the Midwest riverine area before domestication of native seed plants, and it remained the case in the Great Lakes region, much of the Northeast and Atlantic seaboard, and most of the Southeast south of the latitude of the southern border of Tennessee until maize was intensified between ca. A.D. 800 and A.D. 1000.

The archaeobotanical record includes many native fruits: persimmons (*Diospyros virginiana*), plums and cherries (*Prunus* spp.), sumac (*Rhus* spp.), elderberries (*Sambucus canadensis*), blueberries (*Vaccinium* spp.), strawberries (*Fragaria virginiana*), blackberries (*Rubus* spp.), and others. Tubers are occasionally preserved, most often the groundnut (*Apios americana*), and we suspect that edible underground plant parts of many species were routinely gathered but rarely deposited in a state that would be preserved and recognizable. This is also true of leafy greens, which were probably important, especially in early spring when stored resources were running out and new seeds and fruits were unavailable.

THE ADOPTION OF MAIZE

An article published in 1976 by Charles Cleland refined the Focal-Diffuse Model of subsistence change in the Eastern Woodlands. In Cleland's model, the shift to maize agriculture transformed diet breadth from broad and generalized to narrowly specialized on the primary staple: corn. Archaeobotanical information gathered over the past twenty years makes this model seem somewhat simplified, but the end result—an agricultural system dominated by one staple crop more than ever before—still holds. Maize was intensified between A.D. 750 and A.D. 1000 in many parts of the East (Johannessen 1988, 1994). In the American Bottom area of western Illinois during this time, the ubiquity of maize rose from almost zero to being present in 70% to 80% of flotation samples. Maize did not, however, replace the native crops that supported increasingly large and well-integrated communities during the Emergent Mississippian period (A.D. 800–1000). It seems clear that more time and effort was being put into agricultural pursuits, and maize was finally accepted into the native farming systems during this phase of intensification, but increased quantities of maygrass, chenopod, knotweed, and other native crops were grown as well (Lopinot 1991, 1994).

The Visitors' Center at Cahokia and many published articles stress the importance of maize in stocking granaries of the elite and supporting dense populations at Cahokia and other early Mississippian town-mound centers, but they frequently fail to point out that the cropping system of the time was diversified, with maygrass and chenopod seeds outnumbering maize fragments in many features. A recent series of stable carbon isotope ratios from Cahokia does not show that early Mississippians—even those in seemingly high status contexts—ate consistently high quantities of maize (Buikstra et al. 1994). No granaries filled with charred corncobs or kernels have been found at the Cahokia site, and no works of art, whether ceramic or carved shell or stone statuary, indicate that maize had symbolic meaning in the iconography of chiefs. The stone sculpture known as the Keller Figurine is a possible exception. Found during excavations at the BBB Motor Site near Cahokia, this female figure is carved in a kneeling position over "a series of contiguous rectangles, some of which have vertical lines enclosed in shallow arcs on their upper portions" (Emerson 1982:8). These items have been interpreted as ears of corn or possibly a mat of bundled reeds (ibid.), but they bear no strong likeness to either. By contrast, the squashes on the Birger Figurine, found at the same site and also dating to the Stirling Phase (A.D. 1050–1150), are depicted in such clear botanical detail that they can be attributed to the taxon *Cucurbita argyrosperma* ssp. *argyrosperma*, familiar to many eastern North Americans as the green striped cushaw (Fritz 1994b). Not until after A.D. 1200, when the population of Cahokia was declining, does maize assume a position of ascendancy over the native seed crops in this part of the Mississippi River Valley.

In short, a diversified and presumably more resilient and stable agricultural strategy persisted at Cahokia for 400 years after initial intensification of maize. Wild (or managed but not cultivated) plants and animals also continued to be important. Flotation samples from the American Bottom during the early Mississippian period have exceptionally low frequencies of nutshell, but the possibility exists that preprocessed acorn meal and hickory oil were funneled into the heavily populated and cleared bottomland from wooded parts of the valley margin and adjacent upland. Persimmons, grapes, and other fruits are well represented here, as they are at virtually all Mississippian sites. C. Margaret Scarry (1986) proposes that the abundance of some fruits increased as trees were managed at the edges of fields and in fallow land. The typical profile for Mississippian subsistence across eastern North America in general includes a mixture of cultigens, nuts, fruits, weedy annuals, and animals, with deer, turkey, raccoon, and sometimes fish dominating faunal assemblages. Although archaeobotanists do not apply diversity indices to their data very often, and I have not gone through the literature and done so, my impression is that the richness component of Mississippian diets was at least as great as it had been during the preceding period in most regions. In terms of evenness, however, maize becomes increasingly dominant at many sites, especially after A.D. 1200.

To return momentarily to the level of genetic diversity, farmers of the Eastern Woodlands can be credited with breeding several varieties of corn that granted their own societies storable surpluses and benefited the U.S. economy as well. Eastern 8-row, the ancestor

of Northern Flint, seems to have been developed in what is now
the northeastern United States and southeastern Canada at approximately 600 or 700 A.D. (Crawford and Smith 1997). Modern genetic
relationships indicate that maize from the Southwest was carried
across the Plains and that a restricted gene pool or founder effect,
combined with human selection, resulted in the robust and uniform
variety grown by eastern Algonkians, Iroquoians, and farmers of
the southern Great Lakes and eastern prairies. This Northern Flint
became one ancestor of modern Corn Belt Dent hybrids (Brown and
Anderson 1947; Doebley et al. 1986). In the central Mississippi River
Valley and most of the Southeast, however, corncobs exhibit a
greater degree of variability in terms of size, shape, and number of
rows of kernels (Fritz 1992). Paul Mangelsdorf (personal communication, 1982) referred to the desiccated Ozark rockshelter assemblage
as "a mongrel lot." Farmers of southern latitudes seem to have
produced more varieties than the early and late season types recognized by early Europeans (cf. Swanton 1946).

ECOSYSTEM-LEVEL BIODIVERSITY:
THE VARIED HUMANIZED LANDSCAPE

Population density at contact in the Eastern Woodlands was relatively low by New World standards. Douglas Ubelaker (1988)
estimates that approximately 19 people per 100 square km lived in
the Northeast in A.D. 1500 and that 22 people per 100 square km
occupied the Southeast region. Even so, early European accounts
in both areas describe numerous towns and villages, some of which
had hundreds of occupants, large fields where crops were grown,
patches of managed land where other types of activities were conducted, and well-traveled paths connecting settlements.

Eastern agriculture is traditionally thought of as shifting cultivation or slash-and-burn farming. With the exception of a few
places where ridging or dramatically raised hilling were practiced

(Gallagher and Arzigian 1994), no significant alteration of the natural topography occurred. The geographer William Doolittle (1992) has recently argued persuasively that this categorization of the farming as "extensive" understates the degree of intensity involved. Fields in what is now the eastern United States were large enough to be permanently open for decades rather than constantly shifting. Within a field, some plots would be in crops while others were in fallow, but no part of the field would necessarily revert to forest as long as the settlement remained close. Gilbert Wilson's Hidatsa colleague Maxidiwiac (Buffalo Bird Woman) described this type of system as having flourished in the middle and late 1800s in the upper Missouri River drainage, where large communal fields on river terraces were subdivided into sizable family plots. Women from the various households of the village agreed upon boundaries between these contiguous family plots, which measured as large as 180 by 90 yards. Soil fertility was carefully monitored, and plots were left to rest when necessary. The hoe and digging stick technology was labor intensive, but the women loved their fields and pampered their crops, even singing to them, and most of the work was appreciated for the comradeship, the natural beauty, and the emotional satisfaction it afforded (Wilson 1987).

Large agricultural fields that were open for many years were only one of the humanly altered ecosystem types in the East. Julia Hammett (1992 and this volume) has published a masterful summary of ethnohistoric data pertaining to aboriginal landscapes in what is now the southeastern United States, stressing the importance of prescribed burning and other means of thinning or clearing vegetation. Hammett (1992:1) demonstrates that the Southeastern Indians "created and maintained a mosaic of managed patches that yielded high subsistence returns and ensured the short-term stability of their anthropogenic ecosystem." Seven types of anthropogenic patches include hunting camps, fields/gardens, edge areas/ meadows, old fields, parklands/orchards, wetlands/swamps/ marshes, and waterways. Prescribed burning was especially critical in managing hunting camps, meadows, and parklands/orchards. Hammett (1992:34) makes it clear, however, that these patches were limited in size and in location, with burned hunting zones situated "in forested areas away from settlements, probably less than 3 mi wide," and the meadows, parklands, and orchards located in close proximity to (within several miles of) established settlements. Claims that Indian-set fires created the vast expanses of "park-like" forests described by early explorers (Day 1953; Guffey 1977) are not well supported by available evidence. I agree with Hammett (1992:35) that it is probable that "extremely large, expansive open areas were the result of occasional natural wild fires." The Indian-managed groves were more discrete and localized. They would have been places kept free of brush by understory burning, where production of desirable resources was enhanced by removing economically useless trees and thinning out individual nut and fruit-bearing trees in order to favor the heaviest producers.

Early European travelers in the Eastern Woodlands made clear distinctions between open areas in the vicinity of Native settlements and denser forests in uninhabited areas that separated polities. Chronicles of the Hernando De Soto expedition of 1539–43, for example, include many descriptions of fields, open woods, and clusters of farmsteads strung for miles along river terraces near the civic-ceremonial centers of the most successful Mississippian chiefs of the day (Clayton et al. 1993). De Soto wisely sought out these centers in order to take advantage of the surplus stores of food and burden bearers needed by his army of hundreds, and he spent as little time as possible in the sparsely inhabited or uninhabited regions between them. Nevertheless, the existence of "wilderness" regions is documented. En route to the province of Cofitachequi, for example, the entire expedition was lost for so many days on the Coastal Plain of Georgia that their supplies of grain ran out. Conditions became alarming by the ninth day of what had been expected to be a four-day march, and it took several more days before one of the Spaniards who had been sent out came back with news of a good-sized Indian settlement. In the meantime, De Soto "and all his men experienced great vicissitudes and extreme need" (Robertson 1993:80–81).

Garcilaso de la Vega, although not always reliable in terms of exactly what happened when, gives an intriguing explanation of why the Indians themselves were lost. De Soto accused their leader of deceit, saying that "it was not credible that, having had perpetual warfare with one another, they would not know the public and secret roads that passed from one province to the other." The leader responded that:

> neither he nor any of his Indians had ever been where they were at present and that the wars these two provinces had waged had never been in open battle between two forces, one taking an army to the territory of the other, but only at the fisheries on those two rivers and the other streams that they had left behind them and at the hunting grounds, between the parties that both sent out through those woods and uninhabited districts that they had passed. Meeting at these hunting grounds and fisheries, they killed and captured one another as enemies. . . . (Shelby 1993:274)

Mary Helms (1992:189) points out that warfare and hunting had both ideological and ecological significance, "for in traditional societies both activities are typically conducted in locales geograph-ically and cosmologically beyond (outside) the settled, inhabited areas of the polity taking the initiative in such affairs." In the Eastern Woodlands of North America, then, ideological factors embedded in the traditions governing intergroup conflict combined with economic practices (hunting and fishing) to produce ecological consequences: spacing of population concentrations to leave room for expanses of forests. Given the low overall densities of popula-tion in eastern North America (Ubelaker 1988), it is important to remember the difference between heavily managed patches and those beyond. I. D. Campbell and Celina Campbell (1994), for example, examine the archaeological, palynological, and historical evidence available for southern Ontario, homeland of the Huron and other Iroquoian-speaking farmers, and conclude:

> Any impact the prehistoric inhabitants of Southern Ontario may have had on their environment was likely of short duration. The forest succession on their old fields would likely have reverted to an essentially natural forest in a few decades in most areas. The maximum area disturbed would have been less than 3.2 percent of Ontario south of the Canadian Shield. Although they may have had a local impact where their populations were most concentrated, . . . prehistoric populations had no significant lasting effect on the landscape. (Campbell and Campbell 1994:135)

Biologists and anthropologists currently face the challenge of assessing the scale of the impacts—whether beneficial or detrimental—that people of the past had on their landscapes and resource bases. With exceptions including Campbell and Campbell (1994), there seems to be a current trend in the direction of overreacting against our former tendency to ignore the fact that American Indians made ecological changes, now attributing to them the drastic alteration of virtually every square meter of prairie, savanna, and forest in the East. In spite of the fact that we cannot often determine which ancient fires were set by people rather than by lightning and usually lack the chronological precision to establish prehistoric fire frequency for any given region and period, American Indians are now cast as yearly torchers of everything in sight from the day they first set foot on this continent at the end of the last Ice Age. In California and the Pacific Northwest, there is excellent ethnographic evidence for intensive fire management by indigenous peoples (e.g., Turner 1991), but eastern North America is very different from the West in terms of climate, vegetation, and population density at contact. In addition, we must constantly guard against pushing our current notions of "Man the Ecological Disaster" into all phases of the past. The fact that humans today are rapidly exterminating species and creating resource imbalances should have no bearing whatsoever on debates such as Pleistocene Overkill or deforestation as the cause of Cahokia's decline.

I conclude with a warning to watch out for people tied to industries with contemporary economic motives who manipulate the past in order to serve their profit-oriented purposes. Having been hit with lawsuits that prevent or curtail the spraying of chemical herbicides and massive mechanical clear-cutting, some foresters in eastern North America are turning to large-scale burning and slightly modified forms of even-aged management in order to convert forests that include high proportions of mixed hardwood species to low-diversity stands of commercial conifers. The hired ecologists who prepare reports and legal depositions have latched onto the fact that American Indians did a good deal of burning in order to justify current practices. A recent statement by a forester (Dr. Thomas M. Bonnicksen) at Texas A & M University, prepared for use by timber industry intervenors in a federal lawsuit, described U.S. Forest Service even-aged burning practices as "merely mimicking pre-settlement conditions because American Indians burned forests frequently for more than 60 reasons" (Forest Reform Network, June 27, 1996). The purpose of the testimony was to contend that American Indians practiced frequent burning and therefore the U.S. Forest Service is justified in burning the National Forests at its own frequent rate as well as clear-cutting those forests. Using the same tactics, an employee (David Graney) of the Ozark–St. Francis National Forest testified in federal court that "every two to five years . . . this entire Ozark region burned over" in the course of extensive fire management by American Indians (*Call of the Wild* 1996:9). Those who challenge these highly debatable statements are accused of clinging to out-dated notions of Noble Savages living in a forest primeval.

Clearly, the issue of native biodiversity has more than mere academic relevance.

ACKNOWLEDGMENTS

I would like to thank Wayne Elisens and Paul Minnis, organizers of the conference on "Biodiversity and Native North America," and the administration of the University of Oklahoma for bringing scholars and interested members of the public together to discuss such a critical and timely topic.

REFERENCES CITED

Anderson, Edgar. 1952. *Plants, Man, and Life*. Berkeley: University of California Press.

Asch, David L. 1994. Prehistoric Plant Husbandry in West-Central Illinois: An 8000-Year Perspective. In *Agricultural Origins and Development in the Midcontinent*, edited by William Green, pp. 25–86. Office of the State Archaeologist Report 19. Iowa City: University of Iowa.

Asch, David L., and Nancy B. Asch. 1985. Archeobotany. In *Smiling Dan: Structure and Function at a Middle Woodland Settlement in the Illinois Valley*, edited by B. D. Stafford and M. B. Sant, pp. 327–401. Archeological Center Research Series 2. Kampsville, Ill.: Center for American Archeology.

Asch, David L., and Nancy Asch Sidell. 1992. Archeobotany. In *Early Woodland Occupation at the Ambrose Flick Site in the Sny Bottom of West-Central Illinois*, edited by C. R. Stafford, pp. 177–293. Archeological Center Research Series 10. Kampsville, Ill.: Center for American Archeology.

Brown, William L., and Edgar Anderson. 1947. The Northern Flint Corns. *Annals of the Missouri Botanical Gardens* 34(1):1–28.

Buikstra, Jane E., Jerome C. Rose, and George R. Milner. 1994. A Carbon Isotopic Perspective on Dietary Variation in Late Prehistoric Western Illinois. In *Agricultural Origins and Development in the Midcontinent*, edited by William Green, pp. 155–70. Office of the State Archaeologist Report 19. Iowa City: University of Iowa.

Call of the Wild. 1996. Newsletter of the Newton County Wildlife Association (Jasper, Arkansas) 7(4).

Campbell, I. D., and Celina Campbell. 1994. The Impact of Late Woodland Land Use on the Forest Landscape of Southern Ontario. *Great Lakes Geographer* 1(1):21–29.

Clayton, Lawrence A., Vernon J. Knight, and Edward C. Moore (eds.). 1993. *The De Soto Chronicles.* Tuscaloosa: University of Alabama Press.

Cleland, Charles E. 1976. The Focal-Diffuse Model of Subsistence Change in Eastern North America. *Midcontinental Journal of Archaeology* 1:59–76.

Conard, N., D. L. Asch, N. B. Asch, D. Elmore, H. E. Gove, M. Rubin, J. A. Brown, M. D. Wiant, K. B. Farnsworth, and T. G. Cook. 1984. Accelerator Radiocarbon Dating of Evidence for Prehistoric Horticulture in Illinois. Nature 308:443–46.

Cowan, C. Wesley. 1978. The Prehistoric Use and Distribution of Maygrass in Eastern North America: Cultural and Phytogeographical Implications. In *The Nature and Status of Ethnobotany,* edited by R. I. Ford, pp. 263–88. Anthropological Papers No. 67. Ann Arbor: Museum of Anthropology, University of Michigan.

Crawford, Gary W., David G. Smith, and Vandy E. Bowyer. 1997. Dating the Entry of Corn (*Zea mays*) into the Lower Great Lakes, from the Grand Banks Site, Ontario, Canada. *American Antiquity* 62:112–19.

Crites, Gary D. 1993. Domesticated Sunflower in Fifth Millennium B.P. Temporal Context: New Evidence from Middle Tennessee. *American Antiquity* 58:146–48.

Day, Gordon. 1953. The Indian as an Ecological Factor in the Northeastern Forest. *Ecology* 34:329–46.

Decker-Walters, Deena. 1990. Evidence for Multiple Domestications of *Cucurbita pepo.* In *Biology and Utilization of the Cucurbitaceae,* edited by D. M. Bates, R. W. Robinson, and C. Jeffrey, pp. 96–101. Ithaca: Cornell University Press.

Doebley, John F., Major M. Goodman, and Charles W. Stuber. 1986. Exceptional Genetic Divergence of Northern Flint Corn. *American Journal of Botany* 73:64–69.

Doolittle, William E. 1992. Agriculture in North America on the Eve of Contact: A Reassessment. *Annals of the Association of American Geographers* 82:386–401.

Emerson, Thomas E. 1982. *Mississippian Stone Images in Illinois.* Circular No. 6. Urbana-Champaign: Illinois Archaeological Survey.

Fiedel, Stuart J. 1987. *Prehistory of the Americas*. Cambridge: Cambridge University Press.

Ford, Richard I. 1977. Evolutionary Ecology and the Evolution of Human Ecosystems: A Case Study from the Midwestern U.S.A. In *Explanations of Prehistoric Change*, edited by J. N. Hill, pp. 153–84. Albuquerque: University of New Mexico Press.

Forest Reform Network. 1996. *Newsletter of the Texas Committee on Natural Resources* (Dallas), June 27.

Fritz, Gayle J. 1986. Prehistoric Ozark Agriculture: The University of Arkansas Rockshelter Collections. Ph.D. dissertation. University of North Carolina at Chapel Hill. Ann Arbor: University Microfilms.

———. 1992. "Newer," "Better" Maize and the Mississippian Emergence: A Critique of Prime Mover Explanations. In *Late Prehistoric Agriculture: Observations from the Midwest*, edited by W. I. Woods, pp. 19–43. Studies in Illinois Archaeology No. 8. Springfield: Illinois Historic Preservation Agency.

———. 1994a. Early and Middle Woodland Period Paleoethnobotany. In *Foraging and Farming in the Eastern Woodlands*, edited by C. M. Scarry, pp. 39–56. Gainesville: University Press of Florida.

———. 1994b. Precolumbian *Cucurbita argyrosperma* ssp. *argyrosperma* (Cucurbitaceae) in the Eastern Woodlands of North America. *Economic Botany* 48(3):280–92.

———. 1997. A Three-Thousand Year Old Cache of Crop Seeds from Marble Bluff, Arkansas. In *People, Plants, and Landscapes: Studies in Paleoethnobotany*, edited by K. J. Gremillion, pp. 42–62. Tuscaloosa: University of Alabama Press.

Fritz, Gayle J., and B. D. Smith. 1988. Old Collections and New Technology: Documenting the Domestication of Chenopodium in Eastern North America. *Midcontinental Journal of Archaeology* 13:3–28.

Gallagher, James P. 1992. Prehistoric Field Systems in the Upper Midwest. In *Late Prehistoric Agriculture: Observations from the Midwest*, edited by W. I. Woods, pp. 95–135. Studies in Illinois Archaeology No. 8. Springfield: Illinois Historic Preservation Agency.

Gallagher, James P., and Constance M. Arzigian. 1994. A New Perspective on Late Prehistoric Agricultural Intensification in the Upper Mississippi River Valley. In *Agricultural Origins and Development in the Midcontinent*, edited by William Green, pp. 171–88. Office of the State Archaeologist Report 19. Iowa City: University of Iowa.

Gremillion, Kristen J. 1997. New Perspectives on the Paleoethnobotany of Newt Kash Shelter. In *People, Plants, and Landscapes: Studies in Paleoethnobotany*, edited by K. J. Gremillion, pp. 23–41. Tuscaloosa: University of Alabama Press.

Guffey, Stanley Z. 1977. A Review and Analysis of the Effects of Pre-Columbian Man on the Eastern North American Forests. *Tennessee Anthropologist* 2(2):121–37.

Hammett, Julia E. 1992. Ethnohistory of Aboriginal Landscapes in the Southeastern United States. *Southern Indian Studies* 41:1-\50.

Heiser, Charles B., Jr. 1976. *The Sunflower*. Norman: University of Oklahoma Press.

Helms, Mary W. 1992. Political Lords and Political Ideology in Southeastern Chiefdoms: Comments and Observations. In *Lords of the Southeast: Social Inequality and the Native Elites of Southeastern North America*, edited by A. W. Barker and T. R. Pauketat, pp. 185–94. Archeological Papers No. 3. Washington, D.C.: American Anthropological Association.

Hunter, Andrea. 1992. Utilization of *Hordeum pusillum* (Little Barley) in the Midwest United States: Applying Rindos' Co-evolutionary Model of Domestication. Ph.D. dissertation. University of Missouri at Columbia. Ann Arbor: University Microfilms.

Johannessen, Sissel. 1988. Plant Remains and Culture Change: Are Paleoethnobotanical Data Better Than We Think? In *Current Paleoethnobotany*, edited by C. Hastorf and V. Popper, pp. 145–66. Chicago: University of Chicago Press.

———. 1994. Farmers of the Late Woodland. In *Foraging and Farming in the Eastern Woodlands*, edited by C. M. Scarry, pp. 57–77. Gainesville: University Press of Florida.

Lopinot, Neal H. 1991. Archaeobotanical Remains. In *The Archaeology of the Cahokia ICT-II: Biological Remains*, by N. H. Lopinot, L. S. Kelly, and G. R. Milner, pp. 1–268. Illinois Cultural Resources Study No. 13. Springfield: Illinois Historic Preservation Agency.

———. 1994. A New Crop of Data on the Cahokian Polity. In *Agricultural Origins and Development in the Midcontinent*, edited by William Green, pp. 127–53. Office of the State Archaeologist Report 19. Iowa City: University of Iowa.

Lopinot, Neal H., Gayle J. Fritz, and John E. Kelly. 1991. The Archaeological Context and Significance of *Polygonum erectum* Achene Masses from the American Bottom Region. Paper presented to the 14th Annual Meeting of the Society of Ethnobiology, St. Louis.

Newsom, Lee A., S. David Webb, and James S. Dunbar. 1993. History and Geographic Distribution of *Cucurbita pepo* Gourds in Florida. *Journal of Ethnobiology* 13:75–97.

Petersen, James B., and Nancy Asch Sidell. 1996. Mid-Holocene Evidence of *Cucurbita* sp. from Central Maine. *American Antiquity* 61:685–98.

Raven, Peter H., Linda R. Berg, and George B. Johnson. 1994. *Environment*. Fort Worth: Saunders College Publishing.

Riley, Thomas J., Gregory R. Walz, Charles J. Bareis, Andrew C. Fortier, and Kathryn E. Parker. 1994. Accelerator Mass Spectrometry (AMS) Dates Confirm Early *Zea mays* in the Mississippi River Valley. *American Antiquity* 59:490–98.

Robertson, James A. (trans. and ed.). 1993. True Relation of the Hardships Suffered by Governor Hernando De Soto and Certain Portuguese Gentlemen during the Discovery of the Province of Florida, Now Newly Set Forth by a Gentleman of Elvas. In *The De Soto Chronicles*, edited by L. A. Clayton, V. J. Knight, Jr., and E. C. Moore, 1:25–219. 2 vols. Tuscaloosa: University of Alabama Press.

Scarry, C. Margaret. 1986. Change in Plant Procurement and Production during the Emergence of the Moundville Chiefdom. Ph.D. dissertation. University of Michigan. Ann Arbor: University Microfilms.

Shelby, Charmion. 1993. La Florida, by the Inca. In *The De Soto Chronicles*, edited by L. A. Clayton, V. J. Knight, Jr., and E. C. Moore, 2:25–559. 2 vols. Tuscaloosa: University of Alabama Press.

Smith, Bruce D. 1992. *Rivers of Change: Essays on Early Agriculture in Eastern North America*. Washington, D.C.: Smithsonian Institution Press.

Smith, Bruce D., C. Wesley Cowan, and Michael P. Hoffman. 1992. Is It an Indigene or a Foreigner? In *Rivers of Change: Essays on Early Agriculture in Eastern North America*, by B. D. Smith, pp. 67–100. Washington, D.C.: Smithsonian Institution Press.

Smith, Bruce D., and V. Funk. 1985. A Newly Described Subfossil Cultivar of *Chenopodium* (Chenopodiaceae). *Phytolologia* 57:445–49.

Swanton, John R. 1946. *The Indians of the Southeastern United States*. Bureau of American Ethnology Bulletin 137. Washington, D.C.: U.S. Government Printing Office.

Turner, Nancy J. 1991. "Burning Mountain Sides for Better Crops." In *Aboriginal Landscape Burning in British Columbia*, edited by Kenneth P.

Cannon, pp. 57–73. *Archaeology in Montana*, Special Issue, 32(2). Bozeman: Montana Archaeological Society.

Ubelaker, Douglas H. 1988. North American Indian Population Size, A.D. 1500–1985. *American Journal of Physical Anthropology* 77:289–94.

Watson, Patty Jo. 1985. The Impact of Early Horticulture in the Upland Drainages of the Midwest and Midsouth. In *Prehistoric Food Production in North America*, edited by R. I. Ford, pp. 73–98. Anthropological Papers No. 75. Ann Arbor: Museum of Anthropology, University of Michigan.

Watson, Patty Jo, and Richard A. Yarnell. 1986. Lost John's Last Meal. *Missouri Archaeologist* 47:241–55.

Whittaker, Robert H. 1972. Evolution and Measurement of Species Diversity. *Taxon* 21(2/3):213–51.

Wilson, Gilbert L. 1987. *Buffalo Bird Woman's Garden: Agriculture of the Hidatsa Indians* (orig. 1917). St. Paul: Minnesota Historical Society Press.

Wilson, Hugh D. 1981. Domesticated *Chenopodium* of the Ozark Bluff Dweller. *Economic Botany* 35:233–39.

Wilson, Hugh D., John Doebley, and M. Duvall. 1992. Chloroplast DNA Diversity among Wild and Cultivated Members of *Cucurbita* (Cucurbitaceae). *Theoretical and Applied Genetics* 84:859–65.

Wymer, Dee Ann. 1992. Trends and Disparities: The Woodland Paleoethnobotanical Record of the Mid-Ohio Valley. In *Cultural Variability in Context: Woodland Settlements of the Mid-Ohio Valley*, edited by W. Seeman, pp. 65–76. *Midcontinental Journal of Archaeology*, Special Report, No. 7.

Yarnell, Richard A. 1969. Contents of Human Paleofeces. In *The Prehistory of Salts Cave, Kentucky*, edited by P. J. Watson, pp. 41–54. Reports of Investigations No. 16. Springfield: Illinois State Museum.

———. 1974. Plant Food and Cultivation of the Salts Cavers. In *Archeology of the Mammoth Cave Area*, edited by P. J. Watson, pp. 113–22. Orlando: Academic Press.

CHAPTER NINE

ETHNOHISTORY OF ABORIGINAL LANDSCAPES IN THE SOUTHEASTERN UNITED STATES

JULIA E. HAMMETT

Drawing upon early ethnohistorical evidence of the southeastern United States, this study examines the nature of human disturbance and the techniques and methods that Indians of that region used to alter or modify their physical environment. The specific results of their actions are examined to determine what type of mutualistic relationships or "patches" they initiated or maintained. These findings are compared with the habitat conditions and preferences of their important food crops in order to evaluate their effectiveness and their intentionality. Finally, implications of this study for understanding changes in human behavior and for purposes of resource management are proposed.

Reprinted from Julia E. Hammett. 1992. Ethnohistory of Aboriginal Landscapes in the Southeastern United States. *Southern Indian Studies* 41:1–50.

THE SETTING

A Patchy and Disturbed Ecosystem

Ecologists long have recognized the role of disturbance in increasing the net productivity in an ecosystem (Odum 1959), yet until recently most theoretical works on communities have been framed with concepts like steady state, homeostasis, and equilibrium. During the past few years, interest in the dynamics of an ecosystem has grown, and the process of natural disturbance and patch dynamics has become the focus of attention (Pickett and White 1985). A "patch" has been described by John Wiens (1976:83) as an area "distinguished by discontinuities in environmental character states from [its] surroundings." This description has intentionally been made flexible so that boundary conditions relevant for the organism under study can be applied. In this sense, patchiness must be "organism defined" (Wiens 1976:83; Winterhalder 1981:152). Patches are discrete enough to be isolated for purposes of study, yet they vary in terms of spatial and temporal qualities and in diversity, density, and productivity. For human groups, we may add that patches are perceived as discrete spaces where specific resources are concentrated.

Due to dynamic interactions within patches, each organism contributes somewhat to the makeup of the patch. From this standpoint, relatively highly mobile organisms such as vertebrates can be considered patch producers (Wiens 1985). For example, herbivores affect the frequency and distribution of food resources by differential grazing patterns. Granivores bury caches of seeds that may affect plant distributions. Burrowing animals can contribute significantly to the disturbance regime of their local environment. These types of disturbance activities contribute immensely to on-site "heterogeneity of the vegetation as a whole and maintain a state of non-equilibrium patch structure" (Wiens 1985:187).

In general, various types of natural disturbance increase the heterogeneity or patchiness of the ecosystem. A relatively small disturbance such as a tree fall has an effect on many organisms in the general vicinity. Ecologists have noted that such a disturbance opens a space in the forest from the forest floor to the treetops. This space is called a "canopy gap," and it has an important role in ecological rejuvenation of the affected area. The rejuvenation is often associated with changes in availability of other resources, namely, light and soil nutrients, which affect the general makeup of biotic communities. This in turn affects the heterogeneity of the site (Denslow 1985:310–11). Julie Sloan Denslow has recognized that the scale of natural disturbance both temporally and spatially, the ability of various species to exploit the gap, and other environmental factors may affect habitat heterogeneity as well. Conversely, major catastrophic disturbances such as volcanic eruptions or large wildfires can lead to greater homogeneity—that is, large areas having similar environmental conditions such as soil type and plant and animal distributions.

Like other ecologists, those who have concentrated on humans have acknowledged the importance of disturbance, and to a certain extent they have examined spatial concentrations that could be considered patches. In fact, much attention has been devoted to developing models and theories about the human role in creating and maintaining secondary successional plant and animal associations or anthropogenic communities (Bye 1981; Ford 1985). Human disturbance often simulates other types of physical disturbance, but human disturbance may also change the interactions between community neighbors through processes of repetition and intensification.

David Rindos (1984) has noted that through time these processes may produce mutualistic relationships that can lead to domestication. In such cases, two organisms co-evolve in a relationship he has described as "symbiotic" (Rindos 1980:753).

Humans can take the role of instigator in creating or managing patches in order to enhance their net productivity in terms of human gain. When studying patch dynamics, the anthropogenic ecosystem becomes a "shifting mosaic" (Bormann and Likens 1979; Pickett and

White 1985) of patches of various degrees of human and nonhuman derivation and maintenance. S. T. A. Pickett and P. S. White (1985:5) have noted that the term "shifting mosaic" connotes "a uniformity of patch distribution in time and space such that an overall landscape equilibrium of patches applies." They argue that such equilibria are to be expected where (1) feedback occurs between community characteristics and disturbance events; (2) patch size is small relative to the homogeneous landscape unit; and (3) disturbance regimes are stable. I argue here that the situation in the southeastern United States immediately prior to European contact was an example of a shifting mosaic of patches. Thus, the patch concept provides a tool with which to explore the landscape and the land-use pattern of any human group.

Humans have an impact on the ecology of any region they inhabit. The extent of their impact is a by-product of their technology, their numbers and density, and the history of past environmental events. Archaeological evidence suggests that, overall, the environmental impact of aboriginal Americans increased through time as their numbers grew and their technology developed. These trends are consistent with general cultural evolutionary models, although such observations fail to be very explicit.

The Contact period should produce the most information about how humans interacted with their micro-environments because it provides the richest documentation of aboriginal behavior. By examining the letters and journals that have survived from early European explorers and settlers, the interactions between Indians and their environment can be considered more fully than through archaeological work alone.

The region of the Atlantic seaboard, which includes present-day Virginia, North Carolina, South Carolina, and northern Georgia (see map 9.1), has been selected for study because there were early contacts here between Native peoples and the Spanish and English. The study area encompasses three basic geographic zones—the Coastal Plain, the Piedmont, and the Appalachian Highlands—and

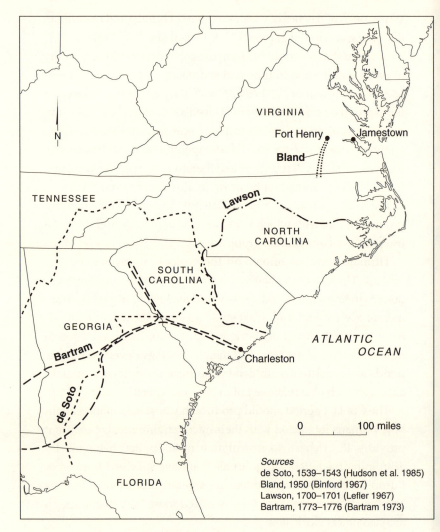

Map 9.1. The study area, showing routes of Spanish and English explorers and traders.

several cultural groups, including Algonkian, Siouan, Muskogean, and Iroquoian-speaking peoples. This diversity of cultural groups and environments should have fostered variation in cultural adaptations to different environmental conditions.

Some general questions are considered here: (1) In what ways did the Native inhabitants alter the natural vegetation of their region? (2) How did the Native inhabitants perceive their actions? (3) To what degree were their actions intentional or unintentional? (4) What were the cumulative effects of their actions? (5) What were the accrued benefits (or detriments) of their actions?

HISTORICAL ACCOUNTS

The primary sources of information for this study were drawn from observations made by early explorers, traders, and settlers from Spain and England (see table 9.1). Like most sources of cultural information, historical documents are loaded with distortions, biases, and contradictions; consequently, it is necessary to recognize their strengths and weaknesses if they are to prove useful. An important key to understanding the limitations of such documents is to determine the cultural context of the writerthe writer's background and intentions in keeping these records. By understanding these factors, a more realistic evaluation of the interpretive value of the documents can be made.

It should be noted from the outset that the Europeans who first "discovered" the American continents were not looking for a new land but for a passage to the other end of the world known to Europe. Their realization of this discovery is perhaps best demonstrated in the use of the terms "Old World" and "New World." Their initial impressions suggest they had no conception of the extent of this land mass. Early explorers repeatedly interviewed the Indians regarding a passage across the continent. Their questions and observations revealed their belief that the continent was not

TABLE 9.1
Primary Sources Used in This Study

Source	Dates	Context	Reference
Hernando de Soto	1539–43	Spanish explorer	Varner and Varner 1951
Thomas Hariot	1586	English explorer	Quinn 1955
John Smith	1607–1609	Jamestown settler	Arber 1910
George Percy	1607–1609	Jamestown settler	Percy 1907
Edward Bland	1650	English explorer	Bland 1651
John Lawson	1700–1709	naturalist and surveyor	Lefler 1967
Robert Beverley	1705	Virginia settler	Wright 1947
William Byrd II	1719–32	Virginia planter and trader	Wright 1966
William Bartram	1773–76	artist and naturalist	Bartram 1973

very sizable. For example, several stories were collected in the Carolinas regarding a falls beyond which there was a great sea of salt (Quinn and Quinn 1973:28).

Also, the major European powers during the Contact period—Spain, France, and England—were in competition for global resource control. This competition did not begin or end with their discovery of the New World. The geographic proximity of these political powers in the Old World made them obvious competitors. In regard to the Carolinas, Ralph Lane's narrative of the Roanoke Island settlement claimed that:

> for that the discovery of a good mine, but the goodness of God, or a passage to the Southsea, or someway to it, and nothing els can bring this country in request to be inhabited

by our nation. And with the discovery of any of the two above shewed, it wilbe the most sweet, and healthfullest climate, and then will sassafras, and many other rootes & gummes ther found make good Marchandise and lading for shipping, otherwise of themselves will not be worth fetching. (Quinn and Quinn 1973:331)

European interests in the New World were (1) to find a passage to Asia; (2) to find any riches this new land afforded; and (3) to gain control over the natural resources of this new land.

Naturally, the earliest accounts were richest in information about aboriginal technology because there had been less time for "contamination" by European influences. Also, these descriptions were very detailed because of the uniqueness of the experiences. As time went on and as the novelty of discovery began to wear off, less detailed documentation occurred. By the 1700s, surveyors commissioned to explore interior areas of the Carolinas were instructed merely to report anything found that was new or unlike what had been seen in other villages.

The aim of these reporters is an important factor in evaluating the validity of their claims. In 1539, Hernando de Soto and his men were responsible for assessing the natural riches of the land with the intention of future apportionment and settlement (Varner and Varner 1951:324). They were interested in identifying the individuals and groups who had the most power and wealth and in discovering their sources of wealth. Rumors of riches in the form of gold, silver, and pearls were investigated and Native holdings in the form of land, luxury items, food, and numbers of human subjects were assessed. Information about the environment along their route, particularly near Indian towns, is useful because these were probably fairly accurate depictions of the landscape shortly after the time of first contact.

Among the earliest useful reports by Englishmen were the accounts of Jamestown settlers Captain John Smith and George

Percy in the early 1600s. Young Captain Smith was an adventurer who had seen action in various parts of the world prior to settling in the New World. Less is known of Percy, except that he was a gentleman by birth and a contemporary and adversary of Smith. The original settlers of Jamestown apparently were plagued with dissension, jealousy, and competition from the start. Smith's work was clearly the most exhaustive of the time, and many contemporary and later works, such as those of William Strachey (1849) and Robert Beverley (Wright 1947), drew heavily upon his writings. These early settlers were dependent upon the continuing support of financiers in England, and it suited their purposes to portray the countryside as attractively to the English eye as possible so that their sponsors would believe their investments were worthwhile. Also, these early pioneers were encouraging other potential settlers to join their ranks. This led them to emphasize or embellish what they considered to be the good qualities of the Americas and to downplay or neglect to mention the bad.

Captain Smith's encyclopedic accounting of Virginia surely suffers from these biases, but the subject matter and detailed descriptions of Indian customs and agricultural techniques make his work a valuable asset for the present study. To a great extent, the well-being and survival of Smith and the other settlers was dependent upon the hard-won lessons of the Indians. From this standpoint, Smith and the settlers benefited from their accurate observations of Indian subsistence technology.

Both Edward Bland and George Percy provided accounts of exploratory trips away from the English settlements. It is difficult to conceive of a way they could have benefited from distorting the truth, but intrinsic biases due to English upbringing and attitudes, and perceptions of the landscape as seen through English eyes, must be taken into account.

John Lawson, a surveyor and naturalist at the turn of the eighteenth century, was the first explorer in the region with any obvious background in the natural sciences. Nevertheless, one researcher has questioned the accuracy of Lawson's observations due to his apparent exaggerations in the form of agricultural propaganda (Lindgren 1972). Lawson's (Lefler 1967) report is the first extensive documentation from the interior part of the Carolinas; this fact, coupled with the subject matter of his observations, makes his information of considerable value.

William Bartram's (1973) observations in the 1770s were too late to record many impressions of aboriginal conditions in the central Piedmont areas, although his training as a naturalist and an artist prepared him to make detailed observations of the landscape. At times, his artistic background led him to romanticize his accounts, yet other aspects of his reports, such as detailed and thoughtful descriptions of plant succession in ancient Indian fields, provided noteworthy documentation.

In southern coastal Virginia near Jamestown, the early settlers found "by chance" upon walking into the woods:

> a pathway like an Irish Pace: We traced along some foure miles, all the way as wee went, having the pleasantest Suckles, the ground all flowing over with faire flowers of sundry coloured and kinds, as though it had been in any Garden or orchard in England. There be many Strawberries, and other fruits unknowne. Wee saw the woods full of Cedar and Cypresse trees, with other trees, which issued out sweet Gummes like to Balsam. We kept on our Way in this paradise. At length, wee came to a Savage Towne. (Arber 1910:lxviii)

This passage demonstrates some of the biases inherent in this kind of documentation. Critics might rightly argue that such accounts are too inaccurate to be considered of real value. But if the biases are recognized, perhaps some information can be gained from this type of literature. For this particular quote, several questions come to mind: (1) What part of the description is due to propaganda? (2) Has the writer embellished the experience to make it more attractive to his audience? (3) Could the environment have been as attractive and productive as this writer reported? These questions are reconsidered later in this chapter.

Comparisons were made to "an Irish Pace" and "any Garden or orchard in England." It may be productive to examine what these images would have meant to a person back in England reading this account. In a study devoted to early colonial gardens in New England, Rudy Favretti (1974) has suggested that the garden of the Plymouth settlers can best be visualized by recalling the cottage gardens of England. These gardens typically had "a central path of grass or gravel with irregular beds on either side. The plants within these beds were well cultivated and the beds maintained neatly, but no order of plant material prevailed. Vegetables, useful flowering plants, and herbs grew side by side without regard to kinds, height, or balance. The main characteristics of these gardens were informality and neatness, with little actual design" (Favretti 1974:5).

Favretti (1974:7) adds that the more formal English manor garden was more the prototype of the wealthier people of Massachusetts. This garden "was actually a formal garden informally planted." Apparently, the climate of Great Britain produced "a lush plant growth that favored informality in the use of plants. The English, too, unlike the French, favored informality in the execution of the garden plan" (Favretti 1974:7).

With this seventeenth-century English model of a garden in mind, we will examine early accounts of southeastern North American landscapes and aboriginal land-use and management strategies.

INDIAN ENVIRONMENTAL MANAGEMENT: TECHNIQUES AND STRATEGIES

Indians of this region practiced a combination of hunting, fishing, plant collecting, and gardening strategies. Food resources that the Indians relied upon regularly are called crops. It is assumed that, in order to ensure harvests, the Indians may have encouraged or protected most crop resources. Information on preferred habitat conditions of these animal and plant crops must be considered in order to evaluate the effectiveness of the aboriginal management and harvest strategies.

BURNING AND CLEARING

Fire ecologist P. J. Viro (1974) has identified three kinds of forest fire: (1) wildfire; (2) swaling; and (3) prescribed burning. Wildfires are uncontrolled and natural fires that normally occur in drier seasons and can be very destructive. "Swaling" is a term for a type of agricultural burning in which fields are periodically left fallow and then subsequently burned and tilled again. Viro's work centers on northern Europe, but he notes that "swaling was formerly practiced on a very large scale in the forested parts of the world" (1974:8). Swaling has been more commonly referred to in the anthropological literature as "swidden" or "slash-and-burn" agriculture and also has been documented in tropical parts of the world including Indonesia (Geertz 1963), New Guinea (Rappaport 1968) and various other parts of southeast Asia and Oceania (Johnson 1972), and the Amazon Basin of South America (Meggers 1971). One would expect to find a version of this system in forested parts of North America. Viro's (1974:8) final category, "prescribed burning," is "a means of preparing and improving a forest site for a new generation of trees." Here this category is broadened to include the enhancement or increase in any set of resources, plant or animal, that is considered desirable by the burners.

Two additional categories of fire are also relevant to the current study: (1) fire hunting, a form of communal hunting drive (described below); and (2) domestic fire, which is used for food preparation, heating, and other domestic purposes. Domestic fire is probably of minor importance in terms of its direct effects on the overall landscape except where fire escapes from a domestic setting and becomes a wildfire or where the need for wood for domestic purposes becomes great enough to make a substantial impact on the surrounding environment. This last type of impact would tend to increase gradually as a function of length of occupation and the size of the human group. It is expected that, under most conditions, domestic fires had much less impact on the landscape than the other categories previously described.

Hunting with Fire

Fire drives for hunting game were an important use of burning in the Southeast prior to contact. In a survey of the ethnohistoric literature for the Eastern Woodlands, Gregory Waselkov (1978) found evidence for four techniques of deer hunting: (1) stalking; (2) the use of a decoy while stalking; (3) the use of surrounds or drives to water; and (4) the use of surrounds or drives involving fire. The use of fire was associated with only some forms of communal drives.

Characteristically, these fires were made in the form of a ring around an area so that the deer would be driven to the center. They were low brush fires that probably were carefully controlled to enable the hunters to contain the game so they could be killed in such a way that their coveted skins would not be burned or damaged. Control over the fire would have been critical in order to capture the game without losing control of the fire. Fire was used to capture rabbits, deer, bear, turkeys, and "what wild Creatures the Parts afford" (Lefler 1967:17, 127, 215).

Prescribed Burning

Prescribed burning is a technique for clearing areas and enhancing certain resources. For areas farther to the north in New England, there is good evidence that fire was used to stimulate vegetation.

In 1656 Adriaen Van der Donck (1846:150), writing about New Netherlands, noted:

> The Indians have a yearly custom of burning the woods, plains and meadows in the fall of the year, when the leaves have fallen, and when the grass and vegetable substances are dry. . . . Those places which are then passed over are fired in the spring in April. This is done . . . to render hunting easier [for stalking], to thin out and clear the woods of all dead substances and grass, which grow better in the ensuing spring . . . to circumscribe and enclose the game . . . and because game is more easily tracked over burned parts of the woods.

In Massachusetts, Thomas Morton (1632) found that "[t]he Savages . . . burne it [the woods] twize a yeare, viz: at the Spring and the fall of the Leafe."

It appears that the practice of prescribed burning extended to the study area as well. In 1709, Lawson noted for Carolina:

> When these Savages go a hunting, they commonly go out in great Numbers, and oftentimes a great many Days Journey from home, beginning at the coming in of the Winter, that is when the Leaves are fallen from the Trees, and are become Any. 'Tis then they burn the Woods, by setting Fire to the Leaves, and Wither'd Bent and Cross, they do with a Match made of the black Moss that hangs on the Trees in Carolina, and is sometimes above six Foot Long. In Places, where this Moss is not found, (as towards the Mountains) they make Lintels of the Bark of Cypress beatn, which serves as well. (Lefler 1967:215)

William Byrd II described the same practice in early November of 1728 in the area of northern North Carolina and southern Virginia (Wright 1966).

Agricultural Clearing

On April 28, 1607, George Percy, one of the Jamestown settlers, entered these notes in his log: "We marched to those smoakes and found that the Savages had beene there burning downe grasse, as we thought either to make their plantation there, or else to give signes to brign their forces together, and so to give us battell" (Arber 1910:lxii–lxiii; Percy 1907:10–11). Other early settlers in coastal Virginia described this method of clearing trees: "The greatest labour they take, is in planting their corn, for the country naturally is overgrowne with wood. To prepare the ground they bruise the bark of the trees neare the roote, then do they scortch the roots with fire that grow no more. . . . The next yeare with a crooked peece of wood, they beat up the woodes by the rootes, and in that moulds they plant their corne" (Arber 1910:61; Strachey 1849:116).

William Byrd's *Natural History of Virginia*, first published in 1737, provides a description of how "one may clean and clear the land [of coastal Virginia] very easily and conveniently" by the technique used by the Indians:

> when the trees are full of sap, and skin about three or four feet of bark from the trunks, which causes them to dry up, so the foliage falls down. This no sooner happens than they begin at once to work the soil and to sow it with grain, or whatever they wish, which soon spring forth and produces manifold fruit. When the aforementioned trees have become quite withered by the removal of the bark, they then go and cut a broad strip from the nearest green trees, which are standing there, [to a point] as far as they wish to clear, in order to prevent the whole forest from burning. They then set fire to the dry trees, which burn immediately. Thus in a short time a very large section of land can be cleared and made neatly available for planting, [a practice] which saves

the planters very much trouble and expense. (Beatty and Mulloy 1940:92–93).

Similar evidence is lacking for agricultural clearing in the Piedmont.

Gardening

Some plants can be classified as staples, whereas others supplemented the diet or provided some other value to general subsistence, such as medicine or dye. All of these plants, staple or supplemental, may be considered to have been more or less crop plants, because in order to ensure harvests they were planted or at least encouraged. The crop plants are divided into field crops, tree crops, and other crops.

Field Crops

Field and garden crops included corn, beans, squash, sunflowers, gourds, tobacco, possibly maypops, Jerusalem artichokes, sumpweed, maygrass, little barley, and chenopods. The best descriptions of field crops are from the early Jamestown settlers, who considered such information vital to their own survival in coastal Virginia. Captain Smith (Arber 1910:62) noted that the Virginia Indians began to plant in April, but their chief planting occurred in May. They continued planting until the middle of June. This type of successional planting appears to have been common in North America and is considered a security measure against late and early frosts. Such a technique also spreads out the harvest period since not all fruits ripen simultaneously: "What they plant in April they reape in August, for May in September, for Iune [June] in October" (Arber 1910:62).

There is good documentation of interplanting numerous crops in their fields. In 1607, Smith described this manner of planting near the southern Virginia coast: "They make a hole in the earth with a sticke, and into it they put 4 graines of whet and 2 of beanes. These holes they make 4 foote one from another. Ther women and children do continually keep it with weeding, and when it is growne midle high, they hill it about like a hop-yard" (Arber 1910:62). Smith (Arber 1910:63) also noted that in May "also amongst their corne they plant pumpeons (pumpkins) and a fruit like unto a muske millen, but lesse and worse; which they call Macocks (probably squash)." In 1586, along the Carolina coast, Thomas Hariot (Quinn 1955:1:337–42) described a similar practice of interplanting fields of maize with beans, cucurbits, sunflowers, and small-seed crops (discussed below). Reasons or benefits for this practice were suggested. Smith (Arber 1910:cxii) noted that "when the wheat [corn] doe growe up havinge a straw as bigg as a canne reede the beanes runn up theron like our hopps on poles." In 1705, Robert Beverley (Wright 1947:141) of southern Virginia added that "Several kinds of Creeping Vines bearing Fruit, the Indians planted in their Gardens or Fields because they wou'd have Plenty of them always at hand; such as, Musk-melons, Water-melons, Pompions, Cushaws, Macocks, and Gourds."

According to Captain Smith (Arber 1910:63), the Virginia Indians also planted "*Maracocks*, a wild fruit like a lemmon, which also increase infinitely: they begin to ripen in September and continue till the end of October." This is contrary to the statement made by Robert Beverley: "The Maracock, which is the Fruit of what we call the Passion Flower, our Natives did not take the Pains to plant, having enough of it growing every where; tho' they eat it with a great deal of Pleasure" (Wright 1947:143). From these two conflicting accounts it would seem that maypops, which thrive in disturbed field areas, were encouraged and possibly even planted whenever they did not occur substantially as volunteer plants.

There is no direct evidence that the Indians of the region added fertilizer to their fields. In New England, the "traditional" Indian technique of adding a fish to a corn hill dates back to the Pilgrims and an Indian named Squanto in 1621. It now appears that Squanto learned this technique from Europeans when he had been kidnapped some years earlier. At that time, he visited England and various other European settlements in the Old and New Worlds (Ceci 1982).

There is a little information on field rotation, another strategy for maintaining a high crop yield. This technique necessitates the rotation of fields, which leaves some areas fallow so that their nutrients may be regenerated through the process of old field succession. Bartram (1973:353) noted a place that "had formerly been a very flourishing settlement, but the Indians deserted it in search of fresh planting land, which they soon found in a rich vale but a few miles distance over a ridge of hills." Similarly, much farther to the north in 1609, Adriaen Van der Donck (1846) observed the practice of rotating fields in the area called New Netherlands.

Tree Crops

The strongest evidence for orchards or tree crop management comes from Bartram in 1773 near a place called Wrightsboro, Georgia, located 80 miles west of Augusta and probably just south of Athens, where he found old Indian settlements with accompanying fields:

> I observed, in the ancient cultivated fields, 1. Diospyros (persimmon), 2. gleditsia triacanthos (honey locust), 3. prunus chicasaw (chickasaw plum), 4. Callicarpa (beauty berry), 5. morus rubra (red mulberry), 6. juglans exalta (hickory), 7. juglans nigra (black walnut), which inform us, that these trees were cultivated by the ancients, on account of their fruit, as being wholesome and nourishing food. These are natives of the forest, yet they thrive better, and are more fruitful, in cultivated plantations, and the fruit is in

great estimation with the present generation of Indians, particularily juglans exalta, commonly called shell-barked hiccory. (Bartram 1973:38)

Further in his journey, somewhere along the Altamaha River, Bartram climbed a high shore where a venerable oak grew near an ancient Indian field encircled with an open forest of stately pines. The field, "verdered over with succulent grass, and chequered with coppices of fragrant shrubs, offered to my view the Myrica cerifera (wax myrtle), Magnolia glauca, Laurus benzoin (spicebush), Laur. Borbonia (redbay), Rhamnus frangula [buckthorn], Prunus Chicasaw, Prun. laurocerasus (carolina laurel cherry), and others" (Bartram 1973:49). In the "ancient famous town of Sticoe," Bartram (1973:343) found "old Peach and Plumb orchards; some of the trees appeared yet thriving and fruitful."

While traveling up along the Altapaha (Altamaha River), presumably near the same area Bartram visited two hundred years later, Hernando de Soto's men found a province of "peaceful and domesticated" people where there were "very large mulberry trees, although they had seen them elsewhere, the other were nothing in comparison to these" (Varner and Varner 1951:269). About two leagues from a town in the province of Cofachiqui, probably near present-day Camden, South Carolina (Hudson et al. 1985:724), de Soto's men found "a pretty place, cooled by great groves of mulberries and other trees heavy with fruits" (Varner and Varner 1951:296). Further on in that same province

they journeyed a full league in garden-like lands where there were many trees, both those which bore fruit and others; and among these trees one could travel on horseback without any difficulty for they were so far apart that they appeared to have been planted by hand. During the whole . . . league [they] spread out gathering the fruit and noting the fertility of the soil. In this way they came to Talomeco, a town of five hundred houses situated on an eminence overlooking a gorge of the river. (Varner and Varner 1951:314)

In southern coastal Virginia near Jamestown, an area that had a relatively dense Indian population, the early European settlers observed:

> Wheresoever we landed upon this River, we saw the good-liest Woods as Beech, Oke, Cedar, Cypresse, Walnuts, Sassa-fras, and Vines in great abundance, which hang in great clusters on many Trees, and other Trees unknowne; and all the grounds be spred with many sweet and delicate flowres of diverse colours and kinds. There are also many frutes as Strawberries, Mulberries, Rasberries, and Fruites unknowne. (Arber 1910:lxviii–lxix; Percy 1907:171)

The proximity of this described scene to actual Indian villages is difficult to determine; however, recall the quote in the introductory section that described a view "as though it had been in any Garden or orchard in England" (Arber 1910:lxviii) as they approached an Indian town.

Other Crops

Several other plants not considered field or tree crops were nevertheless very important to the economy of Native groups in the study area. Many of these crops thrive in open areas. These include a small-seeded plant called mattoume, a woody evergreen shrub called yaupon, and various types of fruit and berry bushes, including blackberries, huckleberries, raspberries, and strawberries. Some of the herb and root crops are found in areas of greater shade and moisture, such as marshes, swamps, bogs, or more mature forests.

With the exception of yaupon, there is no evidence that any of these other crops were planted. The leaves of this shrub were commonly used for a tea known as the Black Drink. Yaupon prefers maritime and coastal plain environments, although it has been documented as far into the interior as Oklahoma, Arkansas, Tennessee, and Kentucky (Merrill 1979). Its dispersal outside of its native environment was due primarily to trade. There is, however, some evidence that it was transplanted to settlements in the Piedmont and the Appalachian highlands that were out of its normal range (Merrill 1979). James Adair observed that it grew along the sea coast of the two Carolinas, Georgia, and Florida. "The Indians transplant, and are extremely fond of it" (Adair 1775:128). In the vale of the Cherokee town of Jore, William Bartram saw "a little grove" of yaupon, which he said was the only place in the Cherokee country that he had seen it grow. According to him, "the Indians call it the beloved tree, and are very careful to keep it pruned and cultivated" (Bartram 1973:357).

Several small-seed crops have been identified archaeologically (Gremillion 1984; Yarnell and Black 1985). These include sumpweed (*Iva annua*), maygrass (*Phalaris caroliniana*), little barley (*Hordeum pusillum*), and possibly chenopod (*Chenopodium bushianum*). Unfortunately, there is little historic documentation of their use. Lawson (Lefler 1967:83) identified lambsquarters (*Chenopodium* sp.) but failed to indicate whether or not the Indians used it. There are only a few actual accounts of specifically identified small-seed crops. Thus, their identity remains partially conjecture. In 1586, along the coast of the Carolinas, Thomas Hariot described one such plant: "There is an herbe which in Duch is called Melden. Som of those that I describe it unto take it to be a kinde of seed thereof they make a thicke broth, and pottage of a very good taste: of the stalke by burning into ashes they make a kinde of salt earth, wherewithall many use sometimes to season their brothe; other salte they know not. Wee ourselves used the leaves also for pot-hearbes" (Quinn 1955:1:340; Sturtevant 1965:66). William Sturtevant suggests this plant probably was either *Amaranthus* sp. or *Chenopodium* sp.

Captain Smith noted a plant called mattoume that "groweth as our bents do in meddows." Smith said the seed was much like rye although much smaller. "This they use for a dainty bread buttered with deare suet" (Arber 1910:58). This small-seed may have been one or more of the seed plants mentioned above. The plant's habit of growing as "bents" suggests that it probably was a stiff, grasslike plant, such as little barley or maygrass.

Many known crops, such as berries, also occurred in these open areas. In the Congaree area near present-day Columbia, South Carolina, Lawson found "great copses of many Acres that bore nothing but Bushes, about the Bigness of Box-trees; which [in the season] afford great Quantities of Small Blackberries, very pleasant Fruits, and much like our Bluest or Huckleberries, that grow on Heaths in England" (Lefler 1967:34). A little past the Congaree he found old fields "now spread with fine bladed Grass, and Strawberry-Vines" (Lefler 1967:38).

Bartram (1973:354–55) made a field trip into the mountains near Cowe (in western North Carolina), where he and his comrade were delighted to find "a most enchanting" if somewhat fanciful view:

> a vast expanse of green meadows and strawberry fields; a meandering river gliding through, saluting in its various turnings the swellings, green turfy knolls, embellished with pasterres of flowers and fruitful strawberry beds; flocks of turkies strolling about them; herds of deer prancing in the meads or bounding over the hills; companies of young, innocent Cherokee virgins, some busy gathering the rich fragrant fruits, other having already filled their baskets. (Bartram 1973:354–55)

Smith claimed that another berry, called "Ocoughtanamnis," was "very much like unto Capers." These grew in "the watry valleyes" (Arber 1910:58).

Herbs, roots, and other types of plants with high water content
are difficult to recover archaeologically, although occasionally seeds
from these plants have been identified. Of the herbs, Captain Smith
mentioned several, including "Violets, Purslin, Sorrell, . . . besides
many we used whose names we know not [that] are commonly
dispersed throughout the woods, [and are] good for brothes and
sallets [salads]" (Arber 1910:58). Their chief root crop, which Smith
called Tockawhoughe, "groweth like a flagge in low muddy
freshes" (Arber 1910:58).

SCHEDULING

According to Captain Smith, the coastal Virginia Indians recognized five seasons of the year: (1) Papanow (winter); (2) Cattapeuk
(spring); (3) Cohattayough (summer); (4) Nepinough (the earing of
their corn); and (5) Taquitock (the harvest and fall of leaf). Major
feasts and sacrifices occurred from September until the middle of
November, when "they have plenty of fruits as well planted as
naturall, as corne greene and ripe, fish, fowle, and wilde beastes
exceeding fat" (Arber 1910:61). Shortly afterward, the Indians made
excursions to the mountains, where they would burn and hunt. It
is probable that burning and other clearing types of activities took
place in the late fall and spring in the mountains and near coastal
and piedmont settlements as well. Smith provided this synopsis of
their seasonal dietary round:

> In March and Aprill they live much upon their fishing,
> weares; and feed on fish, Turkies and squirrels. In May and
> Iune they plant their fieldes; and live most of Acornes,
> walnuts, and fish. But to mend their diet, some disperse
> themselves in small companies, and live upon fish, beasts,
> crabs, oysters, land Torteyses, strawberries, mulberries, and
> such like. In Iune, Iulie, and August, they feed upon the

rootes of Tocknough, berries, fish, and greene wheat. (Arber 1910:68)

This schedule would allow the concentration of people at spring and fall in times of plenty so that the major tasks of harvesting, clearing, and planting could be accomplished, as well as allowing groups to split into smaller units in times of scarcity if necessary.

Although most of the information pertaining to management and scheduling of food crops has been drawn from an area of coastal southern Virginia, it is fairly safe to conjecture that similar types of strategies, with modifications, were used throughout the study region. Evidence from the other areas is not as extensive as Smith's account, but the details we do have fit well into his general scheme. A diagram is provided to illustrate the annual seasonal round of subsistence activities and available food crops (see fig. 9.1).

HABITAT, RANGE, AND DISTURBANCE

These crops were among the many plants and animals mentioned by early explorers (see table 9.2 for plants and animals reported from several Late Prehistoric and Protohistoric sites of north-central and western North Carolina).

PLANTS

The field and garden crops are not discussed in detail here, other than to note that they were placed in open, disturbed areas created and maintained by humans. Most of the important crop plants were dependent upon such areas and would not have survived in less-disturbed habitats. Some of these crops, such as maypops, were volunteer plants, meaning they did not have to be planted; however, most such crops relied upon humans for their propagation.

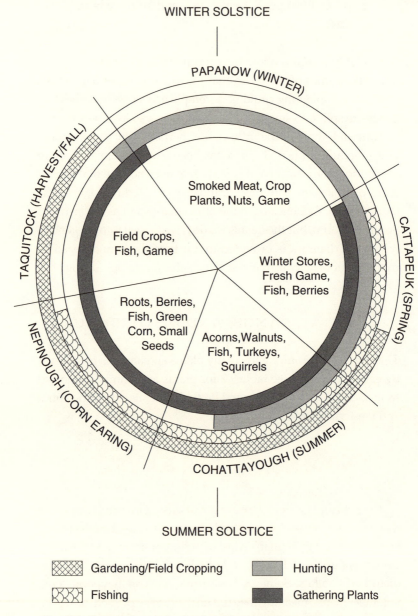

WINTER SOLSTICE

PAPANOW (WINTER)

TAQUITOCK (HARVEST/FALL)

CATTAPEUK (SPRING)

NEPINOUGH (CORN EARING)

COHATTAYOUGH (SUMMER)

Smoked Meat, Crop Plants, Nuts, Game

Field Crops, Fish, Game

Winter Stores, Fresh Game, Fish, Berries

Roots, Berries, Fish, Green Corn, Small Seeds

Acorns, Walnuts, Fish, Turkeys, Squirrels

SUMMER SOLSTICE

Gardening/Field Cropping   Hunting

Fishing   Gathering Plants

Fig. 9.1. Seasonal round of subsistence activities for coastal Virginia Indians ca. 1607.

TABLE 9.2

Animals and Plants Mentioned by Early Explorers or Identified from Late Prehistoric and Protohistoric Archaeological Sites in North-Central and Western North Carolina

Animals/ Plants	Scientific Name	Historical Reference	Archaeological Reference
ANIMALS			
Beaver	*Castor canadensis*	Lefler 1967	Holm 1985
Black Bear	*Ursus americanus*	Lefler 1967	Holm 1985*
Bluejay	*Cyanocitta cristata*	Lefler 1967	Holm 1985
Buffalo	*Bison bison*	Lefler 1967	—
Catfish	Various genera	Lefler 1967	Holm 1985
Cottontail Rabbit	*Sylvilagus floridanus*	Lefler 1967	Holm 1985*
Deer	*Odocoileus virginianus*	Lefler 1967; Bartram 1973	Holm 1985*
Elk	*Cervus elaphus*	Lefler 1967	—
Fox	*Vulpes vulpes*	Lefler 1967	Holm 1985
Horse[a]	*Equus caballus*	Lefler 1967	Holm 1985
Killdeer	*Charadrius vociferus*	Lefler 1967	Holm 1985
Lesser Scaup	*Aythya affinis*	—	Holm 1985
Mink	*Mustela vison*	Lefler 1967	—
Mountain Lion	*Felis concolor*	Lefler 1967	Holm 1985
Muskrat	*Ondatra zibethicus*	Lefler 1967	—
Opossum	*Didelphus virginiana*	—	Holm 1985
Otter	*Lutra canadensis*	Lefler 1967	—
Passenger Pigeon	*Ectopistes migratorius*	Lefler 1967	Holm 1985
Pig[a]	*Sus scrofa*	Lefler 1967	Holm 1985
Quail	*Colinus virginianus*	Lefler 1967	Holm 1985*
Raccoon	*Procyon lotor*	Lefler 1967	Holm 1985
Skunk	*Mephitis* spp.	Lefler 1967	Holm 1985
Sparrow	Various genera	Lefler 1967	Holm 1985
Squirrel	*Sciurus* spp.	Lefler 1967	Holm 1985*
Sucker	Various genera	Lefler 1967	Holm 1985
Toad & Frog	Various genera	Lefler 1967	Holm 1985
Turkey	*Meleagris gallopavo*	Lefler 1967; Bartram 1973	Holm 1985*
Turtle	Various genera	Arber 1910; Lefler 1967	Holm 1985
Wildcat	*Felis rufus*	Lefler 1967	—

TABLE 9.2 (continued)

ANIMALS/ PLANTS	SCIENTIFIC NAME	HISTORICAL REFERENCE	ARCHAEOLOGICAL REFERENCE
Wolf/Dog	*Canis* spp.	Lefler 1967	Holm 1985
Woodpecker	Various genera	Lefler 1967	Holm 1985
PLANTS			
Bean	*Phaseolus* spp., various legume genera		Wilson 1977; Gremillion 1984
Beauty Berry	*Callicarpa americana*	Lefler 1967; Bartram 1973	—*
Bramble (Blackberry)	*Rubus* spp.	Lefler 1967	Wilson 1977; Gremillion 1984*
Buckthorn	*Rhamnus caroliniana*	Bartram 1973	—
Cedar	*Juniperus virginiana*	Arber 1910; Lefler 1967	—
Chenopod	*Chenopodium berlandieri*	Lefler 1967	Gremillion 1984*
Cherry	*Prunus* spp.	Lefler 1967; Bartram 1973	—*
Chestnut	*Castanea dentata*	Lefler 1967	—*
Corn	*Zea mays*	Arber 1910	—
Cypress	*Taxodium distichum*	Arber 1910; Lefler 1967	—*
Crabapple	*Malus* spp.	Lefler 1967	—
Grape	*Vitis* spp.	Lefler 1967	Wilson 1977; Gremillion 1984*
Hawberry	*Viburnum* spp.	Lefler 1967	—
Hawthorn	*Crataegus* spp.	Lefler 1967	Wilson 1977, Gremillion 1984
Hazelnut	*Corylus* spp.	Lefler 1967	Wilson 1977*
Hickory	*Carya* spp.	Lefler 1967	Wilson 1977; Gremillion 1984*
Honey Locust	*Gleditsia triacanthos*	Lefler 1967; Bartram 1973	—*
Huckleberry/ Blueberry	*Gaylussacia* spp./ *Vaccinium* spp.	Lefler 1967	Wilson 1977; Gremillion 1984
Little Barley	*Hordeum pusillum*	—	Gremillion 1984*
Maygrass	*Phalaris caroliniana*	—	Gremillion 1984*
Maypops (Maracocks)	*Passiflora incarnata*	Arber 1910	Wilson 1977; Gremillion 1984*
Mattoume	unknown	Arber 1910	—*

TABLE 9.2 (continued)

ANIMALS/ PLANTS	SCIENTIFIC NAME	HISTORICAL REFERENCE	ARCHAEOLOGICAL REFERENCE
Mulberry	*Morus rubra*	Varner & Varner 1951 Arber 1910; Lefler 1967 Bartram 1973	—*
Oak Acorn	*Quercus* spp.	—	Wilson 1977; Gremillion 1984*
Peach[a]	*Prunus persica*	Lefler 1967	Wilson 1977; Gremillion 1984*
Persimmon	*Diospyros virginiana*	Lefler 1967	Wilson 1977; Gremillion 1984*
Pine	*Pinus* spp.	Lefler 1967; Bartram 1973	Wilson 1977
Plum	*Prunus* spp.	Lefler 1967	Wilson 1977; Gremillion 1984*
Pokeweed	*Phytolacca americana*	Lefler 1967	Wilson 1977
Purslin (Purslane)	*Portulaca* spp.	Arber 1910; Lefler 1967	—*
Raspberry	*Rubus* spp.	Arber 1910; Lefler 1967	—*
Sassafras	*Sassafras albidum*	Arber 1910; Lefler 1967; Bartram 1973	—
Sorrel	*Rumex* spp.	Arber 1910	—*
Spicebush	*Lindera* spp.	Lefler 1967; Bartram 1973	—
Squash	Various cucurbit genera	Arber 1910	Wilson 1977; Gremillion 1984*
Strawberry	*Fragaria virginiana*	Arber 1910; Lefler 1967; Bartram 1973	—*
Sumpweed	*Iva annua*	—	Gremillion 1984*
Sunflower	*Helianthus annuus*	Lefler 1967	Wilson 1977*
Sweet Maple	*Acer saccharum*	Lefler 1967	—
Tobacco	*Nicotiana rustica*	Arber 1910; Lefler 1967	—
Tockawhoughe (Root Crop)	unknown	Arber 1910	—*
Violet	*Viola* spp.	Arber 1910	—*

TABLE 9.2 (continued)

ANIMALS/ PLANTS	SCIENTIFIC NAME	HISTORICAL REFERENCE	ARCHAEOLOGICAL REFERENCE
Walnut	*Juglans* spp.	Arber 1910; Lefler 1967; Bartram 1973	Wilson 1977; Gremillion 1984*
Wax Myrtle	*Myrica cerifera*	Lefler 1967; Bartram 1973	Wilson 1977
Yaupon	*Ilex vomitoria*	Lefler 1967; Bartram 1973	—*

[a] Introduced by Europeans.
* Mentioned in text.

Other field and garden crops, such as some of the small-seeded crops, may have been field followers, relying on the open disturbed edge areas between fields and other types of patches. Thus, in a sense these edge areas should also be considered a kind of patch. The domestic status of these small-seeded crops has been discussed elsewhere (Yarnell 1983) and will not be dealt with here. However, it is important to note that in general these small-seeded crops prefer open, grassy (meadowy or marshy) types of conditions.

The nut-tree crops include hickory nuts, walnuts, hazelnuts, and acorns. All of these are more productive in open or edge areas, where they receive ample sunlight and space (Smith and Hawley 1962:32; Talalay et al. 1984:340). For example, open-grown hickories produce about eight times more nuts than closed-canopy, old-growth hickories. The roots of *Juglans nigra* even produce a toxin called juglone that inhibits other walnuts from growing nearby (Talalay et al. 1984:341–42).

According to Charles Deam (1921), the hickories typically are highly susceptible to fire, so that other means of clearing might have been employed in order to create sufficient openings for these trees, while protecting them from fire damage (cited in Talalay et al. 1984:338). No evidence is available for the susceptibility to fire of the walnut trees and hazelnut shrubs. Laurie Talalay et al. (1984:343) have suggested that the characteristic small thickets of hazelnut would be relatively rare prehistorically except around natural openings or where disturbed areas had been created by slash-and-burn agricultural practices.

The numerous species of oaks in the study area and the difficulty in identifying acorns to species present extreme problems for establishing preferred habitat conditions based on their presence historically or archaeologically. Furthermore, Karl Petruso and Jere Wickens (1984) have noted the difficulty in determining criteria for evaluating acorn productivity: even trees of the same species may vary considerably in their productivity. They observed two generalizations: (1) trees that are good producers in any given year tend to be good producers overall; and (2) productivity of a given tree appears to be dependent upon the surface area of its crown. This would suggest that, in general, oaks are more productive in open areas. Another important observation for tree crops is that older trees tend to produce less than younger mature trees (Petruso and Wickens 1984:371). In other studies, Silas Little (1974) and Edward Komarek (1974) have noted that many of the oaks, including *Quercus virginiana*, *Quercus laevis*, and *Quercus myrtifolia*, have strategies such as crown or stump sprouting that allow them to survive and often thrive (in terms of productivity) in conditions of frequent brush or low-intensity fires. *Quercus prinus*, however, has a low tolerance for fire.

Fruit trees include plum, cherry, persimmon, peach, and mulberry. Persimmon is a native that occurs in dry deciduous forests, pinelands, and old fields (Radford et al. 1968:826). The peach tree was introduced historically. Its rapid dispersal in Native North America, which is demonstrated through observations by John Lawson (Lefler 1967) in 1701 and William Bartram (1973) in old fields in 1773, was likely due to the Indians' previous knowledge of its relative, the plum. Lawson noted that both peach and mulberry were "spontaneous" (Lefler 1967:115, 117), presumably meaning they grew from seed with little or no encouragement.

Although Bartram (1973:38) was certain the Chickasaw plum was native to America, he stated in a footnote that he saw it only in old, deserted Indian plantations, never wild in the forests. He suspected it was brought from "beyond the Mississippi, by the Chicasaws." Similarly, Radford et al. (1968:569) note that the Carolina laurel cherry is "believed to be rare as a native plant, more abundant as an escape from cultivation." Overall, the *Prunus* spp. appear to prefer open or edge areas. Little evidence is available of their reactions to burned areas. *Prunus pennsylvanica*, the fire or pin cherry, prefers cleared or burned areas (Radford et al. 1968:568).

The brambles (*Rubus* spp.), including blackberry, dewberry, and raspberry bushes, "occur in colonies or 'patches' in open and edge situations" (Munson 1984:469). Similarly, one species of strawberry (*Fragaria virginiana*) generally prefers old fields and edge areas (Radford et al. 1968:534–35).

ANIMALS

Citing numerous studies in North America, J. F. Bendell (1974) noted some of the animals that favor areas opened by fires, including white-tailed and black-tailed deer, jack rabbits, moose, black bears, brush rabbits, hares, elks, blue geese, muskrats, beavers, coyotes, and cougars. Because fires produce higher numbers of game on which to prey, humans can also be considered animals that benefit, at least indirectly, from this process.

At a more basic level, animals react indirectly to the responses of plants to environmental conditions. For this region in general, the short-term effects of burning are to "increase protein, phosphorus and calcium content of the grasses, to enhance their palatability and to improve the composition of the rangeland for animals. . . . [N]utritive qualities do not last more than a few months after spring burning, but this is usually the time when livestock and plants need extra protein and minerals" (Komarek 1974:260–61).

In an exhaustive study of the literature on fire ecology and game management, Paul Mellars (1976) found that many factors contribute to the productivity of game animals, including the intensity (i.e., heat and duration) of the fire, the type of vegetation burned, and the periodicity of burning. Much of this section is based on his sources. R. D. Taber and J. L. Murphy (1971) have noted that prescribed burning generally tends to increase the carrying capacity of herbivores by (1) markedly improving soil fertility by releasing a rich supply of nutrients (i.e., rapid recycling of nutrients); (2) allowing a greater penetration of sunlight; and (3) fire pruning, which encourages vigorous sprouting of shrubs and mature trees.

In a study carried out in a mixed oak forest in Pennsylvania, R. F. Ribinski (1968) observed an area where a substantial overstory of tree canopy had been destroyed. Two years later, the browse accessible to white-tailed deer was ten times that available in adjacent unburned sections. After two more years, the browse availability had been reduced to half that available two years earlier.

I. McT. Cowan et al. (1950:250) observed that clearing and burning can lead to a marked improvement in the nutritive properties of forage, although these changes are short-lived. In a study in Maryland, J. B. DeWitt and J. V. Derby (1955) noted a deciduous forest that had been completely cleared in 1942 using a low-intensity, "reburn" prescribed fire. Rapid increase in protein content of four out of the five plant species selected for the study was found, but the beneficial effects of this fire had largely disappeared by the following year. A hot, uncontrolled fire in 1950 produced substantial increases (10–26%) in protein, with more increase the following year. Also, there was a slight decrease in fiber content, but no consistent changes of ash, ether extract, or nitrogen-free extract (Mellars 1976:19).

Naturally increased available browse has an effect on the population of herbivores. Increases in available browse due to disturbance caused by burning and logging have been correlated with increased numbers of large mammals, including moose, black-tailed deer, white-tailed deer, red-tailed deer, and sheep (Mellars 1976:22–23). For example, J. A. Cumming (1969:259) found that tree felling and burning of pine forest in New Jersey increased the white-tailed deer population from approximately six per square mile to thirty-eight per square mile. Critics have cautioned that this increase may be due in part to a diversion of game from other less-productive areas (Taber and Dasman 1957). One study on moose in a contained area demonstrated that, although diversion may be one factor, overall increase in total numbers also occurred (Mellars 1976; Spencer and Chatelain 1953:546). This may be because of an overall improvement in general health due to better forage (Einarsen 1946).

Range managers have developed recommendations of "optimal areas of burns" for various animals. For deer, the ideal range must include patches of burned areas interspersed with areas of older growth of various stages (Cowan 1956:605; Hendricks 1968:225; Mellars 1976:26–27). The older growth provides equally essential protection from predators, winter cold, and summer heat. Similarly, "spot burning" has been recommended for such game birds as quail, turkey, and prairie chicken (Mellars 1976). Too few small patches, however, make for overbrowsing of the more desirable browse and permit undesirable browse of the overstory, which causes range deterioration (Hendricks 1968:227).

In the southern forests, research has demonstrated that the season of burn affects the productivity and variability of available forage. Using 20-year measurements, C. E. Lewis and T. J. Harshbarger (1976:18) found that the "best" burning cycle for deer and turkeys was periodic winter burnings. For quail, they recommended annual winter burnings. J. Larry Landers (1981) found that, for quail, annual winter burning provides food (e.g., insects during summer, seeds during fall and winter), brood habitat, and control of parasites. Excluding fires for two to three years allowed the development of roughs for nesting habitat and summer fruit production. Landers also recommended developing thickets for escape cover and providing hard-mast components. Limited evidence suggests that turkeys benefit from prescribed fires in ways very similar to quail (Hurst 1981).

For bear in the southern forests, Robert Hamilton (1981) recommended prescribed burning on a three-year rotation in coastal areas and a five- to seven-year rotation in mixed pine/hardwoods. He added that patch edges (ecotones) between pine or pine-scrub oak ridges and Carolina bays or hardwood swamps should be burned during winter on a medium to long rotation to enhance berry production.

There is very little information on the effects of fire on squirrels. Roy Kirkpatrick and Henry Mosby (1981) have reasoned that since squirrels are dependent upon hardwood forests, and current prescribed burning practices are intended to keep down hardwoods, the practice would be detrimental. Of course, this is only true for the method practiced by range managers in the South today. Since the productivity of some hardwoods, notably many oaks, can be enhanced with small-scale periodic burning, prescribed burning cannot be conclusively proven to be entirely detrimental to the habitat preferences of squirrels.

In summary, current range-management research indicates that a pattern of prescribed burning in small patches, leaving adequate cover and edge areas, can increase the productivity of many game animals. Aboriginally, such a practice would have increased the richness and yield of many important animals and plant crops in the native Southeast.

ABORIGINAL LAND USE
AND MANAGEMENT

BRUSH MANAGEMENT

The major and most basic result of human disturbance in the Southeast, as in most of the nonindustrial world, has been through the process of forest and brush clearing. From an ecological stand-point, the process of clearing has important consequences for the natural environment. Clearing serves to open up an area, to rejuven-ate it so that ecological pioneers or shade-intolerant types of plants and animals may benefit. Fire was a major technological tool used by the Indians for clearing, so it is worthwhile to consider how it operates in detail.

Studies have demonstrated that many factors affect the intensity of burning. Fire-control experts consider fire to be derived from a triad of oxygen, heat, and fuel. Knowledge of this seemingly com-monplace notion is nevertheless critical if one is to use fire as a tool. For purposes here, the focus is on vegetation fires, where the fuel is some form of plant life. The intensity of heat is based on several factors, including the amount of resin and moisture in the fuel. Another factor is the density of the fuel stand, including the amount of dead wood and other litter on the ground. The density and amount of potential fuel at different heights in a stand of wood act differentially to induce the layers to be more or less susceptible to burning. In areas where there is a considerable quantity of surface litter, one would expect a fire to sweep through a stand along the floor level. Where there is adequate combustible fuel, fire will spread up into the major branches of trees or, if the fire gets hot or high enough, it is likely to climb up to the treetops and spread as a crown fire.

The added amount of oxygen available at the tops of the trees contributes significantly to the spread of such a fire. Consequently, different kinds of trees or plant associations react in different ways to fire. For example, if a crown fire gets established in a stand of pines with their high resin content and concentration of needle-laden branches at the tops of the trees, the fire is likely to spread rapidly and can easily get out of control. If low brush and shrubs are maintained by controlled burning, there is less opportunity for an uncontrollable crown fire to occur. Additional factors include various weather conditions such as humidity, temperature, and air currents.

Certain types of vegetation are more suited to repeated burning, clearing, or other types of disturbance. Studies in fire ecology have identified types of plant and animal life that tend to have higher levels of productivity resulting from their residence in areas subject to periodic burning. Such populations or associations of populations may be called "fire subclimax" or "fire disclimax" communities. The incidence and productivity of many organisms are higher in such secondary successional stage (or disturbed conditions) than under conditions closer to a climax-level association.

PATCH MANAGEMENT

In general, prescribed burning, unlike wildfires, produces a patchy landscape, as not all places burn evenly. Some areas miss being burned altogether, and some are completely devastated. The remaining patchwork is a heterogenous mosaic of small patches or associations at various successional levels. This diversity of patches may be one of the most crucial long-term roles of burning. A list of the general types of anthropogenic patches for the study area is provided in table 9.3.

Hunting Camps and
Animal Crop Management

Prescribed burning may have occurred in conjunction with communal hunts when large groups gathered. At this time, the participants would have benefited from having greater numbers of people for both hunting and clearing activities. The use of fire would have served both purposes. Numerous low brush fires, if

TABLE 9.3

Types of Anthropogenic Patches in the Native Southeast.

PATCH TYPE	GENERAL CHARACTERISTICS	IMPORTANT RESOURCES
Hunting Camps	Circular burned patches in forested areas away from settlements; probably less than 3 mi. wide	deer, berries, nuts, turkeys, bears, squirrels, rabbits
Fields/Gardens	Open cleared areas near habitation sites	corn, squash, beans, maypops, sunflowers, small-seed crops
Habitations	Circular areas often surrounded by gardens and orchards	herbs, small-seeded crops
Edge Areas/ Meadows	Open grassy and "weedy" areas bordering settlements and between different patches	small-seed crops, turkeys, other game birds, berries, rabbits, squirrels
Old Fields	Similar to edge areas but more woody brush	same as edge areas plus some young fruit and nut trees (mostly saplings) and shrubs
Parklands/ Orchards	Open forested areas surrounding established settlements	adult nut and fruit trees and shrubs, deer, squirrel, and other small games
Wetlands/ Swamps/ Marshes	Shadier, wetter wooded areas or swamps/marshes	herbs, root crops, berries
Shorelines	In water or adjacent to water's edge	fish, shellfish, turtles, frogs/turtles

controlled, would be unlikely to spread out of control and up into the trees and would have maintained the parklike landscape described by early writers. Thus, the landscape characterized by Indian hunting activities was a series of small patches, each probably no more than a few miles wide. Repeated periodic burning in the vicinity of previous hunts would have had the overall effect of a mosaic of small patches at various successional stages.

Waselkov's (1978) research on deer hunting suggests that fire drives were commonly used by small Piedmont Indian groups only after contact when the deerskin trade became important. He added that, prehistorically, communal drives probably would have been used primarily by larger groups along the coast for annual or special-occasion feasts held by high chiefs.

Waselkov's work (1978) is provocative yet problematic. The most descriptive early account of Indian burning practices comes from the Jamestown settlement near the mouth of the Chesapeake Bay, not coastal Carolina (Arber 1910:61). Our best information from the Piedmont was recorded 100 years later by John Lawson (Lefler 1967:215). There appears to be no earlier evidence for the presence or absence of fire drives in the Piedmont. Where there are good descriptions of coastal groups, there are equally good accounts of individual stalking methods (Arber 1910). This does not discount Waselkov's hypothesis, but it remains to be substantiated by reliable ethnohistorical or archaeological data.

The fire-drive technique was used to collect not only deer, but also other game including bears, turkeys, and rabbits. The evidence indicates that all of these animals have positive feedback responses to certain types of prescribed burning. This suggests that repeated seasonal burning by the Indians was not actually a "hunting" technique but more of a "harvesting" technique. Circular brush burning had the short-term result of entrapping game and the long-term effect of stimulating the foliage preferred by the game, which helped to ensure future harvests in the same vicinity (Kozlowski and Algren 1974; Mellars 1976).

Forested Parklands

Prescribed burning has been associated with the "park-like" setting described by so many early European explorers (Day 1953; Guffey 1977). Stanley Guffey has suggested that the "deserts" referred to by Bartram (1973) and John Smith in 1607 (Arber 1910) on the Coastal Plain may have been maintained by burning. This remains to be demonstrated. It is likely that extremely expansive open areas were the result of occasional natural wildfires, which could have had far-reaching effects if left unchecked during a dry season. Parklike woodlands within several miles of large, well-established settlements were probably due to periodic burning by Indians. This type of landscaping would have had the additional reward of reducing the probability of large wildfires that could devastate their resource areas.

Plant remains from archaeological sites in the Southeast indicate a reliance on various tree crops (Yarnell and Black 1985), and there is some direct historical evidence that the Indians had something approximating European orchards, gardens, or parklands surrounding their settlements. Nevertheless, preconceived notions of early European explorers restricted their abilities to identify other tree management strategies, and they rarely recognized them. Indirect information relating to tree management is found in the descriptions of explorers traveling in the vicinity of well-established Indian villages. These park or woodland areas were full of fruit, nut, and other useful trees, as well as useful understory shrubs such as berry bushes and large and small game.

In areas of dense population and well-established settlements, human selection favored trees considered economically important. The proximity to settlements, population density, and duration of habitation in a specific locality increased these selection pressures. Areas within a few miles of well-established villages would have appeared to the European eye as gardens and orchards. In such cases, whether the Indians deliberately opened areas or planted trees would be less important than the results of their general management strategies.

Field Crop Management

There is good evidence for the use of fire for agricultural clearing along coastal Virginia. Similar evidence is lacking for this practice in the Piedmont. However, given the late date of accounts in the Piedmont, the technique of clearing land may not have been considered noteworthy. Also, field-clearing activities were seasonal and oftentimes may have been missed by travelers. From Lawson's accounts of fall clearing in conjunction with hunting (Lefler 1967), it is safe to assume that Piedmont residents, at least in part, practiced the same tradition of scheduling and burning techniques as their coastal counterparts.

The Indians of this region practiced a series of gardening techniques, including staggered planting times, planting in evenly spaced holes, and interplanting different kinds of crops. These methods appear to have been standard practice through much of the New World. There are several advantages to planting a variety of crops together.

A benefit of interplanting young squash and melon plants between corn and bean plants is that the young seedlings are protected from direct sunlight by growing in the shade of the more mature corn and bean plants. As the vine plants mature, they serve to retain moisture in the soil for all the plants.

Beans are good companion plants to corn because beans are able to produce most of their necessary supply of nitrogen through their symbiotic relationship with the microorganisms called *Rhizobium*. These bacteria, attached to the roots of legume plants such as beans, are effective in "nitrogen fixation" or the conversion of atmospheric nitrogen (N_2) into a form of nitrogen usable by the plants (Hausen-builler 1978). This leaves much of the nitrogen in the soil available for use by other plants, such as corn, that are not able to fix their own nitrogen. Conservation of nitrogen is essential when the soils are naturally nutrient poor or there is repeated cropping without the addition of fertilizer.

Soil ecologist Edward H. Graham (1944:50) has noted that "Southern farmers long ago learned" that the following types of vegetation cover can be cleared and corn can be grown for the specified amount of years without declining yields: longleaf pines (3 years); longleaf and shortleaf pines (5–7 years); mixed oaks and hickories (10–12 years); and shortleaf pines and oaks (12–15 years). After these times, fertilizer must be added to the ground if yields are to be maintained. This is due to the varying rates of depletion of soil nutrients and minerals from the diverse soil types supporting these different types of vegetation.

It is likely that traditional Indian techniques of mixed cropping and plant spacing conserved nutrients to a greater extent than the modern agricultural practices of row planting and monocropping do. Nevertheless, some nutrient depletion eventually would have occurred despite their more highly adapted gardening techniques. This means that in order to maintain high crop yields, the Indians had to practice field rotation or fertilization of their fields. From historical evidence, it appears that field rotation, an alternative to adding fertilizer to the soil, was the solution used by Native Americans for maintaining themselves in a general locality. At times, soil depletion probably caused them to move their settlements to nearby vicinities.

Edge Areas, Old Fields, and "Weedy" Crops

Several small-seed crops, notably sumpweed, chenopod, maygrass, and little barley (Gremillion 1984), have been recovered archaeologically from this region but were not recognized by early explorers as field crop plants. As in the case of tree crops, this was probably due in part to the biases of the European attitude about what constituted a "crop." When they were noted, they were treated as a curiosity (e.g., Quinn 1955:1:340; Sturtevant 1965) or were compared to a smaller version of a larger-seeded grass with which Europeans were more familiar (Arber 1910:58). For these crops, our most substantial evidence for their nature, habit, and development remains in the archaeological record.

For the most part, the adventitious nature of the crop plants, or their preference for open areas, allowed them to thrive in disturbed conditions created by humans. Crops of this sort have sometimes been called "camp followers," as they often occur in disturbed areas in and around habitation sites. Open areas included meadows, old fields, and edge areas between different types of patches.

Wetlands

Plants that needed moister or shadier environments, such as some herb and root crops, were less likely to have been maintained by humans, although ensuring an adequate supply of such resources near habitation sites may at times have necessitated protecting them from fire and other types of disturbance. Whatever the criteria affecting plant dispersal, we can assume that the Indians recognized the habitat conditions of these plants, because they regularly relied upon them. They would have taken certain steps to control such conditions in order to ensure the well-being of their crops.

INTENTIONALITY

A question remains: how purposeful was this anthropogenic patchwork of the Native Southeast? In November 1728, William Byrd II noted that the "atmosphere was so smoaky all round us . . . from the fireing of the Woods by the Indians, for we were now near the Route the Northern Savages take . . . to War" (Wright 1966: 257–58). Byrd considered these fires to be due to campfires left burning, "which, catching the dry Leaves they ly near, soon put the adjacent Woods into a flame." He added that his men had recently seen evidence of a fire that had gone out of control where some people had a small hunting camp. He apparently did not consider the possibility that the fire was deliberately spread from the camp for the purpose of driving game.

It would seem unlikely for people who lived a lifestyle made possible by virtue of fire not to understand the principles well enough to guard against accidental spreading, unless there was little or no reason to prevent this. If there was danger of damage from the fire, a great investment would be made to control for that hazard. It follows that if fires were frequently allowed to get loose, as Byrd suggested, the benefits of this practice of lack of caution probably outweighed the expense. Overall, information on the Indians' level of awareness regarding their actions is essentially absent from the early literature. Such a question apparently was not of interest to the European observers in the sixteenth and seventeenth centuries.

A recent study by Henry T. Lewis (1977) conducted in northern Alberta, Canada, where the traditional practice of burning has endured until the present, sheds light on this question. Lewis found that the Indians of northern Alberta were very cognizant of their actions. They understood fully the complications of timing, environmental conditions, and resultant effects. According to a 76-year-old Cree informant in 1975, "Fires had to be controlled. You couldn't just start a fire anywhere, anytime. Fire can do a lot a harm or a lot of good. You have to know how to control it . . . the country has changed from what it used to be—brush and trees where there used to be lots of meadows and not so many animals as before" (Lewis 1977:15–16). Many of Lewis's informants were able to point to wooded areas that had formerly been maintained as meadows. It is quite likely that their sense of awareness extended throughout North America wherever fire was used, but evidence to substantiate this assumption remains to be found.

Implications

Mellars (1976:36–39) has discussed several cultural developments that may follow from the use of prescribed burning to manage an environment. He has proposed that prescribed burning would lead to a marked reduction in the time and energy costs for harvesting food by (1) increasing productivity (in human terms); (2) reducing travel and search costs by increasing mobility and visibility; and (3) reducing risk (uncertainty). As predictability increased, concentrations of food permitted the formation of larger, more sedentary patterns of residence.

Increased intensification of human-plant-animal relationships would allow influence over sex, age, and relative abundance of different species by varying the type, degree, seasonality, and frequency of burning. Such management policies might lead to emergence of ideas concerning ownership of economic resources and territorial boundaries.

This hypothesis would be difficult to test archaeologically. For the study area, however, it is clear from ethnohistorical records that these Indians practiced a form of resource management. This was done by establishing and maintaining mosaics of patches at a variety of successional stages through periodic burning, clearing, and gardening. Within each patch, greater or lesser heterogenous conditions existed as a result of specific management practices. At a larger scale, variability between these managed patches could have been substantial in comparison to areas less affected by human disturbance in the surrounding landscape of the three subregionsthe Piedmont, the Coastal Plain, and the Appalachian Mountains. Such a strategy increased the productivity and variability of their resource base. Increased environmental graininess on a local scale led to short-term stability for their anthropogenic ecosystem.

There is good evidence for cooperative management practices in the form of hunting, clearing, planting, and harvesting. With seasonal movement between patches to nurture and exploit various resources, it is very probable that the Indians in this region did have some concept of "home range" or "territoriality." This suggests a new meaning of the term "range manager." The Indians created and maintained the range upon which their plant and animal resources, and they in turn, relied.

AN ABORIGINALLY MAINTAINED LANDSCAPE

This study has attempted to characterize the nature and consequences of human disturbance in the study area at the time of European contact. Indians of this region used fire and other techniques of clearing for a variety of purposes. It would appear that disturbance in the form of clearing was localized near settlements, in hunting areas, and along established paths. Length of occupation and human population density were important factors that helped determine the degree of disturbance. Established settlements had many gardens and fields near their houses, which were often surrounded by a zone of economically important trees. Many open areas described by early explorers were actually old fields, meadows, and edge areas that were controlled by prescribed burning. Other types of patches exploited by these Indians included marshes, swamps, and bogs, which also may have burned periodically.

Indian burning and clearing created and maintained a mosaic of patches. On a smaller and more controlled scale, they replicated the same kind of patchy condition that natural events such as natural disturbance can cause. By utilizing fire, they increased the richness and diversity of their environment and decreased the likelihood of wildfires destroying what so many early writers deemed a paradise.

Some of the early writers highly romanticized their reports for many reasons. Nevertheless, a comparison of their observations about landscapes and Indian management strategies with current recommendations of resource and wildlife managers suggests that historic reports probably were relatively accurate for the areas immediately surrounding Indian habitations. Indeed, Indian practices may have produced a much more productive environment (in human terms) than what modern-day occupants are accustomed to seeing. Wildlife and range managers are just beginning to develop recommendations that are consistent with practices that the Native inhabitants developed over hundreds, if not thousands, of years: the welfare of these people was dependent upon their hard-won knowledge.

ACKNOWLEDGMENTS

Several people contributed to completion of this work. My M.A. committee—Dick Yarnell, Bruce Winterhalder, and the late Roy Dickens—devoted a great deal of special attention and contributed to the scholarly refinement of this work. Stephen Davis produced a computerized version of this manuscript that facilitated its subsequent publication. Two ethnohistorians who share my lust for cryptic records—Carole Crumley and Jean Black—helped me to shed some light on what seemed only a ray of hope when the study began.

To my good friends and colleagues—Gayle Fritz, Paul Gardner, Kris Gremillion, Annie Hoim, Dan Simpkins, and Ann Tippitt— thank you for your continual stimulation, criticism, and encouragement. George Holcomb, Dottie Holland, and Patsy Evans provided crucial logistical support during several times of need.

EDITORS' NOTE

This chapter is reprinted with slight modifications from *Southern Indian Studies* 41 (1992). Permission to reprint this work from Drs. Vincas Steponaitis and R. P. Stephen Davis, Jr., is gratefully acknowledged. This is an edited version of Julia Hammett's master's thesis in anthropology, completed in 1986 at the University of North Carolina at Chapel Hill.

REFERENCES CITED

Adair, James. 1775. *The History of the American Indians.* London. Rpt. New York: Johnson Reprint Corp., 1968.

Arber, Edward (ed.). 1910. *Travel and Works of Captain John Smith.* 2 vols. Edinburgh: John Grant.

Bartram, William. 1973. *Travels through North and South Carolinas, Georgia, and East and West Florida.* Savannah, Ga.: Bee Hive Press.

Beatty, Richard C., and William J. Mulloy. 1940. *William Byrd's Natural History of Virginia.* Richmond: Dietz Press.

Bendell, J. F. 1974. Effect of Forest Fire on Birds and Mammals. In *Fire and Ecosystems*, edited by T. T. Kozlowaki and C. E. Algren, pp. 73–138. New York: Academic Press.

Binford, Lewis R. 1967. An Ethnohistory of the Nottoway, Meherrin and Weanock Indians of Southeastern Virginia. *Ethnohistory* 14(3–4):103–218.

Bland, Edward. 1651. *The Discovery of New Brittaine.* London: Thomas Harper. Reprinted by Readex Microprint Corp., U.S.A (1966).

Bormann, F. H., and G. E. Likens. 1979. *Pattern and Process in a Forested Ecosystem.* Berlin and New York: Springer-Verlag.

Bye, Robert A., Jr. 1981. Quelites—Ethnoecology of Edible Greens—Past, Present and Future. *Journal of Ethnobiology* 1(1):109–23.

Byers, Douglas S. 1946. The Environment of the Northeast. In *Man in Northeastern North America*, edited by Frederick Johnson, pp. 3–32. Andover, Mass.: Phillips Academy.

Ceci, Lynn. 1982. Fish Fertilizer: A Native North American Practice? *Science* 188:26–30.

Cowan, I. McT. 1956. Life and Time of the Coast Black-Tailed Deer. In *The Deer of North America*, edited by W. P. Taylor, pp. 523–617. Harrisburg, Penn.: Stackpole.

Cowan, I. McT., W. S. Hoar, and J. Hatter. 1950. The Effect of Forest Succession upon the Quantity and upon the Nutritive Values of Woody Plants Used as Food by Moose. *Canadian Journal of Research* 28:249–71.

Cumming, J. A. 1969. Prescribed Burning on Recreation Areas in New Jersey: History, Objectives, Influences and Technique. *Proceedings of the Annual Tall Timbers Fire Ecology Conference* 9:251–69.

Day, Gordon. 1953. The Indian as an Ecological Factor in the Northeastern Forest. *Ecology* 34(2):329–46.

Deam, Charles C. 1921. *Trees of Indians*. Indianapolis: Indiana Department of Conservation.

Denslow, Julie Sloan. 1985. Disturbance-Mediated Co-existence of Species. In *The Ecology of Natural Disturbance and Patch Dynamics*, edited by S. T. A. Pickett and P. S. White, pp. 307–24. Orlando, Fla.: Academic Press.

DeWitt, J. B., and J. V. Derby. 1955. Changes in the Nutritive Value of Browse Plants following Forest Fire. *Journal of Wildlife Management* 19:65–70.

Einarsen, A. S. 1946. Crude Protein Determination as an Applied Management Technique. *Transactions of the North American Wildlife Conference* 11:309–12.

Favretti, Rudy J. 1974. *Early New England Gardens, 1620–1840*. 3rd ed. Sturbridge, Mass.: Old Sturbridge Village.

Ford, Richard I. 1985. *Prehistoric Food Production in North America*. Anthropological Papers 75. Ann Arbor: Museum of Anthropology, University of Michigan.

Geertz, Clifford. 1963. Two Types of Ecosystems. In *Agricultural Involution*, pp. 12–37. Berkeley: University of California Press.

Graham, Edward H. 1944. *Natural Principles of Land Use*. New York: Greenwood Press.

Gremillion, Kristen J. 1984. Aboriginal Use of Plant Food and European Contact in the North Carolina Piedmont. Master's thesis. Department of Anthropology, University of North Carolina, Chapel Hill.

Guffey, Stanley Z. 1977. A Review and Analysis of the Effects of Pre-Columbian Man on the Eastern North American Forests. *Tennessee Anthropologist* 2(2):121–37.

Hamilton, Robert J. 1981. Effects of Prescribed Fire on Black Bear Populations in Southern Forests. In *Prescribed Fire and Wildlife in Southern Forests*, edited by Gene W. Wood, pp. 129–34. Georgetown, S.C.: Belle W. Baruch Forest Science Institute of Clemson University.

Hausenbuiller, R. L. 1978. *Soil Science*. 2nd ed. Dubuque, Ia.: William C. Brown Co.

Hendricks, J. H. 1968. Control Burning for Deer Management in Chaparral in California. *Proceedings of the Annual Tall Timbers Fire Ecology Conference* 8:219–33.

Holm, Mary Ann. 1985. Faunal Remains from Two North Central Piedmont Sites. Master's thesis. Department of Anthropology, University of North Carolina, Chapel Hill.

Hudson, Charles, Marvin Smith, David Hally, Richard Poihemus, and Chester DePratter. 1985. Coosa: A Chiefdom in the Sixteenth-Century Southeastern United States. *American Antiquity* 50(4):723–37.

Hurst, George A. 1981. Effects of Prescribed Burning on the Eastern Wild Turkey. In *Prescribed Fire and Wildlife in Southern Forests*, edited by Gene W. Wood, pp. 81–88. Georgetown, S.C.: Belle W. Baruch Forest Science Institute of Clemson University.

Johnson, Allen W. 1972. Individuality and Experimentation in Traditional Agriculture. *Ecology* 1:149–59.

Kirkpatrick, Roy L., and Henry S. Mosby. 1981. Effects of Prescribed Burning on Tree Squirrels. In *Prescribed Fire and Wildlife in Southern Forests*, edited by Gene W. Wood, pp. 99–102. Georgetown, S.C.: Belle W. Baruch Forest Science Institute of Clemson University.

Komarek, Edward V. 1974. Effects of Fire on Temperate Forests and Related Ecosystems: Southeastern United States. In *Fire and Ecosystems*, edited by T. T. Kozlowski and C. E. Algren, pp. 251–78. New York: Academic Press.

Kozlowski, T. T., and C. E. Algren (eds.). 1974. *Fire and Ecosystems*. New York: Academic Press.

Landers, J. Larry. 1981. The Role of Fire in Bobwhite Quail Management. In *Prescribed Fire and Wildlife in Southern Forests*, edited by Gene W. Wood, pp. 73–80. Georgetown, S.C.: Belle W. Baruch Forest Science Institute of Clemson University.

Lefler, Hugh T. (ed.). 1967. *A New Voyage to Carolina, by John Lawson*. Chapel Hill: University of North Carolina Press.

Lewis, C. E., and T. J. Harshbarger. 1976. Shrub and Herbaceous Vegetation after Twenty Years of Prescribed Burning on the South Carolina Coastal Plain. *Journal of Range Management* 29:13–18.

Lewis, Henry T. 1977. Maskuta: The Ecology of Indian Fires in Northern Alberta. *Western Canadian Journal of Anthropology* 7(1):15–52.

Lindgren, W. H., III. 1972. Agricultural Propaganda in Lawson's *A New Voyage to Carolina*. *North Carolina Historical Review* 49(4):333–44.

Little, Silas. 1974. Effects of Fire on Temperate Forests: Northeastern United States. In *Fire and Ecosystems*, edited by T. T. Kozlowski and C. E. Algren, pp. 225–50. New York: Academic Press.

Martin, Paul S. 1971. The Revolution in Archaeology. *American Antiquity* 36:1–8.

Meggers, Betty J. 1971. *Amazonia: Man and Culture in a Counterfeit Paradise*. Chicago: Aldine Atherton.

Mellars, Paul. 1976. Fire Ecology, Animal Populations and Man: A Study of Some Ecological Relationships in Prehistory. *Proceedings of the Prehistoric Society* 42:15–45.

Merrill, William L. 1979. The Beloved Tree: *Ilex vomitoria* among the Indians of the Southeast and Adjacent Regions. In *Black Drink: A Native American Tea*, edited by Charles Hudson, pp. 40–82. Athens: University of Georgia Press.

Morton, Thomas. 1632. *New English Canaan: or New Canaan*. N.p.: Peter Force. Rpt. New York: Burt Franklin, 1967.

Munson, Patrick J. 1984. Comments on Some Additional Species, with Summary of Seasonality. In *Experiments and Observations on Aboriginal Wild Plant Food Utilizations in Eastern North America*, edited by Patrick J. Munson, pp. 459–73. Prehistory Research Series 4(2). Indianapolis: Indiana Historical Society.

Odum, Eugene P. 1959. *Fundamentals of Ecology*. 2nd ed. Philadelphia: W. B. Saunders Co.

Percy, George. 1907. Observations Gathered Out of a Discourse of the Plantation of the Southerne Colonie in Virginia by the English, 1606. In *Narratives of Early Virginia, 1606–1625*, edited by Lyon Gardiner Tyler, pp. 5–23. New York: Barnes and Noble.

Petruso, Karl M., and Jere M. Wickens. 1984. The Acorn in Aboriginal Subsistence in Eastern Northern America: A Report on Miscellaneous Experiments. In *Experiments and Observations on Aboriginal Wild Plant Food Utilization in Eastern North America*, edited by Patrick J. Munson, pp. 360–78. Prehistory Research Series 4(2). Indianapolis: Indiana Historical Society.

Pickett, S. T. A., and P. S. White. 1985. *The Ecology of Natural Disturbance and Patch Dynamics*. Orlando: Fla.: Academic Press.

Quinn, David B. (ed.). 1955. *The Roanoke Voyages, 1584–1599*. 2 vols. 2nd series, nos. 104–5. London: Hakluyt Society.

Quinn, David B., and Alison M. Quinn. 1973. *Virginia Voyages from Hakluyt*. London: Oxford University Press.

Radford, Albert E., Harry E. Ahies, and C. Ritchie Bell. 1968. *Manual of the Vascular Flora of the Carolinas*. Chapel Hill: University of North Carolina Press.

Rappaport, Roy A. 1968. *Pigs for the Ancestors*. New Haven: Yale University Press.

Ribinski, R. F. 1968. Effects of Forest Fires on Quantity and Quality of Deer Browse Production in Mixed Oak Forests of Central Pennsylvania.

Quarterly Report of the Pennsylvania Cooperative Wildlife Research Unit 30(5):13–15.

Rindos, David. 1980. Symbiosis, Instability, and the Origins and Spread of Agriculture: A New Model. *Current Anthropology* 21(6):751–72.

———. 1984. *The Origins of Agriculture.* Orlando, Fla.: Academic Press.

Smith, David M., and Ralph C. Hawley. 1962. *The Practice of Silviculture.* New York: Devin-Adair Co.

Spencer, D. L., and E. F. Chatelain. 1953. Progress in the Management of Moose of South Central Alaska. *Transactions of the North American Wildlife Conference* 18:539–52.

Strachey, William. 1849. *The Historic of Travaile into Virginia Britannia.* London: Hakluyt Society.

Sturtevant, William C. 1965. Historic Carolina Algonkian Cultivation of *Chenopodium* or *Amaranthus. Southeastern Archaeological Conference Bulletin* 3:66–67.

Taber, R. D., and R. F. Dasman. 1957. The Dynamics of Three Natural Populations of the Deer *Odocoileus hemionus columbianus. Ecology* 38:233–46.

Taber, R. D., and J. L. Murphy. 1971. Controlled Fire in the Management of North American Deer. In *The Scientific Management of Animals and Plant Communities for Conservation,* edited by E. Duffey and A. S. Watts, pp. 425–35. 11th Symposium of the British Ecological Society. Oxford: Blackwell Scientific Publications.

Talalay, Laurie, Donald R. Keller, and Patrick J. Munson. 1984. Hickory Nuts, Walnuts, Butternuts, and Hazelnuts. In *Experiments and Observations on Aboriginal Wild Plant Food Utilization in Eastern North America,* edited by Patrick J. Munson, pp. 338–59. Prehistory Research Series 6(2). Indianapolis: Indiana Historical Society.

Van der Donck, Adriaen. 1846. A Description of the New Netherlands. In *New York Historical Society Collection Series* 2, vol. 1, chap. 5, pp. 125–242. Reprinted in 1968, edited by T. F. O'Donnel. Syracuse, N.Y.: Syracuse University Press.

Varner, J. G., and J. J. Varner (trans.). 1951. *The Florida of the Inca.* Austin: University of Texas Press.

Viro, P. J. 1974. Effects of Forest Fire on Soil. In *Fire and Ecosystems,* edited by T. T. Kozlowski and C. E. Algren, pp. 7–46. New York: Academic Press.

Waselkov, Gregory A. 1978. Evolution of Deer Hunting in the Eastern Woodlands. *Mid-Continental Journal of Archaeology* 3(1):15–34.

Wiens, John A. 1976. Population Responses to Patchy Environments. *Annual Review of Ecology and Systematics* 7:81–120.

————. 1985. Vertebrate Responses to Environmental Patchiness in Arid and Semiarid Ecosystems. In *The Ecology of Natural Disturbance and Patch Dynamics*, edited by S. T. A. Pickett and P. S. White, pp. 169–96. Orlando, Fla.: Academic Press.

Wilson, Jack H., Jr. 1977. Feature Fill, Plant Utilization and Disposal among the Historic Sara Indians. Master's thesis. Department of Anthropology, University of North Carolina, Chapel Hill.

Winterhalder, Bruce. 1981. Environmental Analysis in Human Evolution and Adaptation Research. *Human Ecology* 8(2):135–70.

Wright, Louis B. (ed.). 1947. *The History and Present State of Virginia, by Robert Beverley*. Chapel Hill: University of North Carolina Press.

————. 1966. *The Prose Works of William Byrd of Westover*. Cambridge, Mass.: Belknap Press of Harvard University Press.

Yarnell, Richard A. 1983. Prehistoric Plant Foods and Husbandry in Eastern North America. Paper presented at the 48th Annual Meeting of the Society for American Archaeology, Pittsburgh.

Yarnell, Richard A., and M. Jean Black. 1985. Temporal Trends Indicated by a Survey of Archaic and Woodland Plant Food Remains from Southeastern North America. *Southeastern Archaeology* 4:93–106.

List of Contributors

Robert A. Bye, Jardín Botánico, Instituto de Biología, Universidad Nacional Autónoma de México, Apartado Postal 70-614, 04510 México D.F., MEXICO. e-mail <rbye@mail.ibiologia.unam.mx>.

Wayne J. Elisens, Department of Botany and Microbiology, University of Oklahoma, Norman, OK 73019. e-mail <elisens@ou.edu>.

Richard I. Ford, Museum of Anthropology, University of Michigan, Ann Arbor, MI 48109. e-mail <riford@umich.edu>.

Catherine S. Fowler, Department of Anthropology, University of Nevada, Reno, NV 89557-0006. e-mail <csfowler@scs.unr.edu>.

Gayle J. Fritz, Department of Anthropology, Washington University, St. Louis, MO 63130. e-mail <gjfritz@artsci.wustl.edu>.

Julia E. Hammett, Department of Social Science, Truckee Meadows Community College, Reno, NV 89512. e-mail <jhammett@tmcc.edu>.

Walter H. Lewis, Department of Biology, Washington University, St. Louis, MO 63130. e-mail <lewis@biology.wustl.edu>.

Edelmira Linares, Jardín Botánico, Instituto de Biología, Universidad Nacional Autónoma de México, Apartado Postal 70-614, 04510 México D.F., MEXICO. e-mail <mazari@mail.ibiologia.unam.mx>.

Paul E. Minnis, Department of Anthropology, University of Oklahoma, Norman, OK 73019. e-mail <minnis@ou.edu>.

Gary Paul Nabhan, Arizona–Sonora Desert Museum, 2021 North Kinney Road, Tucson, AZ 85743. e-mail <gnabhan@desertmuseum.org>.

Sandra L. Peacock, School of Environmental Studies, University of Victoria, Victoria, B.C. V8W 2Y2, CANADA. e-mail <peacock@sfu.ca>.

Enrique Salmón, Baca Institute, Department of Anthropology, Fort Lewis College, Durango, CO 81301. e-mail <salmon_e@fortlewis.edu>.

Nancy J. Turner, School of Environmental Studies, University of Victoria, Victoria, B.C. V8W 2Y2, CANADA. e-mail <nturner@uvic.ca>.

INDEX

Acacia (*Acacia*), 44
Acalypha (Euphorbiaceae), 53
Adaptation: human, 4–5, 15–18, 253
Africa, 88
Agriculture, 13–14, 16, 56–57, 60–61, 109, 184, 196, 199–200, 216, 256–59, 277; prehistoric, 9, 12–14, 56, 212–16, 231–37, 257, 262–72, 284–88. *See also* Domestication process; Anthropogenic ecology
Agroecology. *See* Agriculture
Aguaruna Indians, 82, 90, 92–93
Alcohol, 59–61, 193–95
Alder (*Alnus*), 143
Algae. *See Cryptomeris, Graciliaria, Halymenia, Rhodymenia*
Algonkian Indians, 236, 253
Aloe (*Aloe*), 64
Alumroot (*Heuchera*), 145
Amphibians, 107, 183, 273. *See also* listings by individual genus
Amuzgo Indians, 47, 49, 50
Animals: domesticated, 185, 196, 273; wild, 35, 38–40, 107, 123, 183–85, 218, 211, 260, 273–74, 278–81, 285. *See also* Anthropogenic ecology, livestock, ecological effects of; listings by individual genus
Antelope (*Antilocarpa*), 38–39

Anthropogenic ecology, 8–9, 31, 51–65, 109, 113, 115–16, 118–21, 134, 146, 162, 199–200; burning, 7, 30, 112–15, 134, 154–56, 162–64, 167, 171, 238, 240, 249–51, 259–61, 276–79, 281–83, 285–87, 289, 290, 292; coppicing/ pruning, 30, 112–13, 115, 134, 150, 154, 238; distribution, 54–55, 57–58, 277; livestock, ecological effects of, 100, 120–21, 168–69, 211, 217; pre- historic, 9, 116, 214, 236–40; soil dis- turbance/digging, 30, 55, 148, 150, 158, 162, 164, 200, 214, 262; various other effects, 134, 146, 162, 199–200
Apache Indians, 192, 211
Apple (*Malus*), 274
Arborvitae (*Thuja*), 143
Archaeological site ecology, 216–19
Archaeology. *See* Prehistory
Arrowroot (*Sagittaria*), 141, 168–69
Asia, 79, 88, 259
Asparagus (*Asparagus*), 150
Aspergillus (fungus), 75
Avalanche lily. *See* Fawn lily
Ayuuk Indians. *See* Mixe Indians
Aztec Indians. *See* Nahua Indians

Bald cypress (*Taxodium*), 44, 274
Balsam-of-Peru (*Myroxylon*), 44

Balsam-root (*Balsamorhiza*), 140–41, 145, 147, 149–50, 153, 166

Barberry family (Berberidaceae), 108. *See also* genera by common name

Barley (*Hordeum*), 13, 225–27, 230, 232, 263, 268, 274, 288, 196–97

Bartram, William, 254, 257, 264–65, 268–69, 278

Basketry. *See* Weaving

Bean (*Phaseolus*), 12, 38, 53, 184, 224–25, 227, 263–64, 274, 287

Bean family (Fabaceae), 108–109, 111, 184. *See also* genera by common name

Bear (*Ursus*), 260, 273, 278, 281, 285

Bearberry (*Arctostaphylos*), 141–42, 183

Beardtongue (*Penstemon*), 142

Beargrass (*Nolina*), 59, 198

Beautyberry (*Callicarpa*), 265, 274

Beaver (*Castor*), 273, 278

Begonia (*Begonia*), 63

Bighorn sheep (*Ovis*), 35–39, 117, 123

Biodiversity, 5, 30–41, 45–46, 50–55, 60–61, 105–107, 183–84, 223–24, 241, 248–50; and importance of indigenous peoples 3–4, 29–41, 108, 134–35, 163–71

Birch (*Betula*), 142–43, 148, 151, 167

Birch family (Betulaceae), 110. *See also* genera by common name

Birds, 35–36, 107, 114, 184, 196, 218, 270, 273, 278, 280. *See also* by individual genus

Biscuitroot (*Lomatium*), 120–21, 140–42, 144, 147, 153

Bison. *See* Buffalo

Bitterroot (*Lewisia*), 120, 140, 157

Blackberry (*Rubus*), 140–41, 233, 274–75, 278

Blazing star (*Mentzelia*), 114

Blue dicks (*Dichelostemma*), 109

Bluejay (*Cyanocitta*), 273

Borage family (Boraginaceae), 110. *See also* genera by common name

Brazilwood tree (*Haematoxylon*), 183, 190

Brine fly (*Ephedra*), 103

Bryoria (lichen), 140

Buckthorn (*Rhamnus*), 88–90, 94, 144, 151, 274

Buffalo (*Bison*), 273

Buffaloberry (*Shepherdia*), 140, 145, 151–53

Bulrush (*Scirpus*), 63, 114, 123, 143, 150

Buttercup family (Ranunculaceae), 110–11. *See also* genera by common name

Byrsonima (Malpighiaceae), 64

Cacao (*Theobroma*), 44

Cacao-flower (*Quararibea*), 44, 54

Cactus family (Cactaceae), 110–11. *See also* genera by common name

Caesalpinia (Fabaceae), 35

Cahokia, 230, 234–35, 241

California, 9, 118, 240

Caltrop family (Zygophyllaceae), 110. *See also* genera by common name

Canada, 83, 88, 133–73, 240, 290. *See also* Eastern North America; listings by individual group names

Canarygrass. *See* Maygrass

Caper family (Capparidaceae), 110. *See also* genera by common name

Cardinal (*Cardinalis*), 36

Carrot family (Apiaceae), 108–109, 111. *See also* genera by common name

Cattail (*Typha*), 114, 124, 141, 143–44, 147, 150

Cattail family (Typhaceae), 110

Cedar. *See* Juniper

Century plants (*Agave*), 12, 30, 57, 59–60, 62, 110, 183–84, 219

Chatino Indians, 47

Cherokee Indians, 268

Cherry (*Prunus*), 140, 143, 151, 155, 183, 216, 264, 274–75, 277

Chestnut (*Castanea*), 233, 274

Chile (*Capsicum*), 36, 184

China, 78

Chinantec Indians, 47–48

Chocolate lily. *See* Fritillary

Choco-Popoloca Indians, 49

Chol Indians, 47–48

Cholla. *See* Prickley pear
Chontal Indians, 36, 47–48, 50
Chuckwalla (*Sauromalus*), 30
Cinquefoil (*Potentilla*), 140
Classification: folk, 34–35, 39–40,
    62–63, 121, 126n.3, 189–91, 208
Clematis (*Clematis*), 144
Cocopa Indians, 30
Cofitachequi, 238, 266
Congaree Indians, 269
Convention on Biological Diversity,
    91–93
Cora Indians, 50
Corn. *See* Maize
Corn lily (*Veratrum*), 90–92, 145
Cotton (*Gossypium*), 183, 216
Cottontail (*Sylvilagus*), 273. *See also*
    Rabbits
Cottonwood (*Populus*), 141–44,
    210–11
Cow-parsnip (*Heracleum*), 141, 147,
    150
Cowpea (*Vigna*), 64
Coyote (*Canis*), 35, 274, 278
Cree Indians, 290
Crop diversity: importance of, 5,
    11–13
Crops. *See* Agriculture; listings by
    common names of specific plants
Croton (*Croton*), 53
Cryptomeria (alga), 39
Cucapá Indians, 49–50
Cuicatec Indians, 49–50
Cultural diversity: importance of, 17,
    46–50, 137, 184, 253
Cultural topography: concept of,
    208–10, 212
Culture change, 3–4, 40–41, 56–57,
    64, 84, 105, 120–21, 123–24,
    137, 166–69, 185, 199, 211, 253,
    255

Deer (*Odocoileus*), 35, 117, 123, 235, 260,
    273, 278, 280, 285
Desert-lavender (*Hyptis*), 184
De Soto, Hernando, 238–39, 252, 255
Devil's claw (*Proboscidea*), 12, 30

Devil's-club (*Oplopanax*), 144
Dock (*Rumex*), 275
Dodder (*Cuscuta*), 110
Dogbane family (Apocynaceae), 148,
    150. *See also* genera by common
    name
Dogwood (*Cornus*), 142, 144, 150
Domestication process, 30, 51–53, 112,
    224–31, 250
Douglas-fir (*Pseudotsuga*), 141–44, 181,
    210

Ear-flower (*Cymbopetalum*), 64
Eastern North America, 6–9, 12–13, 18,
    83–86, 190, 223–41, 248–93
Echinodontium (fungus), 143
Echinopterys (Malpighiaceae), 35
Ecology. *See* Anthropogenic ecology
Elderberry (*Sambucus*), 233
Elk (*Cervus*), 273, 278
Ethnoecology, 29–41. *See also* Anthro-
    pogenic ecology; Knowledge,
    traditional indigenous
Europe, 15, 88, 288
Evening primrose family (Onagraceae),
    111. *See also* genera by common
    name

Fagonia (Zygophyllaceae), 36
False buckwheat (*Eriogonum*), 217
False peyote (*Ariocarpus*), 63
Famine foods, 15
Fawn lily (*Erythronium*), 140, 147, 150,
    153, 155, 162, 166–69
Fiber. *See* Weaving
Figwort family (Scrophulariaceae),
    108–11. *See also* genera by common
    name
Fir (*Abies*), 143–44, 210
Fire. *See* Anthropogenic ecology,
    burning
Fireweed (*Epilobium*), 141
Fish, 39–40, 102, 107, 159, 235, 270–71,
    273
Fishing, 102, 239
Flax family (Linaceae), 110. *See also*
    genera by common name

Flycatcher, silky (*Phainopepla*), 35
Four o'clock family (Nyctaginaceae),
    110. *See also* genera by common
    name
Fox (*Vulpes*), 273
Fritillary (*Fritillaria*), 140, 150
Fuelwood, 119–20, 197, 211, 260
Fungi. *See Aspergillus, Echonodontium,
    Lycoperdon, Monascus*

Gathering: of wild plants, 14–15,
    57–58, 102, 113, 146–54, 184, 196–98,
    211, 275–77
Gayfeather (*Liatris*), 218
Gentian family (Gentianaceae), 110. *See
    also* genera by common name
Gooseberry (*Ribes*), 140, 167
Goosefoot (*Chenopodium*), 11, 13, 217,
    225–26, 230–31, 234, 263, 268, 288
Goosefoot family (Chenopodiaceae),
    108–109, 111, 274. *See also* genera by
    common name
Goose grass (*Paspalum*), 53
Gourd (*Lagenaria*), 226, 263–64
Gracilaria (alga), 39
Grama grass (*Bouteloua*), 217
Grama grass cactus (*Pediocactus*), 217
Grape (*Vitis*), 274
Grape family (Vitaceae), 110. *See also*
    genera by common name
Grass family (Poaceae), 108–109. *See
    also* genera by common name
Greasewood (*Sarcobatus*), 120
Great Basin, 9, 90–91, 99–126
Great Plains, 15, 18
Groundnut (*Apios*), 233
Gymnospermae, 108

Hallucinogens, 63, 196–97
Halymenia (alga), 39
Hand-flower tree (*Chiranthodendron*), 55
Hawkmoth (*Manduca*), 36–37
Hawthorne (*Crataegus*), 142, 148, 274
Hazelnut (*Corylus*), 140, 151, 153, 274,
    276–77
Heath family (Ericaceae), 108. *See also*
    genera by common name

Hickory (*Carya*), 231, 233, 235, 266, 276,
    274
Hidatsa Indians, 15, 237
Hispanics, 36, 56–57, 185, 192, 197, 216
Holly (*Ilex*), 267, 276
Honey locust (*Gleditsia*), 265, 274
Hopewell, 232
Hopi Indians, 13
Horse (*Equus*), 273
Horse purslane (*Trianthema*), 38
Horsetail (*Equisetum*), 144–45
Horsetail family (Equisetaceae), 108,
    110. *See also* genera by common
    name
Huastec Indians, 47, 49, 55, 61
Huave Indians, 49–50
Huckleberry (*Gaylussacia*), 274;
    (*Vaccinium*), 140, 151, 153–54, 167,
    169, 233, 274
Huichol Indians, 47, 49, 63
Hunting, 102, 113, 117, 159, 211, 239,
    259–61, 270, 283, 285, 287
Huron Indians, 240

Iguana (*Ctenosura*), 30
Indian-blanket (*Gaillardia*), 144
Indian-hemp (*Apocynum*), 143, 148,
    150, 170
Indigo (*Indigofera*), 183
Insects, 36, 37, 103, 107, 135, 183, 188
Intellectual property rights, 17, 74–94
International Cooperative Biodiversity
    Group, 80–82, 93–94
Iris family (Iridaceae), 110. See also
    genera by common name
Iroquoian Indians, 236, 253

Jimson weed (*Datura*), 36, 63, 190
Jonas Indians, 49–50
Juniper (*Juniperus*), 114, 142, 144, 181,
    217, 267, 274

Kapok (*Ceiba*), 44
K'iche' Indians. *See* Quiché Indians
Killdeer (*Charadrius*), 273
Kiskadee (*Pitangus*), 35–36
Knapweed (*Centaurea*), 168

Knotweed (*Polygonum*), 13, 227, 230, 232, 234
Knotweed family (Polygonaceae), 108–109, 111. *See also* genera by common name
Knowledge: traditional indigenous, 5, 10, 16–17, 29–41, 80–94, 102–105, 156–58, 185–201; traditional indigenous, loss of, 4–5, 7, 9–10, 31–33, 40–41, 56, 63–64, 119–21, 124–25

Laborador tea (*Ledum*), 141
Land Management. *See* Anthropogenic ecology
Larch (*Larix*), 141
Laurel (*Laurus*), 266, 278
Laurel tree (*Litsea*), 183
Letharia (lichen), 143
Leucaena (*Leucaena*), 54
Lillooet Indians. *See* Stl'atl'imx Indians
Lily (*Lilium*), 140, 166
Lily family (Liliaceae), 108–109. *See also* genera by common name
Linguistic diversity: importance of, 17, 30–31, 121
Livestock. *See* Animals, domesticated; Anthropogenic ecology, livestock, ecological effects of
Lizard's-tail family (Saururaceae), 110. *See also* genera by common name
Loasa family (Loasaceae), 111. *See also* genera by common name
Lovage (*Ligusticum*), 58, 142, 145, 170, 197
Lycoperdon (fungus), 145

Magnolia (*Magnolia*), 266
Maize (*Zea*), 12, 15–16, 184, 190, 193–96, 217, 225, 227, 232–36, 263–64, 274, 288
Mame-Quiché Indians, 49
Manipulated plants. *See* Anthropogenic ecology
Maple (*Acer*), 142–43, 274
Maricopa Indians, 30
Mariposa lily (*Calochortus*), 140
Marshelder. *See* Sumpweed

Materials: use of plants and animals for, 142
Matlatzinca Indians, 49, 50, 61
Maya Indians, 47, 49, 62
Mayapple (*Podophyllum*), 83–88, 94
Maygrass (*Phalaris*), 226, 230–32, 234, 268–69, 274
Mayo Indians, 30, 47, 49, 192
Maypop (*Passiflora*), 263–64, 274, 288, 271
Mazahua Indians, 47, 49, 61
Mazatec Indians, 47–50
Medicinal plants, 10–11, 16, 30, 57–58, 62, 74–94, 102–103, 108, 119, 121, 125, 137, 144–45, 170, 193, 197, 199
Mesquite (*Prosopis*), 35, 40, 115–16
Mexico, 5–6, 12, 15, 29–41, 44–65, 180–201. *See also* listings by individual group names
Miconia (Melastomataceae), 53
Milkweed family (Asclepidaceae), 110. *See also* genera by common name
Mink (*Mustela*), 273
Mint (*Mentha*), 144
Mint family (Lamiaceae), 108–11, 184. *See also* genera by common name
Mistletoe (*Phoradendron*), 35
Mixe Indians, 47–48, 50
Mixtec Indians, 47–48, 50–51, 62
Monascus (fungus), 75
Moose (*Alces*), 278–80
Moreño Indians. *See* Huave Indians
Morning glory (*Ipomoea*), 54, 190
Morning glory family (Convolvulaceae), 63, 110. *See also* genera by common name
Motozintleco Indians, 48, 50
Mountain lion (*Felis*), 273, 278
Mulberry (*Morus*), 265–66, 275, 277
Mushrooms. *See Pleurotis, Tricholoma*
Muskogean Indians, 25
Muskrat (*Ondatria*), 273
Mustard (*Brassica*), 64, 168
Mustard family (Brassicaceae), 108–11
Myth. *See* Oral traditions; Religion

Nahua Indians, 47–48, 50–51, 54–55,
    61–64
Native Seed/SEARCH, 12
"Natural" environments: misapplied
    concept of, 7–8, 16, 160, 207
Nettle (*Urtica*), 144
Nettle family (Urticaceae), 110. *See also*
    genera by common name
Nlaka'pamux Indians, 137–38, 155–57,
    161–62
Nongovernmental organizations, 12, 18
North America, 4–5. *See also* California;
    Canada; Eastern North America;
    Great Basin; Great Plains; Mexico;
    Northwest; Southwest
Northwest, Pacific, 9, 88, 90, 240;
    British Columbia, 133–74
Nutsedge (*Cyperus*), 112
Nuu-Chah-Nulth Indians, 158

Oak (*Quercus*), 54, 181, 233, 235, 265,
    267, 275, 276–77
Oak family (*Fagaceae*), 110. *See also*
    genera by common name
Oats (*Avena*), 120
Ocuitleco Indians, 49–50
Okanagan Indians, 137
Oleaster family (Elaeagnaceae), 110.
    See also genera by common name
Onion (*Allium*), 39, 58, 120, 140, 199
O'oodam, 29–30, 33–37, 40–41, 49–50,
    56, 58, 62, 192
Oral traditions, 35, 37, 117–18, 121, 134,
    159–61, 180–201. *See also* Religion
Orchid family (Orchidaceae), 110. *See
    also* genera by common name
Oregon grape (*Mahonia*), 143, 168–69
Otomí Indians, 47–48, 50–51, 61, 64
Otter (*Lutra*), 273

Packrat (*Neotoma*) 40, 102
Paipai-Kiliwa-Cucapá Indians, 49–50
Paiute Indians, 100, 102–104, 106, 119–21
Palmetto (*Sabal*), 59
Panamint Indians. *See* Timbisha
    Indians
Panic grass (*Panicum*), 12, 184

Papago Indians. *See* O'oodam
Passion flower. *See* Maypop
Pearly Everlasting (*Anaphalis*), 143
Peony family (Paeoniaceae), 108, 110.
    See also genera by common name
Penobscot Indians, 84
Pepper (*Piper*), 53
Peppergrass (*Lepidium*), 184
Persimmon (*Diospyros*), 233, 235, 265,
    275, 277
Peyote (*Lophophora*), 63, 190, 196. *See
    also* False peyote
Phlox family (Polemoniaceae),
    108–109, 111. *See also* genera by
    common name
Physic nut (*Jatropha*), 183
Pig (*Sus*), 196, 273
Pigeon (*Ectopistes*), 273
Pigweed (Amaranthus), 53, 268
Pigweed family (Amaranthaceae), 110.
    See also genera by common name
Pima Indians. *See* O'oodam
Pincushion (*Chaenactis*), 38
Pine (*Pinus*), 54, 59, 112, 115–16,
    121–22, 140–44, 151, 181, 197–98,
    210, 217, 275, 280, 288
Pink family (Caryophyllaceae),
    110–11. *See also* genera by common
    name
Plains. *See* Great Plains
Plantain family (Plantaginaceae), 110.
    See also genera by common name
Pleurotus (mushroom), 55, 141
Pokeweed (*Phytolacca*), 275
Poplar. *See* Cottonwood
Popoluca Indians, 47, 49
Poorwill (*Phalaenptilius*), 36
Porophyllum (Asteraceae), 53
Possum (*Didelphus*), 273
Potato (*Solanum*), 120, 184, 219
Potato family (Solanaceae), 108–109,
    111, 184. *See also* genera by common
    name
Prehistory, 6, 8–9, 11, 14, 40, 55, 60–61,
    64, 166, 207–19, 220–43, 246–93. *See
    also* Domestication process;
    Archaeological site ecology

Prickley pear (*Opuntia*), 40, 57, 141, 181, 219
Prince's pine (*Chimaphila*), 145
Prince's plume (*Stanleya*), 116–17
Psacalium (Asteraceae), 65
Psychotria (*Psychotria*), 53
Pumpkin. *See* Squash
Purépecha Indians, 61. *See also* Tarascan Indians
Purslane (*Portulaca*), 217, 270, 275
Purslane family (Portulacaceae), 111. *See also* genera by common name

Quail (*Colinus*), 273
Quiché Indians, 48–50

Rabbits, 102, 117, 218, 278, 285. *See also* Cottontail
Raccon (*Procyon*), 235, 273
Rarámuri Indians, 47, 49, 54, 56–57, 59, 62–64, 180–201
Raspberry. *See* Blackberry
Religion, 5, 44–45, 52, 63–64, 117–18, 126, 134, 158–61, 180–201, 209–12. *See also* Oral traditions
Reptiles, 30, 38–39, 107, 183, 273. *See also* listings by individual reptile
Rhizobium (bacterium), 287
Rhodymenia (alga), 39
Ricegrass (*Oryzopsis*), 120
Ritual. *See* Oral traditions; Religion
Rocket (*Sisymbium*), 168
Rose (*Rosa*), 142
Rose family (Rosaceae), 108, 111. *See also* genera by common name
Rush family (Juncaceae), 110. *See also* genera by common name

Sac and Fox Indians, 18
Sagebrush (*Artemisia*), 114, 142, 144, 197, 219
St. John's wort family (Hypericaceae), 110. *See also* genera by common name
Saiya (*Amoreuxia*), 30
Sand food (*Pholisma*), 58
Sand Papago Indians. *See* O'oodham

San Juan Pueblo Indians, 211
Sassafras (*Sassafras*), 267, 275
Saxifrage family (Saxifragaceae), 108–109, 111. *See also* genera by common name
Scaup, lesser (*Aythya*), 273
Secwepemc Indians, 137, 147, 149, 153–54, 157
Sedge family (Cyperaceae), 63, 110–11. *See also* genera by common name
Seri, 33–35, 38–40, 47, 50–51
Service-berry (*Amelanchier*), 140, 142, 148, 150, 153, 169
Shaman Pharmaceuticals, 11
Shaving-brush (*Pseudobombax*), 44
Shoshone Indians, 90–93, 100, 103–107, 112, 114, 124
Shuswap Indians. *See* Secwepemc Indians
Silver-berry (*Elaeagnus*), 143
Siouan Indians, 253
Site flora, 216–19
Skunk (*Mephitis*), 273
Smith, John, 254–56, 269–70
Snowberry (*Symphoricarpos*), 145
Soapberry. *See* Buffaloberry
Solandra (Solanaceae), 63
Sorrel (*Oxalis*), 63, 270
Sotol (*Dasylirion*), 59, 181, 197–98
South America, 14, 81–83, 90, 259
Southwest, American (including far–northern Mexico), 13–14, 29–41, 118, 180–201, 207–19, 236
Spice-bush (*Lindera*), 275
Spikerush (*Eleocharis*), 109
Spineflower (*Chorizanthe*), 38
Spring beauty (*Claytonia*), 140, 147, 153–54, 157, 162, 168–69
Spruce (*Picea*), 143
Spurge (*Euphorbia*), 53
Spurge family (Euphorbiaceae), 110–11. *See also* genera by common name
Squash (*Cucurbita*), 12, 184, 217, 225–28, 231–32, 234, 263–64, 268
Squash family (Cucurbitaceae), 108. *See also* genera by common name

Squirrel (*Sciurus*), 270, 273, 281
Stl'atl'imx Indians, 133–73
Storage, 15, 162, 233–35, 238
Strawberry (*Fragaria*), 140, 155, 233, 267, 269–70, 275, 278
Sugarcane (*Saccharum*), 184
Sumac (*Rhus*), 112, 219, 233
Sumac family (Anacardiaceae), 110. *See also* genera by common name
Sumpweed (*Iva*), 13, 225–26, 230, 232, 263, 268–69, 288
Sunflower (*Helianthus*), 12, 225–28, 230–32, 263–64, 275
Sunflower family (Asteraceae), 108–109, 111, 184. *See also* genera by common name

Taos Pueblo Indians, 210
Tarahumara Indians. *See* Rarámuri Indians
Tarascan Indians, 49. *See also* Purépecha Indians
Tepehuan Indians, 49–51, 64
Tewa Pueblo Indians, 212
Thâkiwëa Foundation, 18
Thelypodiopsis (Brassicaceae), 64
Thistle (*Cirsium*), 140, 168
Thompson Indians. *See* Nlaka'pamux Indians
Thryallis (Malpighiaceae), 35
Timbisha Shoshone Indians, 100, 102, 105, 112–15, 117–18, 123–24, 126n.5
Tlapanec Indians, 47
Tobacco (*Nicotiana*), 35, 112, 114, 142, 183, 219, 227, 263, 272
Tojolabal Indians, 47–48
Tortoise (*Gopherus*), 38
Totonac Indians, 47–48, 51, 64
Trapping. *See* Hunting
Tricholoma (mushroom), 141
Turkey (*Meleagris*), 235, 266, 270, 273, 280–81, 285
Turtle, Sea (*Chelonia*), 39
Tzeltal Indians, 47–48, 50
Tzotzil Indians, 47–48, 50

United States. *See* California; Eastern North America; Great Basin; Great Plains; Northwest; Southwest
Ute Indians, 100, 102, 104

Valerian (*Valeriana*), 145, 168
Valerian family (Valerianaceae), 108–109. *See also* genera by common name
Viburnum (*Viburnum*), 153, 274
Violet (*Viola*), 270, 275

Walnut (*Juglans*), 233, 264–67, 270, 276
Washoe Indians, 100, 103, 106
Waterleaf family (Hydrophyllaceae), 111. *See also* genera by common name
Water-parsnip (*Sium*), 141
Wax-myrtle (*Myrica*), 266, 276
Weaving, 30, 57, 59, 150–51, 198
Wheat (*Triticum*), 120, 184, 264
Wheat grass (*Agropyron*), 142, 168
Wild lilac (*Ceanothus*), 144
Willow (*Salix*), 112, 116, 143, 150, 183, 211
Willow family (Salicaceae), 110–11. *See also* genera by common name
Wolfberry (*Lycium*), 219
Woodrat. *See* Packrat

Yampa (*Perderidia*), 120
Yaqui Indians, 49–50, 192
Yarrow (*Achillea*), 145
Yerba mansa (*Anemopsis*), 30
Yew (*Taxus*), 78–79, 142
Yoemem Indians, 30
Yucca (*Yucca*), 181, 197–98

Zapotec Indians, 47–48, 50, 61
Zia Pueblo Indians, 210
Zoque Indians, 47–48